# EXPLORING SCOTTISH HISTORY

## WITH A DIRECTORY OF RESOURCE CENTRES FOR SCOTTISH LOCAL AND NATIONAL HISTORY IN SCOTLAND

2nd edition

Published by the
Scottish Library Association
Scottish Local History Forum
and
Scottish Records Association
1999

**ISBN 0 900649 32 1**

Cataloguing in Publication Data
Exploring Scottish history : with a directory of resource centres for Scottish local and national history in Scotland - 2nd ed. - Hamilton : Scottish Library Association and Scottish Local History Forum, 1999
ISBN 0900649321
I. Title   II. Cox, Michael   III. Scottish Local History Forum IV. Scottish Records Association
941.10072

Cover design by Scott Ballantyne

Printed by Portobello Printers

# EXPLORING SCOTTISH HISTORY

## CONTENTS

| | |
|---|---|
| Introduction  by Michael Cox | 5 |
| Community and Place by Norman S Newton | 7 |
| Family and Social by Mike Seton | 15 |
| Finding out about Scottish History from Books by Michael Cox | 21 |
| Standard Reference Sources by Alan Reid and Brian D Osborne | 23 |
| Background Information and Restrictions | 27 |
| Using the Directory | 29 |
| Abbreviations | 30 |
| Directory | 33 |
| Help from private sources | 209 |
| The Electronic Age | 211 |
| Principal Repositories elsewhere in the United Kingdom and Ireland | 215 |
| Index of Organisations | 218 |
| The Sponsors and Acknowledgements | 229 |

Map of the Counties of Scotland before 1975     11

Photographs:
| | |
|---|---|
| Plan of Aberdeen 1796 | 32 |
| Advertisement for 'McVitie's Digestive Biscuits' in 1928 | 43 |
| Burgess Ticket of James Dewar for Burgh of Dumfries 20 April 1790 | 69 |
| Chartist Poster - Dundee 1842 | 76 |
| House room interior - Glasgow 1909 | 127 |
| Elevation of Bellville House, Inverness 1800 | 151 |
| Postcard showing the Post Office at Craighouse, Isle of Jura c1900 | 159 |
| Men at the coalface in the Westwood Pit, West Calder 1929 | 175 |
| Return of Cottars, Knocknatorran, North Uist 1883 | 199 |

Cover illustration: The Apprentice Pillar, Roslyn Chapel, Midlothian

# INTRODUCTION

During this last decade of the twentieth century Scottish people have shown an increasing interest in finding out about their Scottish history. Since the first edition of *Exploring Scottish History* was published seven years ago, there has been a significant increase in the number of local and family history societies, plus the newer heritage societies, especially in the northern half of the country. Libraries, record centres and museums all report that greater use is being made of their collections and services. In recent years there has also been an increase in the number of people visiting museums, castles, stately homes, heritage centres and art galleries.

Why do we want to find out about our past? Most of us would like to know what happened in our village or town, or the places where our ancestors lived and worked, and, how the social fabric developed at both local and national level. Who were the leaders in society? How did the attitudes and actions of lairds, ministers, 'dominies' and farmers affect ordinary folk? In this century, we have moved from the age of the horse to that of the computer. Changes in society have taken place in every century, but finding out about them is more difficult the further back we go in time. Most people can trace their family back through three or four generations. To be able to trace one's roots back to the seventeenth century needs perseverance and a degree of luck!

Unfortunately, during the past fifty years, only a small percentage of the inhabitants of Scotland have been able to acquire even a basic knowledge of Scottish history due to the vagaries of the education system. As recently as 1997 the Scottish Consultative Committee on the Curriculum recommended that the teaching of Scottish history should be the key component of the teaching of history in our schools - as English history is taught in English schools. In the 1980s, the study of local history became a feature of the curriculum in schools, with children undertaking projects on a wide range of topics. The enthusiasm for this initiative seems to have waned during this decade. However, it did have the effect, in some areas, of parents renewing an interest in the history of their country, especially at a local or family history level, often as a result of helping their children with a 'school project'.

Increasingly, all branches of the media industry are paying some regard to Scottish history. In cinemas we have seen the epic struggles and victories of William Wallace in the film *Braveheart*. Was this more fiction than fact? Better informed were the producers of a television documentary about Martin Martin. Who was Martin Martin? He was a doctor and traveller who wrote about his *Voyage to St Kilda* (1698) and *A Description of the Western Isles of Scotland* (1703). A promised reprint of these two books will help us to find out what life was like in a remote area of the country some 300 years ago. A radio programme, presented by Magnus Magnusson, on Scotland's more formal history sought the assistance of Sir Walter Scott plus a number of Scottish academic historians to tell the tale. Here we were on firmer ground with material from the now extensive and more readily available sources weaved in with observations and explanations from the professional historians.

On St Andrew's Day 1998 we were able to see, on television, the opening of the Museum of Scotland by Queen Elizabeth I - not a typographical error! In this fine building, which took almost fifty years to come to fruition, we can at last see a comprehensive, well displayed, collection of artefacts which all add to our knowledge and appreciation of times past in Scotland. In 1999, we will see the new Parliament of Scotland buildings arise near to Holyrood Palace in Edinburgh, although they will not be ready for occupation by the time the new Members of the Scottish Parliament (MSPs) are elected. As we approach 2007, there will be an ever-increasing number of discussions and assessments on what led up to the Union 300 years earlier. Could Scotland have gone it alone then, and should it go it alone now? Politicians should not forget that is the people of Scotland who will decide Scotland's future.

Telling the history of Scotland and its people during the past 300 years has been made easier for today's researchers because the majority of the records are still to be found in Scotland. This has been mainly due to Scotland having its own legal, ecclesiastical and education systems. There has been a pride in the keeping of records, with many going back to the sixteenth century, a few even earlier. We have the opportunity to look at, even handle, both national and local records at a large number of institutions around the country, to find out what happened to our forebears wherever they lived, and write up their story.

By reading this book and using the directory the reader will be better able to explore his or her Scottish history, either at a local level or over a wider canvas. Two articles look at the main aspects of the history of Community and Place, and, Family and Social. They point the way to finding out about one's family's past and origins; where they lived; the kind of society to be found there over the centuries, and, how it was linked to others in the neighbourhood and the large towns. Information is provided on how to find out about the past through reading or consulting books, and, most importantly, how and where to the find records and material the reader will need to consult.

The greater portion of the book is a Directory providing information on over 350 resource centres for the study of Scottish local and national history in Scotland. There is vast range of material to be found throughout Scotland, with ample support or advice available, to enable anyone to write their Scottish history. We live in an age of instant communication and for our children and grandchildren there will be no lack of records, written, visual, oral and electronic being produced now for them to consult in the future. We can only guess at the means of retrieving and consulting such archival material that will be available to them in 2050!

Michael Cox
Compiler/Editor
December 1998

# COMMUNITY AND PLACE

Community history is a growth industry in Scotland. Since the first edition of Exploring Scottish History, the numbers of local history groups, heritage centres, museums, exhibition centres, theme parks, interpretation experiences, internet sites, oral history projects, and permutations of all of these, have proliferated throughout the land, particularly in the Highlands and Islands.

This is greatly to be welcomed, but standards are patchy, and there have been some frustrations, for both individuals and institutions. The National Museums of Scotland, the Scottish Local History Forum, the Scottish Library Association, Scottish universities, educational agencies and many other national and local bodies have, over recent years, launched initiatives designed to assist local communities in devising ways of understanding their history and presenting it to the world at large.

Some excellent work has been done, but there is a continual demand for advice and training. Many people want to get involved in local history projects in their communities, but are not sure how to go about it. This new and improved edition of Exploring Scottish History can help you get involved - through your local history society, if there is one, or through the local studies section of your local library service.

In most parts of Scotland there are local history classes and lectures on offer, usually in the evenings, and usually sponsored by university extra-mural departments (now disguised under various politically correct nomenclatures) and education authorities. Some universities, including the Open University, now offer Certificates and courses in local studies. The Workers' Educational Association (WEA) in Scotland offers friendly and informal local history courses throughout the country, and in particular are running a wonderful community oral history project, Salt of the Earth, to lead local history into the next millennium.

With so many people interested in local history in one form or another, it is crucially important that we let people know how easy it is to do local history, and how much help is available out there, even in Scotland's remotest communities. Your local library is your starting point, but after that, what to do? Most of us have some fairly basic ideas about local sources for the study of local history - maps, local newspapers, printed books - but exactly where can they be found locally? And, if they are not available locally, where are they?

The problem is one of access, which is improving all the time, and is immeasureably better now than it has ever been before. New technology helps, and there are now internet web sites and CDROMs existing, or in the pipeline, which will bring sources of local history to your computer screen, literally at your fingertips. There are some truly exciting things happening in the new world of techno-history, ranging from Project Pont emanating from the National Library of Scotland's Map Library to comprehensive projects which will assemble together all the local studies material in your area on to one electronic multi-media digital source, with photographs, newspaper text, books and articles, illustrations, old maps, census records, even music and video clips, all in digital format, all retrievable, and all capable of being printed out for public use.

The future is exciting, but as yet not accessible to most people. However, the improvement of access to historical source material has been a major achievement over the last decade, for all of us working professionally in this area. There are two main reasons for this: public demand, and a completely different attitude on behalf of those of us who have been portrayed as the guardians of our nation's heritage.

Public demand has mushroomed in the last few years, as any public librarian, archivist or museum curator knows only too well. Television has discovered history, and programmes such Channel 4's Time Team have occupied a niche in the schedules and have developed a faithful following. Other programmes examine the history of buildings (eg House Detectives), aircraft, canals, railways, industries - commissioning editors in TV companies are seemingly always amenable to new ideas for popular history programmes. We must acknowledge the work of the late Ian Grimble, and more recently of Michael Wood and his tight jeans, in promoting the cause of local history.

Perhaps the media are only responding to a demand or even a need that was already there, but they have focused public attention on history and archaeology in a way that seems light years away from Mortimer Wheeler's pioneering efforts in the 1950s. There has been an increase of leisure time, and a publishing boom in local history books - Scottish bookshops now have bays of Scottish local history material where twenty years ago they might have had one shelf. Even the Scottish educational system seems finally to have rediscovered Scottish history, and school pupils are now amongst the most numerous groups of researchers in Scottish libraries.

Most importantly, professional attitudes have changed alongside public expectations. Local history was once the preserve of the local minister or schoolteacher, with perhaps a couple of rather dotty and eccentric local ladies forming the core of a local history society that owed more to the continuation of Victorian antiquarian traditions than to a response to the revolutionary historic work underway now for a generation in Scotland's universities.

Academics have been notoriously bad at passing on their researches to the masses. For the most part they were simply not interested, and did not see it as part of their role to share their discoveries and reinterpretations of Scottish history with the rest of us. Thankfully this is changing rapidly, and there are plenty of young historians about who have brought a new enthusiasm to academe.

With all this information about, it is no wonder that there is a public demand to learn how to do local history. In a climate of innovation and awareness, the message of local history professionals has to be - come and get it! Once we put many barriers in the way of local historians; now, there is a friendly, welcoming, even patient response from librarians, archivists and museum curators, and the guardians of our heritage have become the enablers and promoters of local initiatives across the land. Even in hard times, with minimal resources, a change of attitude is obvious.

Access to sources will always be a problem, but technology is the answer. While digital technology is gradually increasing, with spectacular results, more mundane technology has been more influential so far - though this will change. Two pieces of equipment familiar to any student of local history have opened up access in ways unimaginable a generation ago: the photocopier, and the microfilm reader.

How did people do local history before the invention of the photocopier? With difficulty, and slowly! Copyright restrictions still apply, but the photocopier has made local history much more portable - not confined to the dingy confines of a particular location open at inconvenient hours. Microfilm has done wonders in giving improved access to source material. We think in particular of the sterling work of the Scottish Newspaper Microfilming Unit - so much local history is embedded in the pages of local newspapers. Once computer technology is used to address the problems of indexing, a gold mine of material can become available. Local newspapers on microfilm can usually be found in your central reference library, or in a local studies department. Sadly, the price of microfilm readers, not to mention the price of reels of microfilm themselves, makes it unlikely that they will be found in smaller communities.

Another piece of equipment which has revolutionised local history is the microfilm reader-printer, making it possible to make prints from a roll of microfilm. Unfortunately, the process is likely to be about 3-4 times more expensive than photocopying, but anybody who has felt their eyesight threatened by hours spent in front of a microfilm reader may consider it money well spent.

It is surprising how many people are intimidated by the simple process of threading a roll of microfilm through a reader. A moment or two of tuition by a member of your library staff will open up whole new avenues of research. And, judging by the number of little old ladies who can be found in front of the nation's microfilm readers, it is a technology that can be easily mastered, a barrier easily demolished.

The other great use of microfilm is, of course, in the study of genealogy, thankfully outside the scope of this article, which is concerned more with community history in its other aspects. However, even family history fanatics - well, some of them - can eventually be persuaded that lurking within the confines of the parish census records of 1841-1891 are not only the answers to their personal lineage but also masses of information of interest to the social historian.

Maps are the skeleton of local history, the bare bones of the historic landscape on which everything else hangs. The originals are often to be found in local archives, from which photocopies (within defined limits) are usually possible. Every area will have its unique range of early maps but there are some common to all areas in Scotland. The Blaeu county maps of 1654, originally published in atlas form, have been reprinted as separate sheets and are frequently available in library and archive map collections. Some libraries may be lucky enough to have a copy of the original, hand-coloured atlas, but don't expect to use original, rare books, or even to see them, except in an exhibition case.

The Blaeu maps should be familiar to anybody doing local history in Scotland, providing as they do a snapshot of the landscape where people lived - though not in 1654, when the engraved maps were published, but of the landscape of Scotland at the end of the 16th century, when the scrappy manuscript maps on which the sublime published maps were based were compiled by Timothy Pont of Caithness, during his perambulations through the whole of Scotland, including the islands.

There are thirty eight sheets containing seventy eight maps, although, unfortunately, there are gaps in the coverage of south east Scotland and the northern Highlands. The originals of Pont's manuscripts are in the National Library of Scotland, but Project Pont has converted them all to digital format, making them available to a wider audience. They are a unique record of place-names, and, surprisingly, of Scottish architecture, for it has recently been noticed that the tiny drawings of castles and big houses are often accurately drawn elevations of the frontages of important buildings, some no longer surviving. Prints, including enlargements, are possible from the digitised database containing Pont's maps.

Another important map source which has become more easily available in recent years is Roy's Military Survey of Scotland, of the period 1747-55. The original, in its various versions, is in the Map Room of the British Library, in London. Generations of Scottish university geography students will be familiar with the bad photocopies which circulated in Scottish university libraries from the 1960s onwards. Now, at last, the British Library is making it much more available, and both coloured and black-and-white prints are easily obtainable, at a price. The map is also available on 35mm coloured slides, at modest cost. Roy's map, drawn as a response to the inadequate mapping available to the British Army during the Jacobite rebellion of 1745-6, is a properly surveyed landscape snapshot of Scotland poised on the brink of an era of great changes in agriculture and the way in which the countryside was organised. It is indispensable in local studies.

Needless to say, illicit copying from either Pont or Roy maps, in whatever form, is strictly forbidden. Nevertheless, legal copies can now be obtained, where not many years ago we could only gape and drool, on rare visits to Edinburgh or London.

For the early 19th century, Thomson's county maps of the 1820s and 1830s, published in atlas form in 1832, are widely available. From the 1860s onwards, Ordnance Survey maps are available. The first edition, published at the scale of six inches to one mile (1:10,560) covers the whole country. A second edition was published around 1900 - the dates vary slightly from one part of the country to another. The settled parts of Scotland were also mapped at the scale of 25 inches to one mile, giving tremendous detail of buildings and landscape features. Even larger scale maps were produced for the centres of some towns and cities.

Maps can be used to trace the development of transport systems - roads, canals and railways, for example. But mostly, they provide a sense of place, something that connects us in our landscape with the people who have lived here before us. They also fire the imagination - courses and lectures which have anything to do with 'old maps' are guaranteed a large audience.

Modern maps, which local historians will also want to consult, are sometimes also found in libraries and archives, but more commonly in the Planning Departments of local authorities. Again, modern Ordnance Survey maps are now widely available in digital form, and indeed, paper copies of really up-to-date maps may not be easy to find.

# Scotland

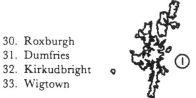

1. Shetland Islands
2. Orkney Islands
3. Sutherland
4. Caithness
5. Ross and Cromarty
6. Nairn
7. Moray
8. Banff
9. Aberdeen
10. Inverness
11. Kincardine
12. Angus
13. Perth
14. Argyll
15. Fife
16. Kinross

17. Clackmannan
18. Dumbarton
19. Stirling
20. West Lothian
21. Midlothian
22. East Lothian
23. Berwick
24. Renfrew
25. Peebles
26. Lanark
27. Bute
28. Ayr
29. Selkirk

30. Roxburgh
31. Dumfries
32. Kirkudbright
33. Wigtown

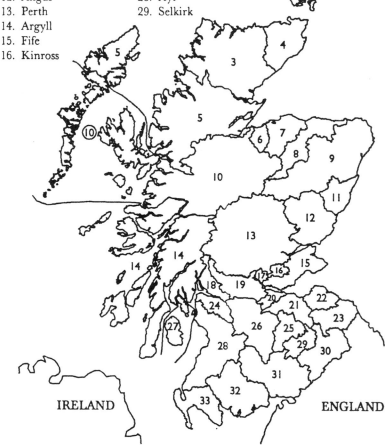

IRELAND

ENGLAND

**Map of the Counties of Scotland 1890 - 1975**

Future researchers - perhaps within the next ten years - will do their map research on computer screens, as part of a multi-media local history package. They will position their mouse on a Poorhouse, and summon up not only photographs of the building but also lists of residents and newspaper accounts of its opening and of Christmas benevolences by local worthies. This is already possible in some lucky places, but it will be some time yet before this new technology is widely available, and until then, map cabinets, ageing indexing systems and the brains of archivists and local studies librarians will continue to serve us well.

Toponomy - the study of place-names - is about as local as local history gets, and is a fascinating area of study in its own right. Our landscape is littered with the linguistic debris of all the different cultures who have lived here, but place-names are evolving all the time, in a rich and often hilarious way - every community will have its own examples. In the Highlands of Scotland, especially on the west coast and islands, and in Orkney and Shetland, Norse influence is everywhere. The Vikings are always good for drumming up interest in local history, though often their place-names are hidden within a later Gaelic shell, and need to be excavated. The Picts in the north east, the Irish Scots in the west and the Angles in the south east all influenced place names in these areas.

Indeed, the layers of place-names in our landscape can be disentangled in much the same way as an archaeologist unravels the layers of history. Sources of place-name studies are often rather ancient, buried in 19th century antiquarian journals or local history tomes, often of dubious scholarship. Nevertheless, these older studies contribute in local knowledge what they sometimes lack in academic excellence and are an essential starting point for anybody interested in their local names. Modern studies, sometimes stultifyingly dull but of major importance, have stimulated the interest of a new generation of academic researchers. The contributions of Ian A. Fraser and W.F.H. Nicolaisen deserve to be mentioned as more lively and accessible than most. Again, local studies librarians can guide you and give you good advice. Anybody doing serious research should coordinate their activities with the School of Scottish Studies, who oversee place-name projects throughout Scotland.

Local newspapers are the life-blood of local history, and often the only source of information, reliable or unreliable. We have already mentioned the microfilm holdings of local newspapers, and if local indexes do not exist, then that is a perfect local history project for some committed researcher, under the guidance of local professionals. Newspapers give us information on what things cost, local trades and industries, leisure activities, buildings, accidents, Royal visits, openings and closings, school prizes, entertainments, churches, railway timetables, schools, public health, crime and much, much more. They also give us information on births, marriages and deaths, though in the last century only the higher echelons of society could afford to publicise such activities. Important public figures and well-known local people will often have obituaries in local papers, from which we can follow further leads to earlier milestones in their careers.

Valuation Rolls, commencing 1855, give a record of who owned a property and the name of the occupier or tenant, and will often be found in local archives. Their survival is patchy but for most areas they can be used from the 1880s onwards. They are often useful in tracing the history of a building and the people who lived in it, though the rather scant information they provide needs to be supplemented from other sources.

In Scottish burghs, but not in country areas, Dean of Guild records can often supply building plans for 19th century housing. When used in conjunction with late 19th century census returns they can give us a real insight into both the overcrowded housing in which most of the population lived and the work force needed to keep mansions and villas operating smoothly.

Within the burgeoning boundaries of current local history activities in Scotland, one area stands out - oral history, or reminiscence work, as it is sometimes called. So much of the 20th century history of Scotland is tied up in people's memories, and more formal historians have come to value and acknowledge the importance of oral history work. The Scottish Oral History Society and the WEA have taken the lead in this area. Projects involving school children and old people need to be carefully managed but can be immensely rewarding.

One word of warning; as a rule of thumb, one hour of memories recorded on tape can generate about six hours work in transcribing, editing, collating, publishing, indexing, cataloguing and storing the results. There are also important questions of confidentiality and of respect for privacy and other people's feelings, and oral history work is best done through an established group, or under the guidance of professionals.

Throughout Scotland there are many people who are well-equipped to contribute to the history of their local communities, but lack either the basic skills, awareness of available materials, self-confidence in their own abilities, or a combination of all three. The hope is that many people who may have dabbled in local history through membership of local societies, non-vocational evening classes, personal interest and reading, or in other ways, may become sufficiently motivated, and sufficiently confident of their own abilities, to pursue their interest.

Local history is best done by local people, but local people can do local history better if they learn a few basic skills and practise them, and learn how to exploit the professional skills of librarians, archivists, writers, teachers and others. There should be no mystery about local history. The sources are mostly now accessible to most of us. It's not 'difficult' either - once you know where things are, and who to ask for them, a lot of the barriers disappear.

Hopefully, technology should no longer be a barrier either. Anybody should be able to read a microfiche, load a microfilm reader, understand a photocopier, and appreciate how your local library service works. Some of us already, and more of us quite soon, will be learning how to grapple with digital technology and computers - intimidating at first, but so easy that a child can do it, as many of them do already, at school and in the home. We can all trace the development of our local communities from early maps, and find out what was happening there from accounts in local newspapers.

If you are not involved already in local history, we hope you will consider joining your local history society, or helping your local archivist or archaeologist, or helping your local librarian with local history enquiries, or offering to help your local tourist board get its brochures right next year!

There is plenty of help available - so search it out, and good luck!

Norman S Newton

# FAMILY AND SOCIAL

As we travel with ever increasing frequency to more and more of those parts of the globe once considered exotic or remote, it certainly seems as though the world is getting smaller. Since we also take with us our creature comforts the urbanised world at least takes on a comfortable familiarity wherever we are with the same hotel rooms, the same cuisine and the same products in the same shops. We feel more secure once we spot the universal logos of Coca Cola or Macdonalds. In the midst of this creeping uniformity it perhaps not surprising that more and more people should seek out something to make their little piece of the earth a little special. Some may put decorative stripes on their Escort, others research their ancestors. What, after all, is the one thing that makes an individual different from others, if not his own history and that of his family.

The surge in interest in family history over the past two decades has been attributed to the television programme Roots. It was certainly a development viewed by many of those who came into contact with it professionally as a rather mixed blessing. Like the National Lottery it has brought benefits to record offices and local history libraries in allowing them to demonstrate a clear need for increased resources. Like the National Lottery it has been sometimes regarded as often undignified and shallow. It has also made "historical research" popular and, despite years of promoting local history to the public at large, many professionals found this sudden popularity uncomfortable and difficult to handle. Nevertheless the demand was clear and intense and in many areas very special efforts have been made to meet it. Over the length and breadth of Scotland family history researchers are probably better catered for now than the local history student ever was or was ever likely to be. Most can now expect to find locally copies of their local census returns, parish registers and part, at least, of the International Genealogical Index (IGI). Some will be fortunate enough to be researching in those parts of the country with special facilities.

Up in the Highlands the local authority took on a professional genealogist both to ease the burden on hard-pressed library staff faced, as many were all over the country, with an area of work they were often unfamiliar with and untrained in; to provide the time and expertise that library staff were unable to give and to bring in a little money to offset the costs of this service.

A little further south, in Moray, a slightly different route was taken. Following in the area's tradition for "sturdy independence" the focus was put on providing the means by which enquirers could find the answers to their questions themselves. The result was (and is) a massive computerised index, named "Libindx" by a dyslexic programmer, which now numbers some 225,000 name, 23,000 place and 13,000 subject entries. Originating in the bringing together of two card indexes, one to some local newspaper files and the other to the names on local headstones, the database now indexes in considerable detail all manner of local history materials including photographs and documents, and not only for personal names or buildings, but also for subjects like living conditions, education, crime or religion. The imminent availability of this invaluable resource on the Internet will give those researching Moray and its inhabitants even more of an advantage over the rest of us than they enjoy at present.

Other parts of the country have been fortunate in having had far-sighted benefactors back in the days when genealogy was the pursuit of scholars and gentlemen, like William Coull Anderson, whose Trust Fund financed the William Coull Anderson Library of Genealogy, formerly in Arbroath, and now in the Angus Archives in Montrose.

Glasgow, because of its size (at least in years gone by) and its history, witnesses more genealogical searches than any other, save Edinburgh. Here the Mitchell Library's Glasgow Room, the focus of most of these enquiries, provides access to the Mormon's Family Search, a CD-based database which includes not only the ubiquitous IGI, but in addition the family history records deposited in the Mormon Library in Salt Lake City as well as the catalogue of the Family History Library there.

Many libraries and archive repositories, East Ayrshire for example with its Tracing Your Family Tree - Sources in East Ayrshire Libraries, have produced more or less detailed guides to the resources they hold, helping to make best use of both researchers' and staff time.

Much of the work in providing research aids has been done by family historians themselves. In the flourishing family history societies devotees have recorded gravestone inscriptions, compiled indexes to census returns and searched out those local records missed by the centralising hand of officialdom. The family historian can be frighteningly enthusiastic and single-minded, exactly the qualities needed to complete tasks of this kind. Despite the heroic achievements so far much more of this kind of work remains to be done and although undertaken for a particular purpose, the fruits of these labours can often be of value to the non-genealogical local history student.

If the family history boom was triggered by one piece of twentieth century technology then it seems certain to be boosted on to an even higher plane by another, the Internet. Already the list of family history sites on the World Wide Web is as long as the proverbial arm. Most of Scotland's Family History Societies are there together with international sites which originate across the Atlantic, such as GenConnect.

The EARL (Electronic Access to Resources in Libraries) Consortium of UK public libraries and associated organisations was established in 1995 to develop the role of public libraries in providing library and information services over the network. It functions through a number of special groups, one of which, the Family History Group has recently launched "Familia", a web-based directory to family history resources in public libraries. The Group plans to develop the site by adding clickable maps, additional information, links to other sites and also to develop a searching mechanism within "Familia".

Even the once (technologically) conservative General Register Office has taken to the Web (www.origins.net), where it provides a fully searchable, pay-as-you-view index of Scottish birth and marriage records from 1553 to 1897, and death records from 1855 to 1897 which can be accessed via a computer from anywhere in the world.

So in these and many other ways much has been done to assist the family historian. Yet the student of "pure" local history need not feel jealous. Much of what has been acquired primarily for genealogists is of value to all and the upsurge in interest in family history has brought with it a rise in the use of local studies generally. After all the best of family historians are not just interested in collecting vast numbers of ancestors or being able to trace their family tree back further than the Joneses. They are keen to find out what they can about the places their forebears lived in, how they lived, how they earned their living, what school they went to, church they attended, games they played or wars they fought in. The most rewarding family history study transmutes into a local history study.

Many local studies libraries doubtless acquired copies of their local census returns in response to demand from family historians. But many others as well as genealogists were then able to discover what a wealth of information on social history the returns contain: information on changing occupations, number of people to a room, where people were born, family size, marriage patterns etc. Although not always reliable in individual detail, particularly in regard to information perhaps personally sensitive, e.g. age, the census returns are an unrivalled source of information on nineteenth century social and economic conditions for even the smallest and most ordinary locality.

The one other resource which can outdo the census in the depth and breadth of information it contains, especially on social issues, is the local newspaper. It has been calculated that there are some 1700 individual newspaper titles held by libraries, universities and newspaper publishers in Scotland. Not so many years ago getting access to your local newspaper was not always easy. They may have been available only in large unwieldy bound volumes or were in such a fragile state as not to be available at all. Since the Scottish Newspaper Microfilming Unit began its work in 1994 great strides forward have been made in making more and more titles readily available to researchers as well as saving some from literal disintegration. Now it is quite normal to find a microfilm copy of the local paper close to its place of publication. The problem for the student has changed. The difficulties of access largely overcome there is now this enormous body of primary material, almost as overwhelming as the super-highway in the amount of information it contains, but presented in a format which positively militates against easy searching. To fulfil their true potential local newspapers need indexes. In some places, Clackmannan and Moray for examples, such indexes exist. If your local newspaper file is not indexed why not approach whoever holds the file, library or newspaper office, and offer to do one. It is a long-term task that needs stamina and commitment and probably more than one person, but it is invaluable work for the future progress of local history studies. It can be done the traditional way, on cards, but there are many database packages available. "Access" is one that is widely used, which can make the initial indexing maybe just a little easier but can make the finished product significantly more useful.

Although the visual image has long been an accepted means of communicating information it is only in quite recent times since television became universally available that the argument for it becoming the prime means could be advanced. Not surprising then that the value of the visual image in local history has only lately come to be fully recognised. Once this happened collections of local photographs began to be assembled, mostly of material already in existence, but occasionally, as with the Fife Local Studies Workshop, producing contemporary photographic surveys. This is an aspect of local studies work where much remains to be done.

With the accelerating pace of change it becomes increasingly vital to record today because by tomorrow it could be gone. It may not always be easy to raise enthusiasm for such work. Most of us can recognise the importance of historic buildings but will find it difficult to see much point in recording a 60s supermarket or pre-war council housing scheme. Indeed we may view the world as better off without them, but that is not the point. We have to approach the history of our locality as a whole not just picking out the quaint or exciting parts. Contemporary photographic surveys then are to be encouraged. With camera technology as it presently is special photographic skills are not needed, although the local camera club could well use such a project as a means of displaying their members' prowess.

Where significant collections had been amassed they had often remained underused. As with newspaper files a photographic collection is so much more valuable if it is indexed in an appropriate way. In Kirkcaldy, where the collection numbers some 10,000 images, they applied video and computer technology, through a system called "Fotofile", to allow quick and easy public access to the images and the information they carry, without having to handle the originals. It is a classic example of the use of new technologies in local studies where the previously incompatible demands of greater access on the one hand and the preservation of unique materials on the other can now both be met. Some of our universities with large collections of historic photographs, such as Aberdeen with its George Washington Wilson collection and St Andrews with the Valentines postcard archive, have digitised these images and have, or are about to, make them available over the Internet, once again combining preservation with improved access.

One area which has perhaps not received its due recognition is oral history. Although perhaps not quite as easy as it might first appear it is still an area where perfectly acceptable results can be obtained by anyone with some patience, an approachable manner and just a smidgen of technical skill. Apart from the obvious advantages of being able to capture accents and dialects as they are spoken as well as those words which may often be peculiar to a very limited area, oral history is a particularly suitable way of recording the everyday history of work, shopping, school or family life. It is also interactive, allowing the interviewer the chance to elicit, for example, how exactly a particular job was performed in a way that written descriptions and even photographs rarely can.

Many local history collections now have a presence on the Internet. At the moment most use it to give a flavour of their holdings, brief guides or contact numbers and opening hours. It has been suggested that there should be a standard, integrated index to all the local history resources in Scotland. Even allowing that the problems of finance and inter-agency co-operation could be solved, the amount of material involved is immense. Such of it as has been indexed has been done so, if in a myriad of different ways by different holders; much of it is unindexed. Similarly, although it is technically feasible it is difficult to foresee a time in the near future when the bulk of the material itself will be available on line. The sheer quantity coupled with a lack of resources ensures that for some considerable time yet the serious student will have to travel to use primary source materials or have them photocopied. Yet signs of the future are there to be seen. In this our universities seem to be taking the lead. Dundee, Edinburgh and St Andrews already have catalogues of manuscripts available on-line. In Edinburgh the stated objective is "to increase awareness and effective use of the Manuscripts held by the University...to create an online finding aid that can be searched across the Internet by scholars across Scotland, the UK and internationally". These can be seen as first steps to what in the longer-term may include online access to the scanned images of particular manuscript items. Indeed there are already sites digitising documents and rare books so that researchers can read the complete text without having either to travel or handle the document itself.

In all this it is easy to forget the good old-fashioned book. Its day seems far from done. Indeed technology, from the photocopier to the computer, has brought book (or pamphlet) production within the capabilities of Everyman and people still buy books, witness the numbers of new bookshops opening up in our town centres. A very acceptable standard of book design and layout can be achieved by anyone with a PC and a cheap Desk Top Publishing package, like Serif's "PagePlus". With these kinds of facilities it is possible to produce a few copies of a fairly short work quite cheaply and even for longer runs where commercial printers have to be involved the costs may not be astronomical. There may even be grants available. The Local History Magazine produces a free History Into Print Information Pack, full of tips and useful information about self-publishing.

If traditional print is not possible then there is always publication on the Internet. Whichever way you choose it is much easier than it ever was to make the results of your own research more widely available.

And then there is the e-book. There are confident forecasts that electronic books will be ubiquitous in five years time. We can all breathe a sigh of relief, though, since industry experts agree that electronic books will not replace printed books. Just as radio survived TV, and film lived on after video, traditional and electronic books will coexist in the future. Beyond that look out for electronic ink.

Many students of local history work alone and achieve superb results. Others prefer to work with the support of a group. Some of these groups are long-established historical societies, others quite new, perhaps resulting from an initiative on the part of a local community education worker. Groups may grow up around a particular project like the Dundee Heritage Trust and HMS Discovery, or they may increasingly find the catalyst they need in the setting up of a community web-page. Projects like the South Ayrshire CyberCentre, which can provide the technical infrastructure, will doubtless encourage the young and not-so-young to delve deeper in to the history of their community. Communities would do well to follow the example of the Glasgow suburb of Hyndland which has its own local history pages on the Web. As Web sites go it is a straightforward but effective design with a judicious balance between text and visuals. It draws its information from both official sources and residents themselves. Although one of the city's more affluent parts Hyndland has neither a long history, scarcely one hundred years, nor an exceptional one, but it clearly has a strong sense of community. After all to function properly as such a community needs to have its own identity. What gives it that identity is its history. Interest in local history fosters community spirit, trust, and pride. The community with an interest in its past will be one with an interest in its present and its future.

Local history has never been more exciting or rewarding. Over recent years an incredible wealth of material has been made accessible to the ordinary man and woman, boy and girl, as never before. Not only is research easier but its results are likely to be much more worthwhile.  Using the technology those results can be presented attractively and professionally and then distributed more widely and at less cost than ever before.  Even if research is not your forte you can make a contribution to your community by carrying out those tasks we have mentioned which will make your local history an even more fertile field for the generations to come.

Mike Seton

# FINDING OUT ABOUT SCOTTISH HISTORY FROM BOOKS

Many people in Scotland only have a limited knowledge of Scottish history. For them and for those who have forgotten what little Scottish history they were taught at school it will be essential that they read a selection of the books listed below. They cover a range of historical topics, some suggest how and where to seek out information and even subjects for projects that could be undertaken by readers when looking at 'their place and community'. All the books should be available in the larger libraries or on inter library loan, with many available at the larger bookshops.

Among the readers of this book will be those who not only 'know their Scottish history' but have engaged in research projects, be they basic or advanced. Information on standard reference sources which historical researchers often need to consult are given later. The subjects covered include bibliographies, biography, religion and law, gazetteers and buildings. Books featured in that section are usually available for consultation in the major local authority and university libraries and in the National Library of Scotland.

## A basic reading list

The first, often reprinted, books to read will provide a thought provoking introduction to Scottish social history are both by T C Smout: *A History of the Scottish People 1560-1830*, published in 1969, and, *A Century of the Scottish People 1830-1950*, published in 1986. Both these books are usually available in bookshops. Another author whose books have been read and studied by many local and family historians is David Moody. His three books should be consulted before the start of any research project. *Scottish Local History* (1986), *Scottish Family History* (1988), and, *Scottish Towns* (1992). Two books which describe the extent of resources to be found in the National Archives of Scotland (former Scottish Record Office), both written by Cecil Sinclair are *Tracing Scottish Local History* (1994), and, *Tracing Your Scottish Ancestors* (1990). Another book of particular interest to family historians is *Tracing Your Scottish Ancestry* by Kathleen B Cory (2nd edition 1996). This book contains illustrations of documents and lists the Parishes in Scotland linked to their County, and Commissariot, with dates of earliest Old Parish Registers (OPRs) and Testaments (Wills).

The next group of books provides more information about Scottish social history. They include: *A Companion to Scottish Culture* (1981), or, *The New Companion to Scottish Culture* (1993), both edited by David Daiches. They cover many aspects of Scottish culture, old and new. I F Grant's book *Highland Folk Ways* (1961) is a social history of life in the Highlands long forgotten in the Lowlands. Isabel Grant was the founder of the Highland Folk Museum in 1934. The books in the series *'Scotland's Past in Action'*, published by the National Museums of Scotland, highlight working and other activities which are part of our social heritage. Books in the *'Discovering'* series, published by John Donald, are reasonably comprehensive guides to fifteen areas in Scotland, providing useful information for local historians. *Studying Scottish History, Literature & Culture* (1996), edited by Ian Donnachie, is an Open University self-study book. The literature section highlights historical and social developments.

The last groups of books in this section are more of a 'technical nature'. They all provide in depth information on the topics covered, which many social, local and family historians will, on occasion, find it necessary to be familiar with. To find out what the area looked like in the past it is necessary to look at old photographs and postcards, where appropriate, but more importantly to study old maps. Virtually all the leading local authority and university library services hold collections of maps. For anyone who has little knowledge of the maps of Scotland the book by Margaret Wilkes, former head of the National Library of Scotland's Map Library is essential reading. *The Scot and His Maps* (1991) is well illustrated and covers maps from the fourteenth to the twentieth century. A book by the late George Oliver, *Photographs and Local History* (1989), takes the reader from taking photographs through to their reproduction. It has many Scottish examples.

All local historians should have some appreciation and knowledge of the wide range and types of buildings to be found in Scotland. The Royal Institute of Architecture in Scotland series *'Illustrated Guides to Architecture in Scotland'*, and, Penguin's *'Buildings of Scotland'* series, together, cover much of the architectural and buildings history across Scotland up to recent times. A background, even detailed, knowledge of Scottish art over the centuries will often make a contribution to any historical research project. There are many books available but Duncan Macmillan's book *Scottish Art 1460-1990* (1991) covers a wide spectrum. Researchers who find themselves looking at original manuscripts before the mid-eighteenth century will find it difficult, sometimes virtually impossible, to read them. A book by Grant G Simpson, *Scottish Handwriting* (1998) has many examples of such writing and provides guidance on deciphering documents.

Most historians will at some time or other wish to look at newspapers of the past. All the local authority history/studies centres have collections of their local 'county' newspapers, with a few having runs of regional and national newspapers. Today, the majority will only be available for consultation on microfilm. For a complete listing of all the newspapers published in Scotland and their location consult *Newplan: Report of the Newsplan Project in Scotland 1994* compiled by Alice Mackenzie.


**General histories of Scotland**

There are three series of books providing general histories of Scotland written by well-known academics. These are *The Edinburgh History of Scotland*, four volumes edited by Gordon Donaldson (1960/70s); the *New History of Scotland Series*, seven volumes (1980s); and, *Modern Scottish History: 1707 to the Present*, five volumes for an Open University/Dundee University distance learning course (1998). For the period before 1707 the *Atlas of Scottish History to 1707* (1996), edited by G B McNeill and Hector L MacQueen provides, by means of maps and text, an outline of Scottish history before the Union.

Michael Cox

# STANDARD REFERENCE SOURCES

The Scottish historical researcher is well served by printed sources covering a wide range of aspects of Scottish life. Notes on a number of the most generally useful of these are given below but there are others, such as the five volumes of MacGibbon & Ross's *Castellated and Domestic Architecture of Scotland* and their three volume *Ecclesiastical Architecture of Scotland* published at the end of the last century, which will prove invaluable to the specialist researcher studying Scotland's architectural heritage.

The starting point for the local historian in Scotland will often be the standard bibliographic sources. *A contribution to the bibliography of Scottish topography* (1917) was compiled in two volumes by Sir Arthur Mitchell and C G Cash. It is a remarkable achievement and constitutes the first modern large-scale bibliography of the country. The first volume comprises a topographical listing by county and 'territories' not limited by the boundaries of a single county - Borders, Galloway and Highlands and Islands. In volume two the arrangement is by subject. An index to places and subjects completes the work.

For many years thereafter, the need for a supplement to this work was felt. *A bibliography of works relating to Scotland, 1916 - 1950*, compiled by P D Hancock and published in two volumes in 1959, endeavoured to meet this need. Again, a topographical approach is adopted in volume one. The subject classification in the second part is more detailed than in its predecessor, however. While consistency with Mitchell and Cash is forfeited to some extent, the themed listing reflects the changes in Scotland during the passage of forty years. Each volume is individually indexed.

While the *British National Bibliography* covers all U.K. publications from 1950 onwards, a separate listing of books and major articles of Scottish interest was not achieved until the establishment of the *Bibliography of Scotland* by the National Library of Scotland. From 1976 to 1987 this was published as series of annual printed volumes. It is now available on the internet and in CDRom format.

The many texts and documents published by Scottish publishing clubs and societies in past years are recorded in C S Terry's *Catalogue of the Publications of Scottish Historical and Kindred Clubs and Societies, 1780-1908* and its continuation to 1927 by C Matheson while the rich holdings of Government and legal documents in the National Archives of Scotland (formerly the Scottish Record Office) are documented in *Guide to the National Archives of Scotland*.

Through the ages the Church has been central to the social and political life of Scotland. *The Fasti Ecclesiae Scoticanae: the succession of ministers in the Church of Scotland from the Reformation* presents a comprehensive listing of ministers with notes about their lives, writings and families. The work is of great value to local historians, biographers and genealogists. Originally published during the third quarter of the nineteenth century, volumes I - VII appeared during 1915 - 1928 as a new edition by Hew Scott. A subsequent three volumes under various editors have brought the coverage up to 1975. Arrangement is by Synod, Presbytery and Parish.

It has been contended that the Fasti is not always a reliable source of information for the Reformation period. In *Scottish parish clergy at the Reformation, 1540 - 1574* (1972) Charles H Haws has sought to address its shortcomings. For the pre-Reformation period the *Fasti Ecclesiae Scoticanae Medii Aevi ad annum 1638* (second draft, 1969) by D E R Watt should be consulted. Several other churches of the reformed tradition produced their own listings of clergy.

Access to the decisions of the supreme civil and criminal courts is conveniently provided by the volumes of *Session Cases*, a work whose extent is somewhat greater than the short title implies. A supplement to each annual volume gives cases decided in the High Court of Justiciary and from 1850 Scottish appeal cases decided in the House of Lords are also covered. A two part index of names of pursuers and defenders provides quick access to this invaluable record. Earlier Scottish civil law appeals before the House of Lords from 1707 are dealt with in David Robertson: *Reports of cases of appeal from Scotland decided in the House of Peers*.

The source of Scots law is provided in the printed volumes of the *Acts of the Parliaments of Scotland* which cover all the legislation enacted between James I's Parliament of 1424 and the Union of the Parliaments in 1707.

The relevance of many of the major British printed reference sources should not be overlooked. For example a vast range of Scots from all historical periods are included in the *Dictionary of National Biography* (DNB) and its supplements and although specialist Scottish biographical dictionaries exist the researcher cannot afford to overlook the DNB. *Who's Who* (for contemporaries) and the eight volumes of *Who Was Who* from 1897 are similarly constructed on a UK basis and repay consultation. *Alumni Oxoniensis*, four volumes listing members of Oxford University from 1500 to 1886, giving parentage, birthplace and year of birth and *Alumni Cantabrigiensis*, eight volumes listing all known students, graduates and office-holders at Cambridge from the earliest times to 1900 both have many entries of Scottish relevance

When searching for information about famous, or notorious, or just significant Scots of past years there are a number of important printed sources which should be consulted. James Balfour Paul *The Scots Peerage* 9 vols., 1904-1914 is, as its subtitle says, 'founded on Wood's edition of Sir Robert Douglas's Peerage of Scotland containing an Historical and Genealogical account of the Nobility of that Kingdom'. It provided a comprehensive account of the great families of Scotland and also provides convenient access to references to them in archival sources such as the Exchequer Rolls, the Register of the Great Seal, etc. There is, in volume 9, an exhaustive index of over 40,000 names referred to in the Peerage and which includes a far wider range of people than might at first be thought to be covered by such a work.

A socially wider ranging biographical source is Thomas Thomson: *Biographical dictionary of Eminent Scotsmen, 1875*. This work is based on Robert Chambers: *Lives of Illustrious and Distinguished Scotsmen 1832* and continues Chambers compilation, taking account both of figures who came into prominence after Chambers' day and also including some historical characters, such as Malcolm Canmore, who were omitted from the earlier work. Strong in its coverage of literary and religious figures a particular value of this work lies in its inclusion of portraits of a number of the major figures discussed.

Tantalising as an example of what might have been, the one issue of Scottish Biographies, published in 1938, gives a snapshot of the great and good of Scotland in that year. A more recent, and successfully sustained, attempt to provide a contemporary Scottish biographical compendium came in 1986 with the publication of **Who's Who in Scotland**, which has been continued to the present date. Like all such sources this is based on information supplied by the subjects so requires to be used with some care.

Numerous regional biographical sources were compiled in the late nineteenth and early twentieth centuries, of which Ernest Gaskell: **Lanarkshire Leaders**, social and political, 1911 may stand as a representative sample.

Specialist biographical sources covering one profession are often surprisingly useful and of more general relevance than might at first be imagined. This is particularly true when the profession is the law, with its involvement in so many aspects of Scottish life. The two senior bodies are both well covered with Francis J Grant: **The Faculty of Advocates in Scotland 1532-1943** giving brief details of advocates, covering their parentage, date of admission to the Faculty, marriage, appointments held and death, while the leading society of solicitors, the Society of Writers to the Signet, is similarly treated in James Stuart Fraser-Tytler: **A history of the Society of Writers to Her Majesty's Signet** which gives a list of members from 1594 to 1890 with details of birth, apprenticeship, admission, offices held and death.

Documents and letters covering a surprisingly wide variety of people have been collected and preserved in the National Library of Scotland and their **Catalogue of Manuscripts acquired since 1925**, (eight volumes to date), and the **Summary Catalogue of the Advocate's Manuscripts** covering earlier material from the National Library's predecessor, the Library of the Faculty of Advocates, will often prove rewarding to the researcher.

The series of **Statistical Accounts of Scotland** form a treasure trove for the local historian. The first **Statistical Account of Scotland** was published during the last decade of the eighteenth century and was compiled by Sir John Sinclair from returns submitted by the minister of each parish in the country. Individual parish accounts vary greatly in length, quality and detail depending upon the interests and energies of their authors. In all cases, they provide a snapshot of life in a Scotland on the edge of great changes and give descriptions of the topography, history, agriculture, industry, way of life, etc, etc. The original publication did not group parishes by county and so each volume contains a gathering of unrelated parishes. A recent reprint by county has rectified this however.

During the 1830s and 1840s a **New Statistical Account** was prepared, again from returns from parish ministers but this time publication was arranged in county volumes, with a more even presentation of material.

A **Third Statistical Account** was tackled in the aftermath of the Second World War, although with less success. Some county volumes appeared during the 1950s, while others have been published only quite recently. Some have largely retained a parish by parish description while others have developed a subject approach alongside accounts of individual parishes.

The three accounts together allow a comparative study of any parish in Scotland during the past two hundred years and so represent an invaluable resource for the investigation of social and economic development and change.

***The Ordnance Gazetteer of Scotland***: a survey of Scottish topography, statistical, biographical and historical was edited by Frances M Groome and published in six volumes, in 1882 - 1885. Although now well over one hundred years old, and while its statistical information is obviously dated , it remains a valuable source for the local historian.

Groome's coverage is encyclopaedic: entries for counties, cities, towns, villages and parishes are accompanied by those for geographical features - hills, rivers, lochs, islands (and even caves); individual buildings and properties find a place also, as do battlefields, historic and prehistoric remains.

Many entries are extensive - the essay on Edinburgh runs to eighty double-columned pages and its own two-page index. Even relatively small communities, however, are given a detailed description of their topography, history, industry and social circumstances. Quotations from literature are often used to capture atmosphere.

While Groome provides a starting point for the study of a locality his use of other sources provides references to further research in published works and Ordnance Survey maps. The Gazetteer is illustrated with coloured county maps, city plans and etchings of buildings and views. It concludes with a 'General Survey' of Scotland compiled from articles prepared by recognised contemporary authorities, allowing local detail to be fitted to the national picture.

Brian D Osborne and Alan Reid

# BACKGROUND INFORMATION AND RESTRICTIONS

The Scottish Library Association (SLA), The Scottish Records Association (SRA) and the Scottish Local History Forum (SLHF), the three organisations that supported the first edition of *Exploring Scottish History*, decided at the beginning of 1998 that it was time to compile and publish a new expanded edition. The main reason for this was the reorganisation of local government in 1995 (see below). This resulted in a significant proportion of local authority library and archive services being relocated, with new staff often having to reassemble collections following the demise of the former local authorities. In addition, other changes which included new telephone and fax numbers, Email and Internet addresses, new people to contact, larger and new collections of material being assembled, meant that a second edition was needed.

Many records and much archival material is linked to the administrative institutions at the time the records were created. It is essential that researchers are able to relate the areas of their studies to the institutions operating during the time spread of their searches. The three main administrative areas, in Scotland, before 1975 were the **Counties**, **Burghs** and **Parishes**. The counties developed from the **Sheriffdoms** of the middle ages, which became known as **Shires** and later **Counties**. In the mid-eighteenth century some changes were made to the shire boundaries. The Local Government (Scotland) Act of 1889 instituted further rationalisation. The map shows the counties for the period 1890-1975. There have been differing types of **Burghs** over the centuries and as towns grew in size their boundaries were altered. However, in 1975, both Counties and Burghs ceased to exist when local government was reorganised with the introduction of a two-tier structure of nine **Regional** and fifty-three **District** councils, plus three **Islands** councils. It was all change again in 1996 when twenty-nine unitary authorities took over local administration on the mainland. The three Islands councils remained.

For most people living outwith the Burghs, the Parish was the administrative area that directly affected their lives. Parish administration had both religious and civil connotations that gradually changed during the latter part of the last century. Parishes had been concerned with ecclesiastical matters such as religious observances and moral behaviour, and civil matters such as the provision of poor relief and education. The three Statistical Accounts of Scotland (see previous chapter) provide the best source of information about parishes for three periods in Scottish history. They were published at the end of the eighteenth century, the 1830s and 1840s and during the period 1951-1993. For a list of the Parishes linked to their Counties and Commissariots, refer to *Tracing Your Scottish Ancestry* (1996) by Kathleen B Cory.

Before referring to the Directory readers should be aware of some of the restrictions placed on certain groups of archival material under 'closure rules', and the basic rules covering copying and copyright constraints.

Two groups of records are **'closed'** (not available to the general public for consultation) **for 100 years**. The most frequently used records in this category are the **Census Records** (Enumerators' Books). In the Directory, under genealogical sources, the reference 'CEN 41-91' shows that the Resource Centre has microform copies of the census returns for the years 1841/1851/1861/1871/1881/1891. This

rule means that researchers will not be able to consult the 1901 census returns until 2001. There may be a delay before all the resource centres who hold genealogical material are in a position to purchase a microform version of the 1901 census. However, if a family has forebears who came from, or, who lived in Ireland, then it is possible to view the 1901 Irish census returns in Northern Ireland and the 1901 and 1911 censuses for the whole of Ireland in the Republic of Ireland.

There is also a **100-year closure period on Health Board records** containing personal information. **Many governmental records are 'closed' for 30 years**. Government Departments and the National Archives of Scotland will advise enquirers which records are affected by these rules.

Every researcher will, at some time, wish to obtain **photocopies, microform and photographic prints** of the material he/she wishes to consult or has been consulting. The Copyright, Designs and Patents Act 1988 affects both the holders of the material and the person wishing to obtain copies of the material. Researchers will need to ascertain the restrictions, discuss their requirements and the costs of obtaining copies with the organisation holding the material. This is especially true in the case of copying photographs and maps.

Under the Act, a 'prescribed' library or archive may do certain things in relation to original works still in copyright which are literary (includes computer programs), dramatic, musical or artistic works. The copyright of such material lasts for fifty years from the death of the author or from the end of 1989, whichever is the later. Exceptions are Crown Copyright, which lasts for 125 years from the year of creation, and, copyright in anonymous works, which runs for fifty years from the year the work was made available to the public.

Under Section 43 of the Act, the material must be available for consultation and not subject to any limitations imposed by a depositor. The library or archive may supply a copy of such material to a member of the public provided that (a) it is required for study or research only, (b) only one copy is supplied, (c) it is paid for at a price not less than the cost attributable to its production, and (d) the copyright holder or depositor has not forbidden copying. The copying of artistic works, which include maps, drawings, paintings and photographs, can be copied in accordance with Section 29 which relates to 'fair dealing'. This is interpreted as no more than 5% of a publication or one article from a journal or magazine. **NOTE: Ordnance Survey maps** less than **50** years old may not be copied without the permission of the Ordnance Survey, Romsey Road, Maybush, Southampton SO16 4GU.

In this electronic age more and more researchers are using **laptop computers** instead of 'pencil and paper' to make notes on what they find when reading archival material, rare books or documents. The larger archive centres usually set aside special places for the use of laptop computers. It is always advisable that researchers contact the library or archive centre they propose to visit to find out if laptop computers can be used and if the designated space(s) have to be booked in advance.

# USING THE DIRECTORY

The information provided in the Directory was supplied by the organisations featured in it between March and October 1998. Inevitably changes will have taken place between the time the information was received and publication. The Scottish Library Association will be pleased to receive information on any changes that have taken place, or, when changes occur in the future. For their address refer to the chapter, The Sponsors. A few of the organisations approached did not wish to be included in the Directory. These were mostly smaller organisations run by volunteers who do not have the resources to deal with enquiries from a distance.

The first and largest part of the Directory features resource centres plus a small number of societies who regularly produce historical publications. The second part lists small societies who collect historical material covering their own area but do not yet have a resource centre.

**The sequence of the Directory entries is by their town/village location in alphabetical order**, except for some smaller organisations to be found in the Western and Northern Isles when the Island name is used. All the organisations can be contacted by telephone, many by fax and increasingly by Email and the via Internet.

The **general summary** provides a brief description of the material held by the resource centre. For small organisations details of any archival material held by them will also be included.

One or two, usually named persons, are given as **Contacts** who can provide information about their collections and/or who can be consulted about specific aspects of the collections. A third Contact, or, more usually the person who should be contacted to arrange an appointment to visit the resource centre, is indicated by an asterisk (*). As most of the Contacts in the public institutions usually work 'office hours' (Monday to Friday 0900-1700), or, in the case of libraries variable hours, **prior contact is advisable (PCA)**. In many cases the Contacts have requested that visits to their institution must be **by appointment only (BAO)**.

An indication is given when **entrance fees** are charged or where **donations** are sought by organisations. Increasingly public institutions and some societies are charging for the time taken by their staff when asked to provide detailed information and/or undertake research projects for people unable to visit them. In 1998, charges for research undertaken by institutions, and, in a few cases, for the consultation of records, varied from £1 to £15 per hour. However media organisations' charges ranged from £40 to £60 per hour. It is imperative that if a reader proposes to ask for work to be undertaken on his/her behalf that a written quotation is obtained in advance. This should indicate what information could be supplied, in what form and at what cost. Usually no charges are made when researchers undertake research work themselves 'on the premises'. This is being made easier by the increasing availability of electronic finding aids.

**Hours of opening** usually refer to the days and times when the resource centre is open to the general public. Some archives, often those within museums, have restricted times for access. These are also indicated.

Brief **location details** are provided, including the proximity of public transport and car parking facilities. Distances up to 0.5 mile from the resource centre are shown as 'nearby' with the actual distance given in miles thereafter. Almost all of the parking and bus routes will be within 0.25 miles, but, bus and rail stations in larger towns are almost always between 0.25 and 0.5 miles from resource centres. Where provided a 'disabled access' is indicated.

The **Primary material** section lists, in summary form, the range of material held by the organisations. More detailed information can usually be provided by the resource centres by means of lists or leaflets.

Today, **Finding aids** are many and various, from hand written and type written lists, card indexes, electronic databases through to CDROMs.

**Leaflets** include lists, leaflets and books relating to the collections and publications featuring aspects of the history of an area. Except for some publicity material all institutions will make a charge for supplying and posting their publications - they will supply a price list on request.

**Reprographics**: Unless indicated otherwise, all the organisations listed in the Directory will be able to supply photocopies, usually A3 and A4, with many offering microform printing and photographic services. These are indicated by the abbreviations R1 - R5 (see the next section). All will supply information about their services and charges on request. Note the information on copyright and copying referred to in the previous chapter.

## ABBREVIATIONS

In order to save space acronyms and abbreviations have been used throughout the Directory. During this decade there has been a significant increase in the amount of genealogical material held by leading libraries and many of the family history and newer heritage societies. As the range of this material is usually the same at most of the locations, albeit covering the immediate area of the location, abbreviations have been used to show this.

| Abbreviation | Expansion |
| --- | --- |
| - (after date) | sequence continues to the present |
| * | Indicates the person to contact to arrange a visit, or, the 3rd Contact in larger organisations |
| # | Indicates a participant in the Scottish Archive Network project |
| B/M/D | Births/Marriages/Deaths |
| BAO | By appointment only |
| BAP | Baptisms |
| BR | Births |
| C | century: 17C = 17th century |
| c | circa |
| CEN | Census records, usually 1841-1891 |
| CH | Christenings |

| | |
|---|---|
| D | Deaths |
| DIR | Directories |
| DIV | Divorce |
| E | East |
| ER | Electoral Registers/Voters Rolls |
| GEN | Genealogical material includes: |
| GRO | General Register Office |
| IGI | International Genealogical Index. |
| | IGI versions in brackets: S - Scotland; E - England; I - Ireland; |
| | GB - Great Britain; UK - United Kingdom; BI - British Isles. |
| incl | include(s)ing |
| IND | Indexes |
| LDS | Church of Jesus Christ of Latter Day Saints; The Mormon Church |
| MAR | Marriages |
| mfiche | microfiche |
| mfilm | microfilm |
| mform | microform (film and fiche) |
| MI | Monument (gravestone) Inscriptions |
| ml | mile(s) |
| MS | manuscript(s) |
| N | North |
| NAS | National Archives of Scotland |
| NLS | National Library of Scotland |
| NMR(S) | National Monuments Record of Scotland |
| NRA(S) | National Register of Archives for Scotland |
| OBITS | Obituaries |
| OPRs | Old Parish Registers, pre 1855 |
| OS | Ordnance Survey (maps) |
| PC | Personal computer |
| PCA | Prior contact/consultation advisable |
| RCAHMS | Royal Commission on the Ancient and Historical Monuments of |
| | Scotland |
| Rd | Road |
| S | South |
| SCRAN | Scottish Cultural Resources Access Network |
| Sq | Square |
| SRO | Scottish Record Office (now NAS) |
| St | Street |
| VR | Valuation Rolls |
| W | West |
| WWI/II | World War One/Two |
| WWW | World Wide Web; Web; Internet |
| **Reprographics:** | |
| R1 | Photocopies A3/A4 |
| R2 | Microfilm (mfilm) copies A4 |
| R3 | Microfiche (mfiche) copies A4 |
| R4 | Microfilm and microfiche copies A4 |
| R5 | Photographic service provided/available, or by arrangement with |
| | a commercial organisation - information supplied on request |
| (b&w,col) | black & white and colour copies |

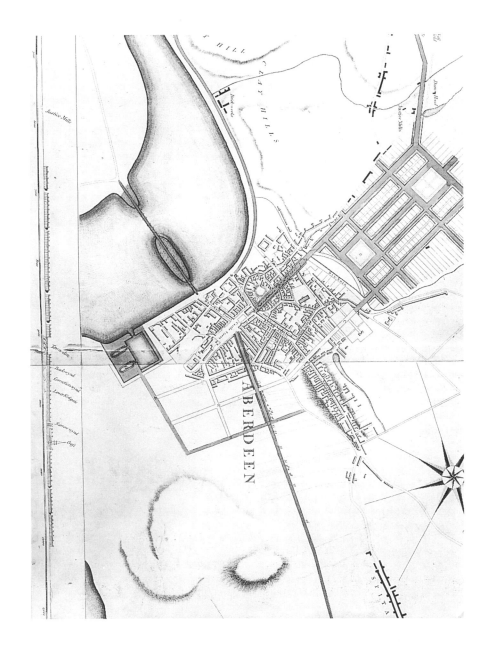

**Plan of Aberdeen c1796 (NAS ref: RHP.2014)**

## Aberdeen

**1 Aberdeen & North East Scotland Family History Society**
**164 King Street, Aberdeen AB24 5BD**
*Tel: 01224 646323  Fax: 01224 639096*
**Email: anesfhs@rsc.co.uk**
**http://www.rsc.co.uk/anesfhs**

Reference library of mainly NE Scotland source material plus some UK, Canada and Australia. Genealogical books covering all Scotland; exchange journals with all Scottish FH Societies.
(1) The Secretary: V Murray
Access: Mon-Fri 1000-1600; Sat 1000-1300; Tue, Fri 1900-2200 (members only). BAO
Charges: Free to members; charges for visitors.
*200 yards N of Castlegate (E end Union St); rail station 0.75 ml, on bus routes, parking nearby; partial disabled access.*
Primary sources: OPRs and Census 1841-1891 for whole of NE Scotland; 1841 Census for all counties north of Nairn. OPR indexes to pre-1855 baptisms and marriages of the Church of Scotland; Indexes to GRO births, marriages and deaths 1837-1900; GRO Consular Birth Indexes in 5 year batches 1849-1994; Consular Marriage Indexes in 5 year batches 1849-1994 and Consular Death Indexes in 5 year batches 1849-1965; UK High Commision Marriage Indexes 1950-1965; IGI 1981 Scotland, 1988 World, 1991 UK & Commonwealth countries. Transcripts for many gravestone inscriptions of NE Scotland (published and MS form).
Finding aids: In-house library catalogue; printed index to Members' Records of Ancestors Charts; computer disk for Index to Gravestone Transcriptions.
Leaflets: Publications list, also on WWW.
Reprographics: R1, R4

**# 2 Aberdeen City Archives & Town Clerk's Library**
**Town House, Aberdeen AB10 1AQ**
*Tel: 01224 522513  Fax: 01224 522491*

Town Clerk's Library; local history books and pamphlets covering Aberdeen and NE Scotland, mainly 19C, c2000 items.
(1) Duty Archivist
Access: Wed-Fri 0930-1630. BAO
*E end of Union St (use Union St entrance); rail & bus stations, bus routes, parking nearby; disabled access.*
Primary sources: City Archives: Archives of Royal Burgh of Aberdeen 12C-1975; Burgh of Old Aberdeen 17C-1891; Burgh of Woodside 19C; deposited

collections include: Aberdeen Congregational churches 1790-1980;
Aberdeen Presbytery 1843-1988, Hall Russell Shipbuilders 19/20C,
Northern Co-operative Society 1860-1980.
Leaflets: Available.
Reprographics: R1, R2, R5

# # 3 Aberdeen City Archives: Old Aberdeen House Branch
## Old Aberdeen House, Dunbar Street, Aberdeen AB24 1UE
### Tel: 01224 481775  Fax: 01224 495830

Archives relate to the former counties of Aberdeen, Banff, Kincardine and
Moray and the City of Aberdeen (education and valuation records only), plus
most of the Burghs in these counties.
(1) Duty Archivist
Access: Mon-Wed 0930-1300, 1400-1630. BAO
*Near King's College, Old Aberdeen, 1 ml N of city centre; bus routes, parking
nearby; disabled access.*
Primary sources: Records of parochial boards/parish councils 1845-1930;
Commissioners of Supply and county councils 17C-1975; town councils
mainly 19C-1975 (Banff from 17C); Schools 19C-1975; valuation and
electoral rolls - varying dates and runs for counties (except Moray) and
burghs, incl. Aberdeen city; Burgh council minutes for Aberchirder, Banff,
Macduff, Old Meldrum, Peterhead, Portsoy, Rosehearty, Stonehaven and
Turriff.
Leaflets: Leaflet gives dates and runs.
Reprographics: R1, R5

# 4 Aberdeen City Council: Museums & Art Galleries
## Section: Aberdeen Art Gallery
## Schoolhill, Aberdeen AB10 1FQ
### Tel: 01224 646333  Fax: 01224 632133

Fine Art Section includes views of Scotland, portraits of eminent Scots,
archive material relating to William Dyce, Sir George Reid and James
McBey. Archaeological Unit hold collections from the City of Aberdeen and
Aberdeenshire, with associated documentation.
(1) Keeper, Fine Art: Jennifer Melville
(2) Keeper, Applied Art: Christine Rew
(*) Keeper, Archaeology: Judith Stones
Access: Mon-Sat 1000-1700, Sun 1400-1700. PCA.
*In city centre; rail & bus stations, bus routes nearby; disabled access.*
Primary sources: Applied Art: photographs of local costume, business
papers (local) relating to haberdashery and dressmaking; some letters on
local suffrage acitivites; Bill Gibb archive of drawings and ephemera.
Archaeological Unit: Archives of excavations in City of Aberdeen since 1973,
incl. reports, plans, photographs.
Leaflets: Archaeological publications lists.
Reprographics: R1, R5

**5  Aberdeen City Council: Reference & Local Studies Department**

**Central Library, Rosemount Viaduct, Aberdeen AB25 1GW**

*Tel: 01224 652512  Fax: 01224 624118*

**Email: refloc@globalweb.co.uk**

Collection covers the City of Aberdeen (minutes & publications of the Council) and the counties of Aberdeen, Banff and Kincardine. Includes c15000 books, pamphlets, newspapers, maps, photographs and genealogical material.

(1) Contact : C Taylor

Access: Mon-Fri 0900-2000; Sat 0900-1700. PCA especially if wishing to consult newspapers not available on microfilm.

*In city centre; beside car park; rail & bus stations nearby, on bus routes; disabled access.*

Primary sources: The extensive local newspaper collection includes Aberdeen's Journal/Aberdeen Journal/Press & Journal (1747-) and Aberdeeen Evening Express/Evening Express(1879-); 2000+ maps 1654- incl. city plans, railway, harbour, road and canal plans, estate and feuing plans, architectural drawings and OS maps; c15000 photographic images 1870-; special collections of fishing craft, farming life, city air raid damage, and George Washington Wilson photographs (see also Aberdeeen University Library entry); ephemera includes theatre programmes, posters, playbills etc. GEN: CEN, OPRs, VR, ER, DIR (1824-1982).

Finding aids: Card index of local printed collection.

Leaflets: Publications list.

Reprographics: R1 (b&w, col), R5

**6  Aberdeen Journals Ltd**

**Lang Stracht, Mastrick, Aberdeen AB15 6DF**

*Tel: 01224 690222 x3172  Fax: 01224 699575*

**Email: editor@pj.ajl.co.uk**

**http://www.presssandjournal.co.uk**

Press and Journal & Evening Express, photographs and cuttings from 1950s covering the north of Scotland.

(1) Librarian: Duncan Smith

(2) Contact : Ken MacKay

(*) Contact : Bob Stewart

Access: Mon-Fri 1300-1600. BAO

*2 ml NW of city centre & rail station; on bus route, parking; disabled access.*

Primary sources: Press and Journal (from 1939) and Evening Express (from 1962) can be seen at the Aberdeen Central Library, Rosemount Viaduct on microfilm.

Finding aids: Card index system for cuttings. From Oct 1997 material on CDRom.

Reprographics: R5

## 7 Aberdeen Maritime Museum: Lloyds Register of Shipping Library
### Shiprow, Aberdeen AB11 5BY
*Tel: 01224 337700  Fax: 01224 213066*

Library houses collections of engineering and shipbuilding drawings; records of Aberdeen's maritime life: ships' documents, Masters Certificates, passengers' diaries; engineering and business records with runs of periodicals.
(1) Assistant Keeper - Maritime History: Catherine Gollogley (Tel: 01224 337713)
(2) Assistant Keeper - Science and Industry: Michael Dey (Tel: 01224 337719)
Access: Museum: Mon-Sat 1000-1700, Sun 1100-1700. Library: Mon-Fri 1000-1200 (BAO).
Charges: Museum admission charges.
*In city centre; rail & bus stations, parking nearby; disabled access arranged.*
Primary sources: c10000 shipbuilding plans - Lewis Shipyard 1920s-1960s, Hall Russell Shipyard 1920s-1980s (with specification books and ships' documentation); Lloyds Register of Shipping 1778-1995; c20000 photographs cover many aspects of Aberdeen's maritime history; periodicals (various) with runs 1911-89; business papers relating to: the granite industry; Davidson & Kay (chemists with ledgers, prescription books 1890s-1960s); William McKinnon & Co (plantation and general engineers c1900-1930); small collection of family photographs (200+) and letter from Royal Family to George Washington Wilson (photographer) - see also Aberdeen University Library entry.
Finding aids: Shipbuilders & plans lists.
Leaflets: Lloyds register leaflet.
Reprographics: R1, R5, limited plan copying.

## # 8 Aberdeen University Library: Department of Special Collections & Archives
### King's College, Aberdeen AB24 3SW
*Tel: 01224 272598  Fax: 01224 273891*
### Email: speclib@abdn.ac.uk
### http://www.abdn.ac.uk/library

The local collection covers all aspects of the culture and history of the NE Scotland 18-20C, incl. books, pamphlets, periodicals, plans, maps and photographs; 3000+ MS and archival collections: the O'Dell collection covers Scottish railways, the MacBean collection of 4000 books, plus articles, pamphlets and prints on the Jacobites; the Simpson collection of c250 books plus pamphlets compiled by Dr W Douglas Simpson, an authority on Scottish castellated architecture; the Thomson, Herald, King collections of pamphlets in almost 1000 vols. were gathered in the 19C by a local landed gentleman, a local newspaper office and a local printer; the pi and SB collections of early printed material (pre 1841) include much of Scottish interest.
Access: Mon-Fri 0930-1630. PCA.

*Within King's College campus, 2 ml N of city centre & main rail & bus stations; on bus route; limited parking; disabled access.*
Primary sources: Local collection: large collection of pamphlets 19-20C runs of several local and other Scottish newspapers, some on microfilm, notably the unique almost complete run of the Aberdeen Journal (indexed to 1861, later Press and Journal); Aberdeen Almanac from 1774, Aberdeen Directory from 1824; local valuation rolls; all material printed in Aberdeen before 1801, emphasis on University. MS and Archives: the University's own archives, from 1495; non-archival collections relating to the three constituent Universities; records of local families, estates, institutions and firms. O'Dell Collection: large collection of printed books, plans and sections; timetables; scrapbooks, incl. MS letters and notes. Some GNSR and LNER archival material. MacBean Collection: contemporary publications; prints of historical and topographical scenes; 19C photographs of Scottish topography. Simpson Collection: 5500 glass lantern slides, mainly Scottish archaeological antiquities. MS additions to author's own works. George Washington Wilson Collection: about 40000 glass photographic negatives, c1860-1908, of most parts of Scotland, serving the tourist trade, but incl. much of social and industrial interest (indexed by place and subject) (see also Aberdeen City Library entry).
Finding aids: Aberdeen University Library catalogue at www.abdn.ac.uk/library/catalog/index.html. Gateway to the Department's digital resources & searchable database of descriptive lists available at www.abdn.ac.uk/library/introduction.hmtl; copies of summary & descriptive lists & Guide to manuscripts & archives available. Aberdeen Journal Index 1748-1861; Misc indexes to local periodicals. Catalogue of pamphlets in the King, the Thomson, & the Herald Collections & the MacBean Collection.
Leaflets: Special Collection and George Washington Wilson Collection leaflets.
Reprographics: R1, R2, R5

## 9    Aberdeen University Library: Queen Mother Library
## Meston Walk, Aberdeen AB24 3EU
*Tel: 01224 272579  Fax: 01224 487048*
## Email: library@abdn.ac.uk
## http://www.abdn.ac.uk/library
The Queen Mother library has a general collection of 19/20C historical and topographical material incl. an extensive collection of OS maps and directories and historical runs of periodicals and record society publications.
(1) Enquiry Desk
Access: Mon-Sat 0900-2200; Sun 1400-2200 (term-time). Mon-Fri 0900-1700; Sat 0900-1300 (vacations). PCA.
*Within King's College campus, approx. 2 ml N of city centre & main rail & bus stations; on bus route, limited parking; disabled access.*
Finding aids: Aberdeen University Library catalogue at www.abdn.ac.uk/library/catalog/index.htm/
Leaflets: Library welcome leaflet.
Reprographics: R1, R5

**10  Aberdeen University Library: Taylor Library**
**Taylor Building, Old Aberdeen, Aberdeen AB24 6UB**
*Tel: 01224 272601  Fax: 01224 273893*
**Email: v.stevenson@abdn.ac.uk**
**http://www.abdn.ac.uk/library**
Library holds historical runs of parliamentary papers.
(1) Contact : Valerie Stevenson
Access: Mon-Sat 0900-2200; Sun 1400-2200 (term-time). Mon-Fri 0900-
1700; Sat 0900-1300 (vacations). PCA.
*Within King's College campus, 2 ml N of city centre & main rail & bus
stations; on bus route; limited parking, disabled access.*
Finding aids: Aberdeen University Library catalogue at
www.abdn.ac.uk/library/catalog/index.html.
Leaflets: Library Welcome leaflet.
Reprographics: R1, R5

**11  Aberdeen University: Centre for Scottish Studies**
**William Guild Building, King's College, Aberdeen**
**AB24 2UB**
*Tel: 01224 272474/272342*
The Centre publishes books & pamphlets on aspects of local history &
historical geography of northern Scotland.
(1) Director: John S Smith (Tel: 01224 272342)
(2) Contact : M Croll (Tel: 01224 272474)
Access: Mon-Tue, Thu-Fri 1000-1400. BAO
*1.5 ml N of city centre, parking nearby.*
Leaflets: Annual journal "Northern Scotland". List available
Reprographics: Photocopies A4.

**12  Aberdeen University: Department of Geography**
**Elphinstone Road, Aberdeen AB9 2UF**
*Tel: 01224 272000  Fax: 01224 487048*
McDonald Collection of 5000 feu & estate plans, mostly of Aberdeen and NE
Scotland.
(1) Cartographic Development Officer: L McLean (Tel: 01224 272324)
Access: Mon-Fri 0300-1200; 1400-1630. PCA..
*On University campus, 1.5 ml N of city centre; parking.*
Reprographics: R1

## 13 The Economic & Social History Society of Scotland
### Dr Andrew Blaikie (Secretary), c/o Dept of Sociology, University of Aberdeen, Aberdeen AB24 3QY
*Tel: 01224 272765  Fax: 01224 273442*
### Email: a.blaikie@abdn.ac.uk
The Society promotes the study of all aspects of the economic, social & cultural history of Scotland. It publishes the refereed "Scottish Economic & Social History" twice yearly.
Leaflets: Publications list available.

## 14 Gordon Highlanders Museum
### St Luke's, Viewfield Road, Aberdeen AB15 7XH
*Tel: 01224 311200  Fax: 01224 319323*
Archive material covers the history of the Gordon Highlanders (75th and 92nd Foot), associated militia and volunteer units, 1794 to present.
(1) Curator: Stuart Allan
(2) Assistant Regimental Secretary: MNB Ross (Tel: 01224 318174)
Access: Mon-Fri 1030-1630. Archive: BAO.
Charges: No charge for research in person. Charges for research by staff.
*1.5 ml W of city centre off Queen's Rd; on bus routes, parking; limited disabled access to archives.*
Primary sources: Miscellaneous manuscript material (soldiers' diaries, letters etc). Photographs, order books, medal rolls to 1902. Incomplete set of war Battalion diaries 1914-18, 1939-45. NB. The collection does not contain official records of individual soldiers' service.
Finding aids: Limited catalogues/card index. (to be computerised).
Leaflets: Museum leaflet.
Reprographics: R1, R5

## 15 Grampian Television Library
### Queen's Cross, Aberdeen AB15 4XJ
*Tel: 01224 846581  Fax: 01224 846800*
Collection of archive news stories and programmes made by Grampian TV since 1961. News film stories from early 1960's (16mm). Programmes made by GTV held since 1960's on 1" Beta.
(1) Contact : Bill Moir
Access: Mon-Fri 0930-1630. BAO
Charges: Search charges.
*W of city centre; rail station 1 ml; bus routes nearby; parking.*
Finding aids: In-house computer system.
Reprographics: Dubs of material available - details/prices on request.

## 16 Macaulay Land Use Research Institute Library
### Craigiebuckler, Aberdeen AB15 8QH
*Tel: 01224 318611   Fax: 01224 311556*
### Email: l.robertson@mluri.sari.ac.uk
### http://www.mluri.sari.ac.uk

Comprises books on historical agriculture & land use pre 1900. Geological, land use & soil maps and surveys.

(1) Contact : Lorraine Robertson (Tel: 01224 318611 x2202)

Access: Mon-Fri 0900-12.30; 1400-16.30. BAO

*W End; on bus route, parking.*

Finding aids: In-house catalogue/index.

Leaflets: Publications list.

Reprographics: R1

## 17 Northern College: Aberdeen Campus Library
### Hilton Place, Aberdeen AB24 4FA
*Tel: 01224 283571   Fax: 01224 283655*
### http://www.norcol.co.uk

Local history collection includes books, pamphlets and some periodicals relating to Aberdeen City and Grampian Region. Maps and plans of Aberdeen and environs in map collection. Primary source material in reserve collection.

(1) Senior Librarian (User Services) (Tel: 01224 283570)

Access: Mon-Fri 0900-2130; Sat 0930-1230 (term-time). Mon-Fri 0900-1700 (vacations). PCA.

*1.5 ml NW of city centre; local rail station, bus routes nearby, parking; disabled access by arrangement.*

Primary sources: Aberdeen Church of Scotland Training College records of classes 1874/5-1905/7, registers of marks 1896/7-1900/1, registers of students 1874-1906, various results, reports, documents, press cuttings 1887-1905; Aberdeen United Free Church Training College registers of marks 1890/5-1906/7, teaching practice record books 1876-1906/8; Aberdeen Training Centre register of students admitted 1906–49, register of students admitted under Chapter V 1907-50, register of students admitted under Chapter VI 1907–49, register of marks 1910-48, minutes of meetings (Aberdeen Provincial Committee) 1905-59, photographs of principals, lecturers and students 1875-1949, press cuttings 1909-59, cuttings of job advertisements 1913-66; Aberdeen College of Education minutes of meetings 1962-87, quadrennial reports 1967/71-1979/83, triennial report 1964/67; Aberdeen T.C. (later College of Education) Demonstration School admission register 1934-68, register of leavers 1925-70, summary registers 1967-70, daily register 1952-57, 1968-70, log books 1888-1970, record books and miscellaneous papers 1846-1970, register of admission etc 1909-34.

Leaflets: Guide to library services (Aberdeen Library).

Reprographics: R1

## # 18 Northern Health Services Archives
## Aberdeen Royal Infirmary, Woolmanhill, Aberdeen
## AB25 1LD
### Tel: 01224 663123/663456

The Health Board's archives contain the records of most of the hospitals and health authorities which once existed or still exist in the Grampian area. These date mainly from the mid/late 19C although some record series date from the 1740s. The archivist also has information on hospital/health records belonging to Highland Health Board.

(1) Archivist: F R Watson (Tel: x55562)

Access: Mon-Fri 0900-1700. BAO

*In city centre; rail & bus stations, bus routes, parking nearby; disabled access.*

Primary sources: Minutes, financial records, patient and staff registers, case notes, nurse training records, annual reports, plans and photographs from over 50 hospitals and nursing homes in the North East; administrative records of bodies set up under various National Health Service (Scotland) Acts (the North-Eastern Regional Hospital Board, Grampian Health Board and their respective constituent boards/units); records of insurance committees, executive councils and local medical committees; some material from local authority health departments incl. annual reports of medical officers of health, registers of notification of infectious diseases and tuberculosis.

Finding aids: In-house - catalogues, card & computerised indexes.

Leaflets: Leaflet notes closure periods of some records.

Reprographics: R1, R5

## 19 The Robert Gordon University: Architecture & Surveying Library
## Garthdee Road, Aberdeen AB10 7QE
### Tel: 01224 263450  Fax: 01224 262889
## Email: library@rgu.ac.uk
## http://www.rgu.ac.uk/library/

A collection of material relating to 25 architects practicing in the Aberdeen area 19-mid 20C, incl. plans, drawings and photographs; and incl. minute book of the Aberdeen Society of Architects early 20C.

(1) Contact : Jim Fiddes

Access: Mon-Thu 0900-2045; Fri 0900-1700; Sun 1300-1645 (term-time). Mon-Fri 0900-1700 (Vacation). PCA.

*2 ml SW of city centre; on bus route, parking; disabled access.*

Finding aids: Indexing underway.

Reprographics: R1

**20 Rowett Research Institute: Reid Library**
**Greenburn Road, Bucksburn, Aberdeen AB21 9SB**
*Tel: 01224 712751 Fax: 01224 715349*
**Email: m.mowat@rri.sari.ac.uk**
**http://www/rri.sari.ac.uk**
18-19C books (120) & journals (13 titles) from the libraries of Sir Archibald
Grant of Monymusk, Collingwood Lindsay Wood of Freeland and others
covering land improvement, agricultural reform/development, animal
husbandry, forestry & gardening.
(1) Contact : Mary Mowat (Tel: 01224 712751 x4336)
(2) Contact : Karen Barclay (Tel: 01224 712751 x4114)
Access: Mon-Fri 0830-1730. BAO
*6 ml NW of Aberdeen off A96; bus routes nearby; parking; limited disabled
access.*
Primary sources: Archival material relating to the early work of the Institute,
incl. books, journals, photographs, ephemera & transcripts relating to the
work of the first Director, Sir John Boyd Orr (1880-1971).
Finding aids: Rowett Research archive lists (also on computer database).
Reprographics: R1

## Airdrie

**21 North Lanarkshire Libraries: Airdrie Library**
**Wellwynd, Airdrie ML6 0AG**
*Tel: 01236 763221 Fax: 01236 766027*
The local collection includes books, pamphlets, business and estate papers,
union and church records, newspapers and photographs covering the Airdrie
and Coatbridge (Monklands) area.
(1) Contact : Margaret Bell
Access: Mon-Tue, Thu-Fri 1000-1900, Wed 0900-1200, Sat 0900-1700.
PCA.
Charges: Genealogical search charges.
*In town centre; rail station, bus routes nearby; disabled access to ground
floor only (no microfiche reader but access possible at other location).*
Primary sources: Airdrie Burgh minutes 1821-1975; Coatbridge Burgh
minutes 1885-1975; records of societies: Airdrie weavers 1759-1964, Airdrie
Female Benevolent 1895-1961, Airdrie Veteran's Club 1941-8, Chapelhall
Reading Room 1851-1925, First of August Friendly 1790-1915 etc;
newspapers include Airdrie & Coatbridge Advertiser 1855-; Mrs Spier's
postcard collection 1905-44; photographs c2000 1860-; maps and plans
1767-1991; GEN: CEN, OPRs VR.
Finding aids: Collections on library catalogue.
Reprographics: R1, R4, R5

Advertisement for 'McVitie's Digestive Biscuits' in 1928
(NAS ref: GD.381/3/30)

## Alexandria

### 22 West Dunbartonshire Libraries: Alexandria Library/Heritage Centre
**Gilmour Street, Alexandria G83 0DA**
*Tel: 01389 753425/759565  Fax: 01389 710550*

Heritage collection includes 600+ photographs 1890s-; newspaper cuttings; OS maps covering the Vale of Leven and Loch Lomondside. GEN: CEN, OPRs, VR, ER.
(1) Contact : Arthur Jones (Tel: 01389 723273)
(2) Contact : Graham Hopner (Tel: 01389 723273)
(*) Contact : Rhoda MacLeod (Tel: 01389 723273)
Access: BAO
*In town centre; rail station, bus routes, parking nearby.*
Finding aids: Card index; information cards.
Reprographics: R1, R5

## Alford

### 23 Grampian Transport Museum
**Alford AB33 8AE**
*Tel: 019755 62292  Fax: 019755 62180*

Collection covers transport development in the North-East of Scotland: Photographs, slides, vehicle manuals, magazines (incl. a complete set of Railway Magazine);
(1) Curator: Mike Ward
Access: Mon-Sun 1000-1700 (Apr-Oct). PCA.
*Off Main St; 25 ml W of Aberdeen; limited bus service, parking; disabled access.*
Finding aids: Indexes for periodicals, technical literature, general & specific subjects.
Reprographics: R5.

## Alloa

### 24 Clackmannan Libraries Archives & Walter Murray Local Studies Collection
**26-28 Drysdale Street, Alloa FK10 1JL**
*Tel: 01259 722262  Fax: 01259 219469*
**Email: clack.lib@mail.easysnet.co.uk**

Collections comprise books, pamphlets, ephemera, slides, photographs, maps (from 1860s), local newspapers plus genealogical material (CEN, OPR, MI, VR, ER, DIR, LISTS, IGI); together with archival records of organisations and individuals.

(1) Information Librarian & Archivist: Ian Murray
(2) Info Librarian & Archivist Asst: Liz McPartlin
Access: Mon, Wed-Fri 0930-1900; Tue 0930-1630; Sat 0900-1230. No
archive material available after 1700 or on Sat.
*In town centre, at rear of Alloa Library; on bus routes, parking at rear;
disabled access.*
Primary sources: Newspapers (microfilm); Clackmannanshire Advertiser
1844-1859, Alloa Journal 1854-1972, Alloa Advertiser 1850-1972, Alloa
Advertiser & Journal 1972-present, Tillicoultry News 1879-1900, Devon
Valley Tribune 1899-1953, Fifeshire Journal 1833-1870; Alloa Circular 1893-
1971; Wee County News 1995-. Local government material from 1660,
mostly pre-1975 County of Clackmannan and burghs of Alloa, Alva, Dollar
and Tillicoultry, plus pre-1975 district councils and post 1975 local
authorities (minutes), Annual Register for County of Clackmannan (later
County Register) 1874-1912; colliery plans and mineral reports; Alloa Grain
Market; Clackmannanshire Agricultural Society; British Women's
Temperance Association (Alloa Branch).
Leaflets: Publications list (over 70 items).
Reprographics: R1 (b&w, col), R4

## Annan

### 25   Historic Resources Centre
### Bank Street, Annan DG12 6AA
### *Tel: 01461 201384   Fax: 01461 205876*
Local history collection includes maps, photographs (1000+) and local
governement records for Annandale and Eskdale.
(1) Contact : Lesley Botten
Access: Mon-Fri 0900-1700. BAO
*In town centre; bus & rail services nearby; disabled access.*
Primary sources: Annan Town Council archives; minutes books (1678-1975);
valuation rolls (1883-1979); and other papers; Dean of Guild Court Plans,
Annan and Lockerbie (1880-1974); some local history books, articles,
photographs and reference materials. MS, photographs relating to
boilermaking by Cochrans Boilers 1898-. Survey of buildings in Annan.
Reprographics: R1

# Anstruther

## 26 Scottish Fisheries Museum
## St. Ayles, Harbourhead, Anstruther KY10 3AB
*Tel: 01333 310628*

Library (c1000vols); photographs (c9000); and documents covering the fishing industry of the past 200 years. Includes boat building plans & drawings from Miller's Boatyard, St.Monans. Some Anstruther local history items.

(1) Curator

(2) Manager

Access: BAO for library & reserve collections

Charges: Admission charges to museum.

*On harbour front; on bus routes, parking opposite; disabled access to museum & library.*

Finding aids: Reference library fully indexed (manual system). Archival material being catalogued.

Leaflets: Publications - guide book and leaflets.

Reprographics: R1, R5

# Arbroath

## 27 Angus Council: Arbroath Library
## Hill Terrace, Arbroath DD11 1AH
*Tel: 01241 872248*

Collection of books covering the Arbroath area, with maps, newspapers, photographs, Arbroath Year Book & genealogical material.

(1) Librarian: Teresa Roby

Access: Mon, Wed 0930-2000; Tue, Thu 0930-1800; Fri-Sat 0930-1700.

*In town centre; rail station, bus routes, parking nearby; disabled access.*

Primary sources: Newspapers: Arbroath Herald 1885-1991; Arbroath Guide 1884-1978; 2000 photographs from 1880; OS maps; 40+ oral history interviews; GEN: CEN,OPRs, MI, VR, ER, DIR(1891-1956), IGI(S).

Finding aids: Subject index; photographs & newspapers partly indexed.

Reprographics: R1, R2, R5

## 28 Angus Council: Signal Tower Museum
## Signal Tower, Ladyloan, Arbroath
*Tel: 01241 875598*

Collection of maps, prints, drawings, photographs, portraits and local history files.

(1) Contact : Margaret H King

Access: Mon-Sat 1000-1700 (Sep-Jun). Mon-Sat 1000-1700, Sun 1400-1700 (Jul-Aug). PCA.

*Former shore base for Bell Rock Lighthouse staff, close to Arbroath Harbour; parking; disabled access (ground floor only).*

Primary sources: Arbroath shipping index; Arbroath trades index 1880-; list of Arbroath burgesses; Shanks Lawnmower archive; Bellrock Lighthouse archive; fishing boat index from present day working backwards.
Reprographics: R1, R5

## Ardersier

### 29  Queen's Own Highlanders
### Regimental Museum Library, Fort George, Ardersier IV1 2TD
#### *Tel: 01463 224380  Fax: 01463 224380*
Correspondence to: Cameron Barracks, Inverness, IV2 3XD. Regimental records and documents, photographs, publications. Does NOT include personal records which are held by Public Records Office, Kew, and Army Records Office, Hayes.
(1) The Curator (on Wednesdays)
(2) The Chief Clerk
Access: Mon-Fri 1000-1800 (Apr-Sep). Mon-Fri 1000-1600 (Oct-Mar). BAO
Charges: Nil (but visitors pay Historic Scotland for admission to Fort George).
*At Fort George 12 ml NE of Inverness; parking & bus route nearby; disabled may obtain chairs by arrangement with Historic Scotland.*
Primary sources: Photograph file and albums; MS diaries, regimental orders and records; letters; some enlistment books; published histories of 72nd, 78th, 79th Highlanders; Seaforth Highlanders; The Queen's Own Cameron Highlanders; Queen's Own Highlanders; Lovat Scouts; Ross Militia; Inverness Militia (most of collection is on microfilm).
Finding aids: Museum computer.
Leaflets: Museum leaflet.
Reprographics: Photocopies A4.

## Ardrossan

### 30  North Ayrshire Libraries: Local History Library
### 39-41 Princes Street, Ardrossan KA22 8BT
#### *Tel: 01294 469137  Fax: 01294 604236*
#### Email: reference@naclibhq.prestel.co.uk
Extensive collection of historical material with emphasis on North Ayrshire (books, maps, photographs and archival material). Includes the Alexander Wood Memorial Library of c4000 vols. covering Ayrshire mostly 18 & 19C.
(1) Local History Librarian: Jill McColl
(2) Reference Librarian: Sandra Kerr
Access: Mon-Tue, Thu-Fri 0930-1700; Sat 1000-1300, 1400-1700. BAO
Charges: Staff search charges.
*In town centre; rail station, bus services nearby, parking; disabled access.*

Primary sources: Primary source material includes: Newspapers - Ardrossan and Saltcoats Herald, Arran and West Coast Advertiser 1853-; Records of: Royal Burgh of Irvine from 16C, Burgh of Millport from 1864; Poor Committee of Irvine minute books 1846-1930; Cunningham of Auchenharvie Papers from 16C, with 18 and 19C coverage of local mining operations, land transactions and correspondence. Collection of photographs and postcards (000s), maps from 1630 incl. OS from 19C. GEN: CEN, OPR, MI, BR, VR, DIR, IGI (BI).
Finding aids: Printed indexes for Cunningham of Auchenharvie papers & the Archive.
Leaflets: List of publications (c30).
Reprographics: R1 (b&w, col), R2

## Ayr

## 31 Ayrshire Archaeological & Natural History Society
## 10 Robsland Avenue, Ayr KA7 2RW
Society publish books on history, archaeology & natural history of Ayrshire.
(1) Publications Officer: R W Brash (Tel: 01292 441915)
Leaflets: Publications list available.

## # 32 Ayrshire Archives
## Ayrshire Archives Centre, Craigie Estate, Ayr KA8 0SS
## Tel: 01292 287584  Fax: 01292 284918
## Email: kwilbraham@south-ayrshire.gov.uk
## http://www.south-ayrshire.gov.uk/archives/archives.htm
The Archive comprises local government records for Ayrshire together with presbytery, parish & estate records.
(1) Archivist: Kevin Wilbraham
(2) Assistant Archivist: Pauline Gallagher
Access: Tue-Thu 1000-1600. BAO
Charges: Charges for detailed historical enquiries.
*Approx.1 ml E of town centre, bus & rail stations; parking; disabled access.*
Primary sources: Official & non-official records, incl. Ayr County Council (1890-1975) and its predecessor bodies, the Commissioners of Supply (1705-1929) and the Highway Authorities (1767-1890); District Council records (1975-1996); Parish records incl. the records of the Parochial Boards and Parish Councils (1845-1930); Burgh records (13C-1975) incl. Ayr, Irvine, Prestwick, Troon, Maybole, Girvan, Darvel, Kilmarnock & Cumnock; Presbytery of Ayr records (c1641-c1980); estate records, incl. the papers of the Duke of Portland (c1800-1900); Kennedy's of Kirkmichael (1432-c1860) and the Hamilton's of Rozelle and Carluie (1734-1920); records of various businesses, societies, institutions 18-20C.
Finding aids: Lists & card index.
Leaflets: Information leaflet; record information sheets.

**33 Ayrshire Sound Archive**
**University of Paisley, Craigie Campus Library, Beech Grove, Ayr KA8 0SR**
*Tel: 01292 886266 Fax: 01292 886006*
Collection of interviews of local people made in the 1980s (c150 cassette tapes)
(1) Contact : Avril Goodwin (Tel: 01292 886265)
(2) Contact : Jack Gibson (Tel: 01292 886266)
Access: Mon-Fri 0900-1900, Sat 0900-1700 (term-time). Mon-Fri 0900-1700 (vacations) PCA.
*Approx. 1 ml E of town centre, rail & bus stations; parking.*
Finding aids: Printed catalogue.

**34 Burns Cottage**
**Alloway, Ayr KA7 4PY**
*Tel: 01292 441215 Fax: 01292 441750*
Collection of Robert Burns books; poems, biographies, manuscripts and correspondence; the Burns Family Bible and historical items.
(1) Contact : John Manson
Access: Mon-Sun 0900-1800 (Apr-Oct). Mon-Sat 1000-1600; Sun 1200-1600 (Nov-Mar). PCA.
Charges: No charge if prior notification; charges for museum.
*In Alloway village, 2 ml S of Ayr; local bus service, parking; disabled access.*
Finding aids: Catalogue of exhibits, etc.
Leaflets: Available.

**35 South Ayrshire Libraries: Scottish & Local History Library**
**Carnegie Library, 12 Main Street, Ayr KA8 8ED**
*Tel: 01292 286385 Fax: 01292 611593*
**Email: jcastle@south-ayrshire.gov.uk**
**http://www.south-ayrshire.gov.uk**
A large collection of books, articles, journals, newspapers, maps, plans, photographs and ephemera relating to Ayrshire and SW Scotland; incl. the Burns Collection (editions of poetry, criticisms, ephemera), Galt Collection (editions of John Galt's works) and the publications of the Ayrshire Archaeological and Natural History Society.
(1) Contact : Jeanette Castle
(2) Contact : Tom Barclay
Access: Mon-Tue,Thu-Fri 0900-1930; Wed, Sat 0900-1700. Advance booking for microfilm reader/printer and PCs. BAO
Charges: Local history search charges.
*Rail station 1 ml, bus station, parking nearby; disabled access possible.*

Primary sources: Local authorities minutes: Kyle and Carrick District Council (1975-1996), Burgh of Ayr (1901-75) and other Ayrshire Burghs, Ayr County Council, plus, more comprehensive records of Burgh of Ayr, incl. charters (from 13C), Poor relief minute book (1872-94), Poor House stent book (1757-1845), index for Sasines (1599-1609); Calendars of confirmation of Wills (1876-1936, 1948-59); maps from 17C; 10000 photographs from 1870s plus postcards; newspapers include: Ayrshire Post 1880- (indexed 1920-60), Ayr Advertiser 1803-, Ayr Observer 1832-1930. GEN: CEN, OPRs, MI, VR, ER, DIR, IGI.
Finding aids: Computerised catalogue.
Leaflets: Publications and general leaflets.
Reprographics: R1, R4

## Barrhead

## 36  Barrhead Community Museum
## 128 Main Street, Barrhead G76 1SG
### *Tel: 0141 876 1994*
Collection includes photographs of Barrhead, Neilston and Uplawmoor area; Barrhead Burgh material includes letter books and Dean of Guild plans (NB. Most Barrhead Burgh material is kept at the Central Library, Paisley).
(1) Contact : John Malden
Access: Mon-Sat 1030-1600 (Apr-Oct). PCA.
*Bus routes, parking nearby; disabled access.*

## Bathgate

## 37  Bennie Museum
## 9-11 Mansefield Street, Bathgate EH48 4HU
### *Tel: 01506 634944*
A collection of material relating to the Bathgate area, incl. local schools, World Wars I & II, railway, distillery, brewery, glassworks, church and buildings.
(1) Contact : W I Millan
Access: Mon-Sat 1100-1630 (Oct-Mar); 1000-1600 (Apr-Sep).
*In town centre; rail station, bus routes, parking nearby.*

## Berwick-upon-Tweed

### 38 Berwick-upon-Tweed Record Office
**Council Offices, Wallace Green, Berwick-upon-Tweed TD15 1ED**
*Tel: 01289 330044 x230  Fax: 01289 330540*
**Email: archives@berwickc.demon.co.uk**
**http://www.swinhope.demon.co.uk/genuki/nbl/northumberlandro/berwick.html**

Most archive material relates to North Northumberland but some overlaps into Scotland. Outline summary of records on WWW.
(1) Borough Archivisit: Linda Bankier
Access: Wed-Thu 0930-1300, 1400-1700. PCA.
Charges: Postal search charge.
*In town centre; rail station, bus station nearby; parking; disabled access to office.*
Primary sources: Marriages at Coldstream Bridge 1793-1797 (indexed transcript); Eyemouth Methodist Church Minute Book of Trustees meetings 1897-1910, 1913-1931; some 20C building plans and sale catalogues of Berwickshire; proceedings of Berwickshire Naturalists Club 1842-1891; River Tweed Commission Assessment Rolls or Schedule of Fisheries in River Tweed and streams running into it 1908-1924, 1926-1938; printed reports and commission re salmon fishing in Scotland and River Tweed mid 19-20C; 2nd ed. OS maps of River Tweed (Coldstream to mouth of river); Lamberton Toll marriages 1833-1849 (printed book). GEN: CEN 1891 Ber/Rox; MI pre 1985 Ber; CH/MAR pre 1855 Ber/Rox; IGI(S).
Finding aids: Family History Resources leaflet; list of genealogical publications
Leaflets: Catalogues in search room.
Reprographics: R1, R5 (limited)

## Bettyhill, By Thurso

### 39 Strathnaver Museum
**Clachan, Bettyhill, By Thurso KW14 7SS**
*Tel: 01641 521418*

Collection of photographs & documents for the Parish of Tongue & Farr; The Ian Grimble Collection of Scottish history books with Gaelic/English material covering the far north of Scotland, the Clan Mackay and the Strathnaver clearances.
(1) Contact : Pat Rudie (Tel: 01641 521418/330)
Access: Mon-Sat 1000-1300, 1400-1700 (Apr-Oct). Other times BAO.
Charges: Admission charges.
*In old parish church at E end of village; minimal bus service, parking nearby; disabled access to library/archive.*
Finding aids: Numerical card indexes & alphabetical lists.

Leaflets: Fact sheets relating to local life and the Strathnaver clearances.
Reprographics: Photocopies A4; dark room with b&w facilities by prior
arrangement

## Biggar

### 40 Biggar Museum Trust (I)
**Moat Park, Biggar ML12 6DT**
*Tel: 01899 221050*
**http://www.biggar-net.co.uk**
Collection includes books, plans, photographs, diaries covering the Upper
Clyde and Tweed valleys and Biggar area.
(1) Contact : Margaret Brown
(2) Contact : Ann Matheson
Access: Mon-Sat 1000-1700; Sun 1400-1700 (Easter-Oct). Mon-Fri 1000-
1600 (Nov-Easter). PCA as collections are in two locations
Charges: Museum admission charges.
*In town centre; bus services nearby, parking; disabled access.*
Primary sources: Town Council letter books; newscuttings 1850-; 23000
photographs of people, events & places from 1843, incl. the George Allen
collection c1937-c1970; architects' plans from 1839; Minute books & records
of Whipman Society 1808-88; Biggar Gala Day 1907- recent; records of
Horticultural Society; Biggar Dramatic Club; Reading & Recreation Club;
Masonic Society records 1726-1800s; local diaries. Books include old & new
Statistical Accounts for Scotland.
Finding aids: Newscuttings indexed; photographs indexed by subjects.
Leaflets: Publications list.
Reprographics: R5

### 41 Biggar Museum Trust (II)
**9 Edinburgh Road, Biggar ML12 6AX**
*Tel: 01889 221497*
**http://www.biggar-net.co.uk**
Collection includes Albion Motors Archives 1899-c1972 plus genealogical
material.
(1) Contact : Brian Lambie
Access: PCA as collections are at two locations. BAO.
*North end of town; bus services & parking nearby.*
Primary sources: Albion Motors Archives comprises minute books, plans,
manuals, photographs & 8000 negatives. GEN: CEN, OPR, MI plus church
discipline & fornication records.
Leaflets: CEN & OPR lists.
Reprographics: R5

## Blackburn

### 42 West Lothian Library Service: Local History Collection
**Connolly House, Hopefield Road, Blackburn EH47 7HZ**
*Tel: 01506 776331  Fax: 01506 776345*
A collection of c4000 books & articles on West Lothian, plus photographs, slides, maps, videos, newspapers & ephemera.
(1) Contact : Sybil Cavanagh
(2) Contact : Evelyn Dunn
Access: Mon-Thu 0830-1700; Fri 0830-1600; first Sat in month 0900-1300.
*0.5 ml from centre of Blackburn; bus routes nearby; parking, disabled access.*
Primary sources: West Lothian Courier 1873-; Linlithgowshire Journal & Gazette 1891-; Midlothian Advertiser 1906-67. Minutes of: Old Burgh, pre 1975 district councils, some parochial boards, West Lothian County Council, West Lothian District Council, West Lothian Council & Lothian Regional Council. 5000 photos from 1890s; old county & OS maps; c100 videos, mostly of old cine films from 1910 incl. Gala days. GEN: CEN, OPR, VR ER. Finding aids: Catalogue of books, articles, maps, videos, photographs & archival materials. Newspapers indexed. For former Livingston Development Corporation Archives, contact Alice Stewart, Archivist, West Lothian Council Archives & Records Management (tel. 01506 460020)
Leaflets: Local History & Family History leaflets. Publications list.
Reprographics: R1, R2

## Blairgowrie

### 43 Blairgowrie Genealogy Centre & Blairgowrie, Rattray & District Local History Trust
**c/o Blairgowrie Library, Leslie Street, Blairgowrie PH10 6AW**
*Tel: 01250 872905  Fax: 01250 872905*
Genealogy collection includes CEN 41-91, OPR, MI, Lists, BR, IGI (GB). *Local history collection includes 700 slides of photographs and postcards; c2000 Barony/Town Council documents (mainly accounts/receipts) 1802-1901; maps: OS 1860s-1900 and some local estates (*collection kept by Adam Malcolm - see below)
(1) Genealogy Centre: John Pitt (Tel: 01250 873468  Fax: 01250 875257)
(2) Local History Material: Adam H Malcolm (Tel: 01250 875212  Fax: 01250 875212)
Access: Mon-Wed, Fri 1400-1600 (Apr-Nov). Other times BAO.
Charges: Genealogy centre admission charges for non Perth/Kinross residents. Search fees charged.
*In town centre; bus route nearby; parking; disabled access.*

Finding aids: Index of paper holdings & slides.

## Blantyre

## 44 David Livingstone Centre
## 165 Station Road, Blantyre G72 9BT
### Tel: 01698 823140  Fax: 01698 821424
Collection of printed material with books and notebooks (1871-73) belonging to or written by David Livingstone (1813-73), incl. original letters (1846-73); social history collection reflecting the history of the building and the Blantyre Area.

(1) Contact : Karen Carruthers

Access: Mon-Sat 1000-1700; Sun 1230-1700. Winter opening hours may be reduced. Appointment only for researchers.

Charges: Museum admission charges.

*Blantyre rail station & bus routes nearby, parking; disabled access (library).*

Finding aids: Card index.

Leaflets: David Livingstone Centre leaflet.

Reprographics: R5, photocopies A4.

## Bo'ness

## 45 Falkirk Council Library Services: Bo'ness Library
## Scotland's Close, Bo'ness EH51 OAH
### Tel: 01506 778520  Fax: 01324 506801
### Email: mscott@falkirk-libsuprt.demon.co.uk
Collection includes books, maps, newspapers, pamphlets, videos and ephemera covering the Bo'ness area.

(1) Contact : Marion Scott (Tel: 01324 506845)

(2) Contact : John Dickson (Tel: 01324 506811)

Access: Mon-Tue, Thu 0930-2000; Wed, Fri-Sat 0930-1700. PCA.

*On the shore road close to harbour; bus routes nearby, parking.*

Primary sources: Newspapers: Bo'ness Journal 1900-39 (gaps); Falkirk Mail 1905-62, Falkirk Herald and predecessors 1845- (gaps); collection of locally published books; local events videos include Bo'ness various years from 1914; OS maps.

Leaflets: Publications list.

Reprographics: R1, R2

## Bonnyrigg

### 46  Bonnyrigg & Lasswade Local History Society
c/o Bonnyrigg Public Library, Polton Street,
Bonnyrigg EH19 3HB
*Tel: 0131 663 6762*

Collection comprises a small photographic archive (prints and slides) plus maps, publications, leaflets and MS material covering the area. McTaggart Collection comprises family history material (000s of photographs, prints of paintings, obituary notices) of the painter William McTaggart 1835-1910. (This is kept at the Midlothian Local Studies Centre, Loanhead).
(1) Chairman: Neil Stewart (Tel: 0131 654 1222)
(2) Secretary: Sheena Johnson (Tel: 0131 663 8048)
Access: BAO
*In town centre; bus routes nearby, parking.*
Finding aids: Local history collection catalogued.

## Brechin

### 47  Angus Council: Brechin Library
St.Ninian's Square, Brechin DD9 7AA
*Tel: 01356 622687  Fax: 01356 624271*

Brechin photographic, map & newspapers collection with some historical documents of area.
(1) Librarian: Amanda Pirie
Access: Mon, Wed 0930-2000; Tue, Thu 0930-1800; Fri-Sat 0930-1700. PCA.
*Central location; bus routes nearby, parking; disabled access.*
Primary sources: Brechin Advertiser 1848-; Brechin & District News 3/10/1952--Jan 1953, Brechin Herald 18/2/1890-12/4/1892; catalogue of names in the Brechin Burgess Records 1707-1975; old Wright's Society of Brechin membership book 1801-1836; St James' Lodge of Free Gardeners Register 1806-1836; commissariot record of Brechin - Register of Testaments 1576-1800; c500 photographs from 1890s; maps from 1820s plus OS; GEN: CEN, OPRs, VR, ER, IND, IGI(S).
Finding aids: Computerised catalogue.
Reprographics: R1, R2

## Bridge of Allan

## 48 W H Welsh Educational & Historic Trust
### c/o Bridge of Allan Library, Fountain Road, Bridge of Allan FK9 4AT
### *Tel: 01786 833680*

Collection of books; 200 photographs mostly late 19C early 20C relating to the Spa; memoirs, scrapbook, articles relating to Dr Welsh, with local history material and memorabilia for Bridge of Allan and district.
(1) Librarian or members of the Trust
Access: Mon, Fri 0900-1230; 1330-1730; Tue, Thu 0930-1230, 1330-1930; Wed 0930-1230; Sat 0900-1200. BAO
*In town centre; bus routes, parking nearby; disabled access.*
Reprographics: R1

## Brora

## 49 Highland Libraries: Brora Library
### Gower Street, Brora KW9 6PD
### *Tel: 01408 621128  Fax: 01408 622064*

Collection of 200+ books covering Brora, Ross and Cromarty etc. Local newspaper Northern Times 1899-.
(1) Librarian
Access: Mon 1800-2000; Tue 1000-1230, 1400-1700; Thu 1400-1700, 1800-2000; Fri 1000-1230, 1330-1630. PCA.
*Rail station, bus route nearby, parking.*
Reprographics: R1

## Buckie

## 50 Buckie District Fishing Heritage
### Heritage Cottage, Cluny Place, Buckie AB56 1HB

Collection comprises records of all sail boats from mid 19C to drifters and modern diesel fishing boats. Over 1000 photographs of boats, the fishing industry and local scenes. Information on boat building yards in the Buckie area. Video and audio cassettes featuring people in the fishing industry past to present.
(1) Contact : Allan Fraser (Tel: 01542 832826)
(2) Contact : Frank McLeod (Tel: 01542 835368)
Access: Mon-Fri 1000-1200, 1400-1600; Sat 1000-1200 (Jun-Sep). Other times BAO.
*Rear of library in town centre; bus route, parking nearby.*
Leaflets: Available.
Reprographics: R5

## Campbeltown

**51 Kintyre Antiquarian & Natural History Society
c/o Campbeltown Museum, Hall Street, Campbeltown
PA28 6BS**
*Tel: 01586 552281  Fax: 01586 551489*
**Email: elizabeth.marrison@virgin.net**
Small collection of books, photographs (20C 300+) and MS relating to
natural history, archaeology, local and family histories relating mainly to
Kintyre but with some Islay material (further photographs and paintings in
the Museum).
(1) Contact : Elizabeth Marrison
(2) Contact : Duncan McMillan (Tel: 01586 552631)
Access: Tue-Fri. BAO
Charges: Donations welcome.
*In town centre; bus route nearby, parking.*
Finding aids: In-house catalogues.
Leaflets: Publications list.

## Carlisle

**52 Border Television Library
Television Centre, Carlisle CA1 3NT**
*Tel: 01228 525101  Fax: 01228 41384*
Local news covering Isle of Man, Cumbria, Northumbria, Borders and
Dumfries & Galloway. Local interest and national programme from 1960.
(1) Contact : Derby Stewart-Amsden
Access: Mon-Fri 0930-1800. BAO
Charges: Search by client is chargeable.
*Off London Rd at southern ring road; bus route nearby, parking.*
Primary sources: Primary TV (all 2" material now housed at National Film
Archive). 1" tape; 16mm film; Beta and Beta SP video tape; Digital Betacam
and DigiPro.
Finding aids: Databases - news & stock since 1987; some archive news;
programme details since 1960 (incomplete). Indexes - paper files - news
1960-1989; programme details.
Reprographics: Photocopies of specific files, database files or programme
catalogue, fees depend on research and handling time.

## 53 Cumbria Archive Service
### Cumbria Record Office, The Castle, Carlisle CA3 8UR
*Tel: 01228 607285*

Although the Record Office is primarily concerned with the records of Cumberland, Cumbria and Carlisle (11C to present) it does hold a miscellaneous collection of Scottish material.

(1) Assistant County Archivist: David Bowcock

(2) Senior Assistant Archivist: Susan Dench

Access: Mon-Fri 0900-1700. PCA.

Charges: Researchers must register for Reader's ticket.

*Near city centre; rail & bus station nearby; parking adjacent; disabled access to ground floor.*

Primary sources: Papers of Saltcoats, Ayrshire colliery and saltpans 1719-31 and Craig & Poundland estates 1789-1837; Methodist Chapels at Dumfries 1876-1981 and Eastriggs 1917-8; Collie, Milne & Kinmont families, Edinburgh 1847-1927; Casebooks of Dr A Graham, Langholm 1769-1800; notebooks, surveys and plans of various mines 1920-65; photographs of Quintinshill Railway disaster 1915.

Finding aids: Typescript lists.

Reprographics: R1, R2, R5

## Carluke

## 54 Carluke Parish Historical Society
### 79 Hamilton Street, Carluke ML8 4HA

Collection comprises over 700 photographs of varying dates; maps incl. all OS maps of Carluke; artifacts & ephemera; records of Carluke Agricultural Society 1861-1962 and material on the sculptor Robert Forrest and the town cinemas.

(1) Contact : Christine Warren (Tel: 01555 773462 (eve)  Fax: 01555 751535)

(2) Contact : Janet Somerville (Tel: 01555 772406)

Access: Sat-Sun. BAO

*In town centre; rail station nearby, on bus route, parking.*

Reprographics: Photocopies A4

## Carnoustie

## 55 Angus Council: Carnoustie Library
### 21 High Street, Carnoustie DD7 6AN
*Tel: 01241 859620*

Collection of printed material about Carnoustie and the South Angus area, plus photographs, maps and newspaper collections.

(1) Librarian: Alasdair Sutherland

Access: Mon, Wed 0930-2000; Tue, Thu 0930-1800; Fri-Sat 0930-1700.

*Main St; bus services, parking nearby; disabled access.*

Primary sources: Photographic collection (400) from 1890; local newspapers; Broughty Ferry Guide, Carnoustie Gazette 1889-1988, Bro'ty Advertiser 1915-1919. OS maps from 1865. GEN: CEN, OPR, ER after 1975, IGI(S)
Reprographics: R1, R2, R5

## Clydebank

### 56 Clydebank Museum
### Dumbarton Road, Clydebank G81 1XQ
### *Tel: 01389 738702  Fax: 0141 951 8275*

Social and industrial history material includes a Singer Sewing Machine archive incl. technical photographs and literature, brochures, instruction manuals mostly 1950s-1970s; plus small collection of material covering shipbuilding and associated trades.
(1) The Curator
Access: Mon, Wed 1400-1630, Sat 1000-1630. Other times BAO. PCA.
*On A814 in former Town Hall; rail stations, parking nearby, on bus routes; disabled access.*
Leaflets: Museum leaflet and videos.
Reprographics: Photocopies A4.

### 57 West Dunbartonshire Libraries: Clydebank Central Library : Local Studies Department
### Dumbarton Road, Clydebank G81 1XH
### *Tel: 0141 952 8765  Fax: 0141 951 8275*

Library contains material relating to Clydebank and district.
(1) Contact : Patricia Malcolm
Access: Mon, Wed, Fri 0930-1700; Tue, Thu 0930-2000; Sat 0900-1700. PCA.
*On A814 beside former Town Hall; rail station nearby, on bus routes; parking nearby.*
Primary sources: Extensive information relating to shipbuilding; Singer Sewing Machine Co and the Clydebank Blitz in WWII; photographs 1890s-; newspaper cuttings; Clydebank Town Council minutes with some Valuation Rolls before 1975; Clydebank District Council minutes 1975-1996; newspapers: Clydebank & Renfrew Press 1891-1921, Clydebank Press 1922-1983, Clydebank Post 1983-.
Finding aids: Publications list.
Reprographics: R1, R5

## Coatbridge

### 58   Summerlee Heritage Park
**Heritage Way, Coatbridge ML5 1QD**
*Tel: 01236 431261   Fax: 01236 440429*
Collection of technical books/journals 1870s-1950s covering coalmining, engineering and boiler-making industries, plus maps and plans of local works incl. Hudsons Boilerworks 1890s-1960s, coal pits and pumping engines late 19C, with wide ranging ephemera and photographs.
(1) Curator: Mathew Hume
(2) Curator: Neil Ballantyne
Access: Mon-Fri 0900-1700. PCA.
*Near town centre; rail stations, bus routes nearby, parking; disabled access.*
Reprographics: R5

## Cromarty

### 59   Cromarty Courthouse
**Church Street, Cromarty IV11 8XA**
*Tel: 01381 600418   Fax: 01381 600408*
**Email: courthouse@mail.cali.co.uk**
**http://www.cali.co.uk/users/freeway/courthouse**
Collection contains a series of public access files of information on the history of Cromarty.
(1) Curator: David Alston
Access: Mon-Sun 1000-1700 (Apr-Oct). Mon-Sun 1200-1600 (Nov,Dec, Mar). PCA. Jan, Feb BAO.
Charges: Donations welcomed.
*In town centre; bus service, parking; disabled access difficult.*
Primary sources: Burgh administration and affairs, mostly 19C, incl. databases of court records, militia lists, gravestone inscriptions, property ownership & shipping. Collection of late 19-early 20C photographs.
Finding aids: Databases (see above); WWW site incl. folklore, shipping & some genealogical sources. Email enquiries welcome.
Leaflets: List (8 books).
Reprographics: R1, R5

# Cumbernauld

## # 60 North Lanarkshire Council Archives
**10 Kelvin Road, Lenziemill Industrial Estate, Cumbernauld G67 2BD**
*Tel: 01236 737114  Fax: 01236 781762*

Collection includes archival material, local authority records, pamphlets, ephemera, manuscripts, plans, slides and photographs covering North Lanarkshire.

(1) Contact : Craig Geddes

Access: Mon-Fri 0900-1700. BAO

Charges: Genealogical search charges.

*SE of town centre; rail station, bus routes nearby, parking; limited disabled access.*

Primary sources: Local authority records: Burghs of Kilsyth 1826-1975, Motherwell & Wishaw 1860-1975, Cumbernauld (with Development Corporation) 1956-, Coatbridge 1841-1975; County Councils of - Dumbarton 1895-1974, Lanark c1900-c1950, Stirling 1917-1974; District Councils - Cumbernauld & Kilsyth, Monklands, Motherwell 1974-1996; North Lanarkshire Council 1996-. Hamilton of Dalziel Muniments c1500-c1895; Drumpellier (1560-1961) & Gartsherrie (1829-1902) Estate papers; Alston papers c1870-1970; Cumbernauld House papers 1706-c1950; Coats estate chartulary, Records of Coatbridge College 1905-55; Airdrie Bowling Club 1852-94; Episcopal churches 1843-1992; and of commercial organisations Etna Iron & Steel Co 1894-1974, Wishaw Co-operative Society 1889-1973, R B Tennant & Co 1898-1955.

Finding aids: In-house: Archives list.

Reprographics: R1, R4, R5, plan copies.

## 61 North Lanarkshire Libraries: Cumbernauld Central Library
**8 Allander Walk, Cumbernauld G67 1EE**
*Tel: 01236 725664  Fax: 01236 458350*

Collection includes books, photographs, maps, newspapers, local authority and community groups and fiction works by local authors. NB some material relating specifically to Kilsyth is kept at the Kilsyth Library, Burngreen, Kilsyth, tel & fax 01236 823147.

(1) Contact : Catriona Wales

Access: Mon-Tue, Thu-Fri 1000-1900; Wed 0900-1200; Sat 0900-1700. PCA.

Charges: Genealogical search charges.

*In the Cumbernauld Centre; bus services, parking; disabled access.*

Primary sources: Reports and minutes of Cumbernauld and Kilsyth District Council 1975-96 and previous authorities, plus community groups in Cumbernauld and Kilsyth; c4000 photographs 1950-; OS maps; minutes of Cumbernauld Subscription Library c1820 and Cumbernauld Southern District

Debating Society c1932; newspapers include Cumbernauld News and Kilsyth Chronicle 1966-; GEN: CEN, OPRs.
Finding aids: Family history search on CDRom.
Reprographics: R1

## Cumnock

**62 East Ayrshire Council Library Service: Local Archives**
**Baird Institute, 3 Lugar Street, Cumnock KA18 1AD**
*Tel: 01290 421701  Fax: 01290 421701*
Local history collection comprises books, magazines, articles, maps, photographs etc covering the history of people and places in E Ayrshire.
(1) Contact : Anne Geddes
Access: Mon-Tue, Thu-Fri 1000-1300, 1330-1630. PCA.
Charges: Staff search charges.
*In town centre; bus station, parking nearby; disabled access difficult.*
Primary sources: The photograph collection includes 1000+ photographs, 100 slides and 1000 postcards 20C; maps mostly OS; newspapers: Ayr Advertiser 1834-1971 (gaps); Cumnock Chronicle 1901-; GEN: CEN, OPRs, MI, some VR & ER, DIR, IGI(S).
Leaflets: Publications leaflets.
Reprographics: R1, R5

## Cupar

**63 Fife Council East Area Libraries: Local History Collection**
**Cupar Library, 33 Crossgate, Cupar KY15 5AS**
*Tel: 01334 412285  Fax: 01334 412467*
http://www.sol.co.uk/w/w.owen/genuki/fif/cupar_lib.htm
Collection of: books, pamphlets, periodicals, newspapers, press cuttings, maps, prints, photographs covering Fife and particularly NE Fife.
(1) Community Librarian: Angela Beattie
Access: Mon-Wed, Fri 1000-1900; Thu, Sat 1000-1700. PCA.
*In town centre; rail station nearby, on bus routes, parking.*
Primary sources: 500 Photographs 1900-; maps from 19C incl. OS; Register of Sasines 18-19C; newspapers - Fifeshire Journal 1833-93; East Fife Record 1856-1916; Fife News 1967-74; Fife Herald 1967-; Courier & Advertiser 1926-89. GEN: CEN; OPRs, VR, BR, IND, IGI.
Finding aids: Newspaper index.
Reprographics: R1, R2, R5

**64 Fife Council Museums (East)**
**County Buildings, St Catherine Street, Cupar KY15 4TA**
*Tel: 01334 412933  Fax: 01334 412933*
**Email: standrewsmuseum@clara.net**
Collection of material relating to E Fife: maps, plans of buildings (100), photographs (1000), postcards and printed ephemera.
(1) Contact : M D King (Tel: 01334 412934)
(2) Contact : M Wood (Tel: 01334 412691  Fax: 01334 412691)
Access: Mon-Fri 0900-1700. PCA. BAO
*In town centre; rail station, bus routes, parking nearby.*
Primary sources: Records and correspondence of the Newburgh Friendly Society 19C; the Anderson family of Newburgh (19C minister/amateur geologist); letters and diaries of Martin Anderson (1854-1932), 'Cynicus' satirical cartoonist.
Reprographics: R1, R5

**65 Fife Folk Museum**
**High Street, Ceres, Cupar KY15 5NF**
*Tel: 01334 828380*
Collection of photographs, slides, postcards, books, newspapers, accounts, old advertisements, catalogues, cuttings & emphemera relating to the social, economic & cultural history of bygone Fife.
(1) The Curator
(2) Contact : R Peterkin (Tel: 01334 828249)
Access: Sat-Thu 1400-1700. Other times BAO.
Charges: Admission charge.
*Near the Cross on the main road; bus services nearby, parking behind museum; limited disabled access.*
Finding aids: In-house catalogues.
Leaflets: Booklets - list available.

**66 Fife Health Board: Purchaser Group Library**
**Springfield House, Cupar KY15 5UP**
*Tel: 01334 656200 x513  Fax: 01334 657579*
**Email: dmcginley@fhblib.demon.co.uk**
Registrar General, local government and public health reports for Scotland and Fife covering various dates from late 19C.
(1) Contact : Dorothy McGinley
Access: Mon-Thu 0900-1700; Fri 0900-1630. BAO
*In grounds of Stratheden Hospital, 1 ml W of Cupar; bus service nearby, parking; disabled access.*
Leaflets: Lists of archive material held.
Reprographics: R1

# Dalkeith

## 67 Dalkeith History Society: Dalkeith History Museum Workshop
### 4 Buccleuch Street, Dalkeith

The Museum Workshop has a collection of photographs, postcards, archival material of societies, research material by members.
(1) Secretary: David R Smith (Tel: 0131 663 1995)
(2) Contact : Lauchlan MacLean (Tel: 0131 663 2349)
Access: Tue 1000-1200. Other times BAO. PCA.
*In town centre, above Citizens' Advice Bureau; bus routes, parking nearby.*
Primary sources: Archives include c500 photographs, c400 slides and 100 postcards of Dalkeith area 1890-; papers of the Dalkeith Scientific Society 1839-1880, Dalkeith Bowling Club 1850-1930, Children's Day Committee 1920s; 'Old Dalkeith Magazine' 1990s.
Leaflets: Publications by members - list.

# Dingwall

## 68 Highland Libraries: Dingwall Library
### Old Academy Buildings, Tulloch Street, Dingwall IV15 9JZ
### *Tel: 01349 863163  Fax: 01349 865239*

A collection of 3000+ books covering the local and family history of Ross and Cromarty.
(1) Librarian
Access: Mon-Fri 0930-1800; Sat 1000-1300.
*In town centre; rail station, bus route, parking nearby,*
Reprographics: R1

# Dollar

## 69 Dollar Museum
### Castle Campbell Hall, Dollar FK14 7AY
### *Tel: 01259 742895  Fax: 01259 742895*

Collection contains books, journals, maps, photographs, postcards and miscellaneous papers relating to people, places and events in Dollar and neighbourhood and particularly to the Devon Valley Railway.
(1) Honorary Curator: Janet Carolan
Access: Sat 1100-1300, 1400-1630; Sun 1400-1630 (Easter-Christmas). Other times by appointment. PCA.
Charges: Donations welcome
*At the top of the Burnside; bus route, parking nearby; disabled access.*
Primary sources: Dollar Magazine 1902-; published 19C reminiscences; minute books of societies and clubs; early guide books, facsimiles of 18-19C

maps; photocopies of some early Dollar Academy archival material and local cemetery inscriptions. Collection of photographs of Devon Valley Railway.
Finding aids: Index to people & places.
Leaflets: Membership leaflet.
Reprographics: Photocopies A4; photographs can be supplied.

## Drymen

### 70 Drymen & District Local History Society
### c/o Drymen Library, The Square, Drymen G63 0BL
### *Tel: 01360 660751  Fax: 01360 660751*

Collection is small and consists of newspaper cuttings; photocopies of local material incl. maps (Drymen and Buchanan); a few monographs, slides and prints. Reference packs for students.
(1) Secretary: Alison Brown (Tel: 01360 660737)
(2) Community Librarian: Marie Elder
Access: Mon, Fri 0930-1300, 1400-1700; Tue, Thu 0930-1300, 1400-1900; Sat 0900-1300. PCA.
*In village centre; parking, on bus route.*
Reprographics: Photocopies A4.

## Dumbarton

### 71 Scottish Maritime Museum: Denny Ship Model Experiment Tank Archives
### Castle Street, Dumbarton G82 1QS
### *Tel: 01389 763444  Fax: 01389 743093*

A complete record of ship model hull tests conducted 1883-1984 at Denny Ship Model Experiment Tank by Messrs Wm Denny & Bros; data for over 1000 ships built by the firm. Graphs of hydrodynamic results, lines plans, staff log books, ships specification books, etc. and details of individual research in naval architecture undertaken in the building.
(1) Documentation Officer: James Grant (Tel: 01294 278283  Fax: 01294 313211)
(2) Curator: Veronica Hartwich (Tel: 01294 278283  Fax: 01294 313211)
Access: Mon-Fri 1000-1600. Access to archive restricted. BAO
Charges: Search charges.
*Opposite Safeway supermarket; rail station, bus routes, parking nearby.*
Finding aids: Catalogue.
Reprographics: R1, R5

## 72 West Dunbartonshire Libraries: Dumbarton Public Library
### Strathleven Place, Dumbarton
### *Tel: 01389 733273/763129  Fax: 01389 733018*
Local Studies Collection contains material relating to the history of the Dumbarton and Vale of Leven areas incl. c1000 books, newspapers 1851-, newspaper cuttings, c12000 photographs, c2500 slides, c1000 maps and archives (MS and printed) 1424-.
(1) Contact : Graham Hopner
(2) Contact : Rhoda MacLeod
Access: Mon, Wed, Fri 0930-1700; Tue, Thu 0930-2000; Sat 1000-1700.
Charges: Genealogical postal enquiry search charges.
*In town centre; rail station nearby, on bus route, parking; disabled access.*
Primary sources: Dumbarton and Lennox Herald 1851-, Helensburgh and Gareloch Times 1880-1980; Dumbarton and Vale of Leven Reporter 1964-; Dumbarton Town Council Minutes 1578-1975 (17C gaps); Helensburgh Town Council Minutes 1807-1975; County Council of Dunbarton Minutes 1895-1975; Dumbarton District Council Minutes 1975-96; West Dunbartonshire Council Minutes 1996-; (some Vale of Leven District Council Minutes c1930-75). Poor Relief records 1847-1962; Sasines Dumbarton and Argyllshire 1617-1780 Testaments for Scotland 1514-1800. GEN: CEN, OPRs, VR, ER, IND.
Finding aids: Card catalogue, lists, indexes.
Leaflets: Publications list.
Reprographics: R1, R5

## Dumfries

## # 73 Dumfries & Galloway Council Archives
### Archive Centre, 33 Burns Street, Dumfries DG1 2PS
### *Tel: 01387 269254  Fax: 01387 264126*
Documents covering life and administration of Dumfries Burgh and Sanquhar Burgh plus Family, Business, Club, Estate and miscellaneous records relating to Dumfriesshire and parts of Kirkcudbrightshire and Wigtownshire; church records of Dumfries; customs records; plans and maps, microfilm of local interest records held elsewhere; small library of reference, local history and genealogical books, pamphlets and research notes.
(1) Archivist: Marion Stewart
Access: Tue-Wed, Fri 0900-1300; 1400-1700; Thu 1800-2100. BAO
Charges: Donations welcomed. Fee based research service.
*In town centre; rail station approx. 0.75 ml, bus station, parking nearby.*
Primary sources: Local authority records - Dumfries Council - minutes 1643-, Dean of Guild records/plans 1777-1975, Sanquhar Council minutes 1714-1975; Nithsdale District Council records 1975-96. Petitions 1655-1833; minutes of railway, gas, waterworks, hospital and bridge committees 1850-1929 and Town Clerk's letter books 1787-1966 for Dumfries. Court Records - books 1506-89, papers 1505-1893, Porteus Rolls 1679-1866, diet books 1658-1825; sasines 1617-1780; Treasurers' accounts 1633-; Service of Heir

Registers 1751-1844; Feu Rolls 1674-1825; shipping, bridge etc dues 1756-1802; c8000 Victorian architectural drawings. Licence records: various 1718-1974; Kirk session (1648-1980s) and customs records (1824-1970s); Estate records: Stewart of Shambellie, Maxwell of Barncleugh, McCartney of Halketleaths, Clerk-Maxwell of Middlebie (c1500-1970s); Clubs, organisations and business records (19/20C); Wesleyan, Secession, Congregational and Catholic church records (18-20C). Police taxes (1795-1887) and records (1844-1973) plus jail books (1714-1839). Newspapers: Dumfries & Galloway Standard and predecessors (1777-1911) and Dumfries & Galloway Courier (1809-1886). Genealogical notes and family trees; GEN: CEN, OPRs, VR, ER, MI, IGI(S).
Finding aids: Lists of collections; shelf lists, holdings guide, 13 subject source lists; indexes: Council (1730-1840) & Kirk Session minutes (18C); Dean of Guild Plans (1893-1975)
Leaflets: Source lists, booklets, leaflets.
Reprographics: R1

## 74 Dumfries & Galloway Family History Society Research Centre, 9 Glasgow Street, Dumfries DG2 9AF
*Tel: 01387 248093*
### Email: kylbet@aol.com
Substantial collection of genealogical books, journals and maps (from 1819) mostly for Dumfries and Galloway, Kirkcudbrightshire and Wigtownshire. GEN: CEN, OPR, MI, IND, IGI(S).
(1) Contact : M Aitken
(2) Contact : J Stoddart
Access: Tue-Fri 1000-1600 (Apr-Oct); Tue-Fri 1100-1500 (Nov-Mar). Every Sat 1000-1300.
Charges: Search charges for non-members.
*W bank of river nearby Buccleuch St Bridge; rail station 1 ml approx., bus station, parking nearby; disabled access.*
Finding aids: GEN mfiche indexes; Dumfries newspapers indexes 1777-1930.
Leaflets: Publications list.
Reprographics: Photocopies A4.

## 75 Dumfries & Galloway Health Board Archives: Crichton Royal Museum
## Easterbrook Hall, Crichton Royal Hospital, Bankend Road, Dumfries DG1 1SY
*Tel: 01387 244000 x4228*
The Archives contain material relating to hospitals in SW Scotland from 1776.
(1) Contact : Morag Williams (Tel: 01387 244228)
Access: Museum: Thu-Fri (all year) 1330-1630 , Sat (Easter-Oct) 1330-1630. Archives: Tue-Fri 0930-1630 (BAO).

Charges: Variable search charges.

*On the S side of town; hospitals bus service, parking nearby; disabled access via rear door.*

Primary sources: Dumfries & Galloway Royal Infirmary Minute books (2 vols missing), annual reports, cash books, ledgers, letter books, staff registers 1777-; Crichton Royal Hospital Crichton Trust documents 1823-, Minute books 1839-, annual reports, case notes 1839-, registers of admission, restraint and seclusion, accident and death, obligants books, Sheriff's warrants, staff registers (19/20C), Cottage hospital material relating to Stranraer, Kirkcudbright, Castle Douglas, Moffat, Langholm incl. minutes, annual reports (incomplete), some letter books, patients registers; infectious diseases hospitals material incl. patient registers for Thornhill, Castle Douglas, Lochmaben, Newton Stewart; photographic collection (700+); hospital plans; Area Health Board minutes; oral archive; hospital magazines 1844-.

Finding aids: Archives list.

Leaflets: Crichton Royal Museum and Gardens and Hospital Records and the Family Historian leaflets.

Reprographics: R1, R5

## 76 Dumfries & Galloway Libraries: Local Studies Collection

### Ewart Library, Catherine Street, Dumfries DG1 1JB

*Tel: 01387 252070/253820  Fax: 01307 260294*

### Email: libs&i@dumgal.gov.uk

The Collection contains material relating to Dumfries and Galloway incl. books, pamphlets, maps, plans, photographs, ephemera, archives and genealogical material.

(1) Reference and Local Studies Librarian: Ruth Airley (Tel: 01387 252070)

(2) Resources Development Librarian: Graham Roberts (Tel: 01387 253820)

Access: Mon-Wed, Fri 1000-1930; Thu, Sat 1000-1700.

Charges: Search charges possible.

*In town centre, just off Edinburgh Rd (A701); on bus route, parking nearby; disabled access.*

Primary sources: 22000 books; 6500 pamphlets; map collection from 1607 includes OS maps; 12000 photographs from 1860s; records of commissioners of supply from 1667; registers of Sasines: index 1617-1780; records of local authorities; Burgh of Dumfries 19/20C, counties of Dumfries, Wigtown and Kirkcudbright 20C, district councils of Nithsdale, Annandale, Wigtown and Stewartry 1975-96, Dumfries & Galloway Regional Council 1975-96, Dumfries & Galloway Council 1996-; newspapers: Dumfries & Galloway Standard with predecessors 1777- (indexed to 1930 & 1983-), Wigtown Free Press 1843-1925 (index); GEN: CEN, VR, ER, IGI.

Finding aids: Computerised catalogue & card indexes.

Leaflets: Research and publications leaflets.

Reprographics: R1, R3, R5

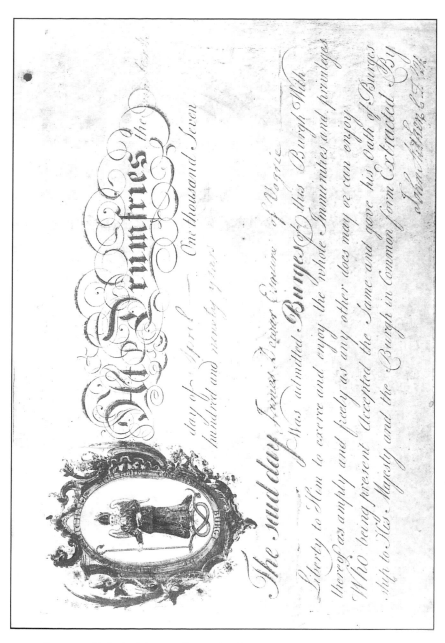

**Burgess Ticket of James Dewar for Burgh of Dumfries 20 April 1790**
**(NAS ref: GD.330/58/19)**

## 77 Dumfries Museum
**The Observatory, Church Street, Dumfries DG2 7SW**
*Tel: 01387 253374  Fax: 01387 265081*
**Email: info@dumfriesmuseum.demon.co.uk**
**http://www.dumfriesmuseum.demon.co.uk**
Books and pamphlets of local interest, 18C, mostly 19 & 20C journals and
books of Scottish & local interest incl. archaeology, social and natural
history, literature (esp.Robert Burns) numismatics etc.; Diaries of William
Grierson
(1) Contact : Siobhan Ratchford
(2) Contact : Elaine Kennedy
Access: Mon-Fri 10.00-1300; 1400-1700. PCA.
*In Church St (W bank of river); rail station 1 ml approx., bus station nearby,
parking; disabled access.*
Finding aids: Card index to library being computerised.
Leaflets: 100 leaflets, list.
Reprographics: R1, R5

## Dunbar

## 78 Dunbar & District History Society
**Dunbar Town House Museum, Dunbar Town House,
High Street, Dunbar EH42 1ER**
*Tel: 01368 863734*
**http://www2.prestel.co.uk/dunbar/ddhs**
Collection includes 1500 photographs of district 1890s-; research reports &
printed works on history of Dunbar; OS maps plus plans of harbour &
railway; some valuation rolls
(1) Contact : Pauline Smeed
Access: Mon-Sun 1230-1630 (end Mar-end Oct); Sat-Sun 1400-1630 (Nov-
Mar). PCA.
Charges: Some research charges.
*Town House in middle of High St; rail station, bus routes & parking nearby;
disabled access.*

## 79 East Lothian Antiquarian & Field Naturalists' Society
**Inchgarth, East Links, Dunbar EH42 1LT**
A collection of books and artefacts of local interest deposited with the East
Lothian Council Local History Centre and Museum Service. Documents
deposited with the NAS(SRO), list available from Local History Centre.
(1) Hon Secretary: Stephen Bunyan (Tel: 01368 863335)
Leaflets: Publications: Transactions East Lothian Antiquarian and Field
Naturalists' Society Vol 1-XXIII; Dunbar Parish Church 1342-1987;
Bibliography of East Lothian - 1936; Bibliographies East Lothian - 1941.

## Dunblane

### 80 Dunblane Cathedral City Museum
### The Square, Dunblane FK15 OAQ

Documents, account books, minute books, plans re Cathedral restoration - much to do with Cathedral affairs but not all.

(1) Honorary Custodian: Marjorie P Davies (Tel: 01786 823440)

(2) Contact : May Swanson (Tel: 01786 824389)

Access: Mon-Sat 1000-1230, 1400-1630 (mid May-early Oct). Other times BAO.

*Opposite Cathedral; rail station, bus routes, parking nearby; disabled access.*
Primary sources: Artefacts, displays, prints, paintings, photographs and documents concerning the Cathedral. A collection of over 6000 communion tokens; library containing local and church history plus proceedings of the Society of Antiquarians of Scotland 1882-1957, and the Bulletin of John Rylands Library 1950-1971. Journal of the Society of Friends of Dunblane Cathedral from 1930.

## Dundee

### 81 Abertay Historical Society
### c/o Archive Centre, 21 City Square, Dundee DD1 3BY
### *Tel: 01382 434494  Fax: 01382 464666*
### Email: iain.flett@dundeecity.gov.uk

Society members undertake research into a wide range of historical topics in the Tayside area.

Leaflets: Publications list available.

### 82 Dundee Arts & Heritage: McManus Galleries
### Albert Square, Dundee DD1 1DA
### *Tel: 01382 432020  Fax: 01382 432052*

Fine Art collection includes local topographical views, portraits and works by local artists; 10000 photographs of Dundee and District 1850-; Archives include a whaling collection and the Mary Slessor (1848-1915) archive.

(1) Facility Manager: Janice Murray

Access: Mon 1100-1700; Tue-Sat 1000-1700. PCA.

*At top of Reform St, rail & bus stations nearby, no parking; disabled access.*
Finding aids: In-house printed indexes.

Reprographics: R5, photocopies A4.

# 83  Dundee City Archives
## Dept of Support Services, 21 City Square, Dundee DD1 3BY
*Tel: 01382 434494  Fax: 01382 434666*
**Email: iain.flett@dundeecity.gov.uk**
**http://dundeecity.gov.uk/dectml/services/archives**

The archives hold the records of the Dundee City Council and its predecessor authorities, family, estate, business, trade union and other private records, plus, records retransmitted from the NAS(SRO).
(1) City Archivist: Iain Flett
(2) Archivist: Richard Cullen
Access: Mon-Fri 0915-1300, 1400-1645. BAO
*In city centre - entry by 1 Shore Terrace; rail & bus stations, parking nearby; disabled access by appointment.*

Primary sources: The official records of the City of Dundee; Burgh Court books 1520-1898; Registers of decrees 1676-1883; Registers of Deeds 1626-1908; Council minute books 1553-1990, and account books 1586-1994; Shipping registers 1580-1713; Education records c1864-1985; Police records 1824-1894; Parochial Board records 1848-1930; Broughty Ferry Police Commissioners/Town Council minutes 1877-1913; Tayside Regional Council: Minutes and reports 1975-1996; Justices of the Peace records for Dundee (1894-1975) & Angus (1791-1974); Customs records: Dundee (1708-1945) and Montrose 1707-1929; Register of Sasines 1639-1812, Protocol book 1571-1608; Church records: Baptist, Congregational, Episcopal, Methodist & Unitarian, mostly 19-20C - Methodist from 1771; plus schools, societies, institutions, utilities mostly from end of 19C. Estate records include: Balgray & Logie Estates (Angus) 1495-1962, Northesk Muniments 1247-1922, Snaigow Estate (Perthshire) 1606-1962, Strathmartine Estate 1537-1889, Wedderburn of Pearsie 1483-1918; Unions: Amalgamated Engineering Union c1920-c1970, Amalagamted Society of Boilermakers 1868-1981, Railway Clerks' Association 1901-87; Shipping: Dundee, Perth & London Shipping Co. 1826-1960, Dundee Port Authority 1814-1986; Business records: Robb Caledon Shipbuilders 1872-1980, Jas Scott & Sons (spinners & jute mfrs) 1861-1969, Victoria Spinning Co 1893-1978, Halket & Adam Dundee Ropeworks 1926-68, David Winter & Son (stationers, booksellers, publishers) 1858-1951; Guild & trades records: Guildry Incorporation of Dundee 1570-1970, Maltmen 1653-1871, Masons 1659-1960, Slaters 1684-1976, Seaman Fraternity 1652-1978, Tailors 1556-1920, Weavers 1557-1951, Wrights 1691-1915.
Finding aids: Card indexes & lists; summaries on WWW, incl. Friends Newsletter.
Leaflets: Summary lists.
Reprographics: Photocopies A4.

## 84 Dundee City Council: Local Studies Library
### Central Library, The Wellgate, Dundee DD1 1DB
*Tel: 01382 434377 Fax: 01382 434036*
Email: local.studies@dundeecity.gov.uk
http://www.dundeecity.gov.uk/dcchtm/nrd/centlib/loc-stud.htm

Collection of 20000+ items include books, pamphlets, newspapers 1803-, 2000 maps and plans, photographs, directories plus c25000 items of ephemera, incl. posters covering Dundee, Tayside and NE Fife.
(1) Contact : Eileen Moran
Access: Mon-Tue, Fri-Sat 0930-1700: Wed-Thu 1000-1900. PCA.
*In the Wellgate Centre; rail station, bus routes, parking nearby; disabled access.*
Primary sources: Includes collection of material relating to Mary Slessor (missionary) and William McGonagall (poet); Whaling logbooks; Tay Railway Bridge disaster; newspapers: Courier and Advertiser and predecessors 1856-, Dundee, Perth & Cupar Advertiser 1805-61, Evening Telegraph and Post and predecessors 1877-; People's Journal 1905-86; the Lamb collection of ephemera - 450 boxes from end 19C; Alexander Wilson Bequest, 4000 glass negatives 1870-1905; Dundee photographic surveys of 1916 & 1991; GEN: CEN, OPRs, MI, ER, OBITS, DIR, IGI(S).
Leaflets: Information sheets and publications list, incl. Tay Valley FHS publications.
Reprographics: R1, R4, R5

## 85 Dundee Registration Office (Births, Deaths & Marriages)
### 89 Commercial Street, Dundee DD1 2AF
*Tel: 01382 435222 Fax: 01382 435224*

Custodial records include B.M.D (Dundee/Angus varying dates); CEN (Tayside and Scotland 1881); OPRs (Tayside 1553-1854), IND (Scotland: OPRs, BMD, CEN 1881-1891, DIV 1984-95). On-line access to GRO, Edinburgh.
(1) Chief Registrar (Tel: 01382 435223)
(2) Senior Registrar (Tel: 01382 435226)
Access: Genealogy searches: Tue-Thu 0930-1130, 1400-1600. BAO
Charges: Search charges.
*In town centre; rail station, bus station, parking nearby.*
Leaflets: Available.

# 86   Dundee University Archives
## Tower Building, University of Dundee, Dundee DD1 4HN
*Tel: 01382 344095   Fax: 01382 345523*
**Email: p.e.whatley@dundee.ac.uk**
**http://www.dundee.ac.uk/archives**

Large manuscript collection of business records: Dundee and Indian jute industry; textile industries; railway and shipping. There are map, plan and photographic collections relating to Dundee, Tayside and Fife.

(1) University Archivist: Patricia Whatley

Access: Mon-Wed, Fri 0900-1700; Thu 0930-2330, 1700-2000, Sat 1000-1300 (term-time). Mon-Wed, Fri 0900-1700; Thu 0930-1330 (vacations). PCA.

Charges: Research service charges.

*In city centre; rail station & bus routes nearby, parking adjacent; disabled access.*

Primary sources: University archives: Records of University College, Dundee c1875-1954; Queen's College, Dundee 1954-1967; University of Dundee 1967-; Dundee Medical School (St Andrews University) c1887-1966; Dundee School of Economics 1928-1954. Papers in University collection include Patrick Geddes (town planning), Robert Alexander Watson-Watt (radar), R C Buist Collection (history of medicine in Angus 16C-). Manuscript Collection: jute industry records in Dundee and India 1820-1948; woollen, linen and engineering industries c1840-1978; John Berry of Tayfield files relating to Hydro Board projects and their effect on the environment 1934-1988, papers of James Dalyell c1814-1873 and John James Dalyell c1853-1873; Joseph Johnston Lee, World War I poet 1898-1948; Peter Carmichael of Arthurstone 1837-1890; Shiell and Small, solicitors, papers relating to local railway companies 1826-1935; local medical associations 1864-1957; Dr William Maxwell Jamieson papers relating to epidemics 1870-1993; Dundee Medical Library 1880-1903; Glasite Church sermons and correspondence 1728-1885; papers of the College and Collegiate Church of the Holy Spirit, Isle of Cumbrae c1850-1926; MS and correspondence of Thomas Campbell, poet 1797-1854; Alexander Scott 1851-1935; Sir Robert Robertson 1894-1949; records of Dundee Stock Exchange Association 1876-1964; John P Ingram shipping notebooks 1767-1980; papers of Wilson family of Alva (woollen manfs); papers relating to James Ballantyne Hannay, diamond research and family affairs 1842-1987; company records Valentines of Dundee Ltd 1896-1982; Dundee Town Council minutes 1880-1940; Methodist Church, Arbroath and Montrose Circuit 1798-1989. Map and Plan Collection from 18C includes technical drawings and plans of factories in Dundee and West Bengal, estate drawings and railway drawings. Photographic Collection: (10000 from end 19C) include industrial and non-industrial photographs, incl. medicine, education, business and the environment. The Peto Collection (c130000 images) has a small proportion taken in the area, best known for portraits of celebrities 1946-70. Brechin Diocesan Manuscripts and Library: Correspondence of Bishop Alexander Penrose Forbes 1844-1874; transcripts of Episcopal registers c1681-1890; records of Diocese of Brechin c1744-1904; Diary and commonplace book of

William Drummond of Hawthornden 1606-1619; records of local Episcopal churches 1756-1977. Tayside Health Board: Extensive records of local hospitals 1811-1979. Kinnear Local Book Collection: 4500 books, pamphlets and periodicals relating to wide range of subjects connected with Dundee, Perthshire, Angus and Fife 17C–20C. Joan Auld Memorial Collection: Over 400 books relating to economic, labour and shipping history of Scotland early 19C-.
Finding aids: Descriptive lists & computerised source lists & catalogue.
WWW site with summary lists of collections, source lists, general information, photographs latest news, links, contact details & publications.
Leaflets: Summary guide.
Reprographics: R1, R4, R5

## 87  Tay Valley Family History Society
### 179 Princes Street, Dundee DD5 6DQ
### *Tel: 01382 461845*
### Email: tayvalleyfhs@sol.co.uk
### http://www.sol.co.uk/t/tayvalleyfhs/

Collection of genealogical books, journals and information covering Tay Valley area (Angus, Fife, Perthshire and Kinross). GEN: CEN, OPR, MI, BR, IND, IGI (S-1992)
(1) Contact : V Smith
Access: Mon 1000-1600, 1900-2100; Tue-Wed, Fri 1000-1600; Thu 1900-2100; Sat 1000-1300. PCA.
Charges: Search charges for non members.
*NE city centre; rail station 1 ml approx., bus station nearby, on bus routes, parking.*
Finding aids: Indexes of individuals on computer database; library catalogue on WWW.
Reprographics: R1, R4

## 88  University of Abertay Dundee: Library
### Bell Street, Dundee DD1 1HG
### *Tel: 01382 308866  Fax: 01382 308880*
### Email: libdesk@tay.ac.uk
### http://www.tay.ac.uk/is/

Library holds the University's archives & records plus a small collection of material relating to Dundee & Tayside.
(1) Contact : Diane Robertson (Tel: 01382 308870)
Access: Mon-Fri 0830-2200; Sat 1000-1700; Sun 1200-1900 (term-time). Mon-Fri 0845-1700 (vacations). PCA.
*In city centre; rail & bus stations, parking nearby; disabled access.*
Reprographics: R1

# EXTRAORDINARY MEETING.

## NATIONAL STRIKE.

### CHARTER.

FOR THE

**A PUBLIC MEETING**

WILL BE HELD

## ON THE MAGDALEN YARD GREEN,

THIS EVENING, AT HALF-PAST SIX O'CLOCK,

For the purpose of consulting the whole of the people in regard to the means which ought to be adopted for carrying their will into operation.

### THE VOICE OF THE PEOPLE IS THE VOICE OF GOD.

*A Collection will be made to Defray Expenses.*

BY ORDER OF THE DELEGATES.

At the GREAT DELEGATE MEETING, held in the School-Room, Pullar's Close, on the evening of Friday the 19th instant, it was decidedly ascertained that the vast numbers of workmen, of all the Trades in Dundee, represented by the assembled Delegates, with the exception of a very few workmen, agreed to STRIKE for the PEOPLE'S CHARTER.—In accordance with the will of the Delegates,

Dundee, August 20, 1842.

PRINTED AT THE CHRONICLE OFFICE, DUNDEE.

**Chartist Poster - Dundee 1842 (NAS ref: ex AD.14/44/81)**

## Dunfermline

### 89 Fife Council Museums (West): Dunfermline Museum
### Viewfield Terrace, Dunfermline KY12 7HY
*Tel: 01383 313838  Fax: 01383 313837*

Local history collections include papers, photographs and books relating to local industries (linen, coalmining etc) and social life.
(1) Museums' Access Co-ordinator
Access: Mon-Sat 0900-1700. PCA.
*In town centre, off East Port; rail & bus stations nearby, parking adjacent; limited disabled access.*
Primary sources: Miscellaneous papers associated with damask linen industry in Dunfermline, incl. pattern books, printed machine catalogues, MS and printed designs, photographs, guildry books; miscellaneous papers concerned with other local industries and social life in the district incl. coalmining material.
Finding aids: Card indexes, accession sheets via staff.
Reprographics: R1, R5

### 90 Fife Council West Area Libraries: Local History Department
### Dunfermline Library, Abbot Street, Dunfermline KY12 7NL
*Tel: 01383 312994  Fax: 01383 312608*
### Email: dunfermline@fife.ac.uk

Local history collection developed from the Dr Erskine Beveridge donation of 60 years ago. It houses books on people, places, events and industries in Dunfermline and West Fife plus articles, journals, maps, plans, photographs and ephemera. Collections include: George Reid Collection of medieval manuscripts and early printed books and the Murison Burns collection.
(1) Local History Librarian: Anne Rodwell
(2) Information Services Librarian: Chris Neale
Access: Mon-Tue, Thu-Fri 1000-1900; Wed, Sat 1000-1700.
*In town centre, off High St; rail & bus stations, parking nearby; disabled access.*
Primary sources: Newspapers: West Fife Echo 1900-1932; Dunfermline Journal 1851-1951 (incomplete), Dunfermline Press (incomplete) 1859-1897, Rosyth & Inverkeithing Journal 1940-1951; directories, almanacs and registers for Dunfermline, Fife and Kinross 1814-1912 collection of Minute Books for various societies, incl. Niffler Society and the Incorporation of Weavers; Dunfermline Abbey Kirk Session records and Extracts from the Burgh records of Dunfermline in the 16-17C; Aberdour Poor Register 1845; church records; trade and work records; Burgh and official records include Baron Court book 1686 & 1708-13, Parochial Board minutes 1848-1930 (gaps); c8000 photographic images end 19C-; early OS maps; estate records; GEN: CEN; OPRs; MI, VR; ER; DIR, LISTS, IND, IGI(S).

Finding aids: Card catalogue & newspaper index, catalogue of photographic collection, map list.
Leaflets: Publications incl. history and family history research booklets.
Reprographics: R1, R4, R5

## Dunning

**91   Dunning Parish Historical Society**
**Old Schoolhouse, Newton of Pitcairns, Dunning PH2 0SL**
**http://www.dunning.mcmail.com**
Collection includes 200 b&w photographs 1890-1940 & 1800 col mostly 1992/3 of parish; research paper; 40 interviews 1990s on tape; 12 videos of reconstructed & retold historical recollections include tattie howkers, tradesmen, evacuees.
(1) Chairman: Ian Philip (Tel: 01764 684269)
(2) Secretary: Patricia Wallace (Tel: 01764 684581)
(*) Vice-Chairman: Elizabeth Fletcher (Tel: 01764 684061)
Access: BAO
*On outskirts of village; parking.*
Leaflets: Newsletters & booklets plus videos.

## Dunoon

**92   Argyll & Bute Library Service: Local Collection**
**Library HQ, Highland Avenue, Sandbank, Dunoon PA23 8PB**
*Tel: 01369 703214  Fax: 01369 705797*
Comprehensive collection of books relating to the district and its inhabitants; postcard collection (1000 1890s-1920s); photographic collection (includes over 2000 pre1914 photographs of Campbeltown). Other primary source material is held by the Council's Archive, Manse Brae Area Office, Lochgilphead.
(1) Local Studies Librarian: Michael Davis
Access: Mon-Fri 0900-1700. BAO
*3 ml N of town centre; infrequent bus service, parking; disabled access.*
Finding aids: Paper & computerised catalogue
Leaflets: Publications list.
Reprographics: R1, R5

## 93 Dunoon & Cowal Heritage Trust: Castle House Museum
### Castle Gardens, Dunoon PA23 7HH
*Tel: 01369 701422*

Small collection of 200 photographs 1860s-; 800 postcards 1890s-; correspondence of societies and some Dunoon Grammar School records 1900-.

(1) Curator: J Stirling
(2) Contact : M Paterson (Tel: 01369 703040)
(*) Contact : K M Allan (Tel: 01369 703033)
Access: Mon-Sat 1030-1630, Sun 1430-1630 (Apr-Oct). PCA.
*Close to pier; bus route, limited parking nearby; disabled access.*

## East Fortune

## 94 Museum of Flight Library
### East Fortune Airfield, East Fortune EH39 5LF
*Tel: 01620 880308   Fax: 01620 880355*
### Email: aes@nms.ac.uk

Wide range of aviation books, photographs, documents, maps, periodicals and manuals.

(1) Contact : Adam Smith
(2) Contact : Colin Hendry
Access: Museum open Mon-Sun 1030-1700 (15 Mar-15 Nov). Library BAO. Charges: No charges to use library.
*At Museum of Flight; Haddington to North Berwick bus calls Easter-Oct, parking; disabled access.*
Primary sources: 5000 photographs on aviation topics with emphasis on Scotland. Large document collection relating to the Museums's collection of aircraft, engines and rockets, and aircraft production in Scotland. Major collection of material about 1920 Lanark Air Show. Large collection of material relating to East Lothian airfields. Large collection of airship related material.
Finding aids: Enquiry service via email.
Leaflets: Museum leaflet.
Reprographics: R1

## East Kilbride

**# 95 South Lanarkshire Council: Archives & Information Management Service**
**30 Hawbank Road, College Milton, East Kilbride G74 5EX**
*Tel: 01355 239193  Fax: 01355 242365*

Records of South Lanarkshire Council and predecessor authorities and of public, private, commercial and community organisations within South Lanarkshire.

(1) Archivist: Frank Rankine

Access: Mon-Thu 0930-1630, Fri 0930-1600. BAO

*Bus routes nearby, parking; disabled access.*

Primary sources: Records of East Kilbride (1960s-75) and Hamilton (late 19C-1975) Burghs (see also Hamilton Library); Hamilton, East Kilbride & Clydesdale District Councils (1975-1996); South Lanarkshire Council (1996-); extensive records of East Kilbride Development Corporation (1947-95) include plans, maps, technical and promotional material and 2000+ photographs; business records include Laurie & Symington, agricultural auctioneers, Lanark 1860s-1960s.

Finding aids: Archive lists.

Reprographics: Photocopies A4.

**96 South Lanarkshire Libraries**
**East Kilbride Central Library, 40 The Olympia, East Kilbride G74 1PG**
*Tel: 01355 220046  Fax: 01355 229365*
**Email: e.k.reference@south-lanarkshire.co.uk**

Collection comprises 2500+ items incl. books, pamphlets, 500 maps, newspapers relating to East Kilbride and district.

(1) Local Studies Librarian: John McLeish

Access: Mon-Tue, Thu 0915-1930; Wed, Sat 0915-1700; Fri 0930-1930. PCA.

Charges: Search charges for mail enquiries.

*In town centre in Olympia shopping complex; bus station, parking nearby; disabled access.*

Primary sources: Newspapers: East Kilbride News 1952 to date; Hamilton Advertiser 1956-1988; Glasgow and East Kilbride Railway Development Association Archives 1963-1980. GEN: CEN, OPRs, IGI(BI).

Finding aids: Library catalogues; indexes for some material.

Leaflets: Genealogical & publications lists.

Reprographics: R1, R4

## Edinburgh

**97 Advocates Library**
**Parliament House, Edinburgh EH1 1RF**
*Tel: 0131 260 5683  Fax: 0131 260 5663*
A specialised law library and a legal deposit library since 1711. The comprehensive collection of Scottish law publications include printed session papers 1707-1868 (3300+ vols). NB. Access to material is available via the Manuscripts Division of the National Library of Scotland.
(1) Senior Librarian: Catherine A Smith (Tel: 0131 260 5637)
(2) R S Librarian: Andrea Longson
(*) Keeper of the Library: Angus Stewart QC
Access: Mon-Fri 0930-1600. BAO
*Off the High St, Waverley rail station, St Andrews Sq bus station, parking nearby; on bus routes.*

**98 The Architectural Heritage Society of Scotland**
**Dr Sean O'Reilly (Director), The Glassite Meeting House, 33 Barony Street, Edinburgh EH3 6NX**
*Tel: 0131 557 0019  Fax: 0131 557 0049*
**Email: glassite@ahss.org.uk**
**http://www.ahss.org.uk**
The AHSS (formerly Scottish Georgian Society) concerns itself with the protection & study of Scotland's architectural history. It has linkages with other similar organisations. It publishes an annual journal "Architectural Heritage" and the twice yearly "Magazine".

**99 Bank of Scotland Archive**
**Operational Services Division, 12 Bankhead Terrace, Sighthill, Edinburgh EH11 4DY**
*Tel: 0131 529 1288  Fax: 0131 529 1307*
Scotland's first bank was established by an Act of the Scots Parliament on 17 July 1695. This Act specified that certain records should be preserved for as long as the bank endured. The archive contains a wealth of material covering the economic development of Scotland.
(1) The Archivists
Access: Mon-Fri 1000-1600. BAO
*On Sighthill Industrial Estate 4 ml W of city centre; bus routes, parking nearby.*
Primary sources: Bank of Scotland records from 1695: lists of proprietors, records of share transfers, minute books, ledgers, correspondence, journals, banknote registers, maps & plans, salary books, branch records, circulars etc.; extensive holdings for the British Linen Bank from 1746 and Union Bank (previously Glasgow Union Banking Co.) from 1830 until their respective mergers with The Bank of Scotland in 1971 and 1955; other bank archives:

Aberdeen Banking Co., Edinburgh Linen Co-Partnery, Edinburgh Stapleary of Yarn, Salton Bleachfield, Caledonian, Central, City of Glasgow, Sir Wm Forbes, Leith, Manchester & Liverpool, Montrose, Northumberland & Durham, Paisley, Perth, Perth United, Ship, Thistle. Mainly MS volumes; The Melville papers 1777-1849; the Bank of Scotland Directories 1960-64; Hunters & Co, bankers, Ayr 1773-1843; Scottish Banks' General Managers' Committee 1764-1971; Bank of Scotland Trading with the Enemy Act (WWI) records 1914-19.
Finding aids: NRA(S) lists Nos 945 & 1110.
Leaflets: List of books covering history of the Bank.
Reprographics: R1

## 100 Bank of Scotland Museum
### Head Office, The Mound, Edinburgh EH1 1YZ
*Tel: 0131 243 5467  Fax: 0131 243 5546*

Small museum which tells the story of nearly 300 years of banking in Scotland from 1695, having a wide collection of Scottish banknotes and forgeries of these notes; early pictures & photographs of the bank and staff; Scottish coins; maps, plans and engravings.
(1) The Bank of Scotland Archive (q.v.) (Tel: 0131 529 1288  Fax: 0131 529 1307)
Access: Mon-Fri 1000-1645 (early Jun-early Sep). Other times BAO.
*In city centre; Waverley rail station & St Andrews Sq bus station nearby, on bus routes.*
Leaflets: Available.

## 101 British Geological Survey
### Murchison House, West Mains Road, Edinburgh EH9 3LA
*Tel: 0131 667 1000  Fax: 0131 667 2785*
Email: mhlib@bgs.ac.uk
http://www.bgs.ac.uk/

The library holds a large collection of books, journals, maps and photographs relating to all aspects of the geology of Scotland. The National Geological Records Centre holds the records and archives of the Geological Survey in Scotland dating from the 1860s, incl. mine plans and borehole records.
(1) Archives: Richard Gillanders (Tel: 0131 650 0307)
(2) Library: Bob McIntosh (Tel: 0131 650 0322)
Access: Mon-Thu 0900-1630; Fri 0900-1600. Archives BAO.
*King's Buildings' campus, 2.25 ml S of Princes St E End; bus routes nearby, parking; disabled access.*
Primary sources: Collection of mine plans (c2500) incl. plans of abandoned mines. Geological Survey photographs (c20000) on geology and scenery throughout Scotland, incl. historical photographs, particularly mining and quarrying (1890s-). Survey archives (from 1860s) incl. field maps, field notebooks, correspondence and biographical material. Mineral resource

records on mineral exploration and extraction. Large collection of borehole records, incl. bore books of coal and iron companies (early 1800s to c1950). Finding aids: Catalogues, database indexes, plans of abandoned coal/oil/shale mines on mfilm aperture cards only.
Reprographics: R1, R5, photocopies A0-A2.

## 102 Chartered Institute of Bankers in Scotland
### 38b Drumsheugh Gardens, Edinburgh EH3 7SW
*Tel: 0131 473 7777  Fax: 0131 473 7788*
### Email: info.ciobs@dial.pipex.com
### http://www.ciobs.org.uk
Library includes a special collection ocvering banking histories, banking documents, Scottish bank notes.
(1) Chief Executive: C W Munn
Access: Mon-Fri 0900-1700. PCA.
*In W End, off Queensferry St; Haymarket rail station, bus routes, parking nearby.*
Reprographics: Photocopies A4.

## 103 The Cockburn Association (The Edinburgh Civic Trust)
### Trunk's Close, 55 High Street, Edinburgh EH1 1SR
*Tel: 0131 557 8686  Fax: 0131 557 9387*
### Email: cockburn.association@btinternet.com
### http://www.cockburn.org.uk
Cockburn Association Annual Reports and minute books 1895-1970 and Newsletters 1971 to date, covering planning/conservation issues in Edinburgh. NB. Reports and newsletters can be seen at the NLS and Central Library in Edinburgh.
(1) Secretary: Terry Levinthal
Access: Mon-Fri 0930-1730. BAO
*Off the High St; Waverley rail station & St Andrews Sq bus station, parking nearby.*
Reprographics: R1

## 104 The Corstorphine Trust: Local History Section
### The Dower House, St.Margaret's Park, Corstorphine High Street, Edinburgh EH12 7SX
*Tel: 0131 316 4246*
Collection features the history of Corstorphine through c1600 photographs from end 19C; documents incl. correspondence on local events, histories of clubs & organisations; some postcards, drawings, paintings, estate & OS maps. GEN: CEN, OPRs.
(1) The Archivist

Access: Sat 1000-1200; Wed 1000-1200 (mid Apr-mid Oct). PCA. Other
times BAO.
*3.5 ml W of W End of Princes St; on bus routes, limited parking.*
Finding aids: In-house catalogue to be computerised.
Leaflets: Publications list.
Reprographics: R1, R5

## 105  Council for Scottish Archaeology
### Karin Peterson (Secretary), c/o National Museums of Scotland, Chambers Street, Edinburgh EH1 1JF
### *Tel: 0131 247 4119  Fax: 0131 247 4126*
### Email: csa@dial.pipex.com

The CSA works to advance the study and care of Scotland's historic
environment. It supports local archaeological action & offers an information
service. Regular publications "Discovery & Excavation in Scotland" &
"Scottish Archaeological News".
Leaflets: List of publications available.

## 106  Cramond Heritage Trust
### The Maltings, The Foreshore, Cramond, Edinburgh EH4

Wide ranging collection of information on Cramond from pre Roman times to
present incl., Cramond Kirkyard records plus photographs and maps,
information on archaeological digs and finds, local people incl. oral tapes.
(1) Contact : K Dods (Tel: 0131 336 2124)
(2) Contact : I Williamson (Tel: 0131 312 6125)
Access: Sat-Sun 1400-1700 (Jun-Sep). Other times BAO. PCA.
Charges: Donations welcomed.
*3.5 ml NW of city centre; bus routes, parking nearby.*
Leaflets: Booklet and leaflet list.
Reprographics: Photocopying and photographic facilities can be arranged.

## 107  Edinburgh Academy
### 42 Henderson Row, Edinburgh EH3 5BL
### *Tel: 0131 556 4603  Fax: 0131 556 9353*
### Email: edacadr@aol.com
### http://www.cybersurf.co.uk/academy

Collection includes files on former pupils & rector's reports, syllabi, classes
etc. from 1824, together with school magazines, old photographs,
memorabilia & former pupils' publications.
(1) Contact : A M Jarman
Access: BAO
*0.7 ml N of Princes St; Waverley rail station 1 ml, bus routes nearby, parking.*
Finding aids: Apply through archivist.
Reprographics: R1

**108 Edinburgh Archaeological Field Society**
**c/o K R Murdoch, 21 Marchbank Gardens, Balerno,**
**Edinburgh EH14 7ET**
*Tel: 0131 539 6776*
**Email: postmaster@scifi.abel.co.uk.**
**http://www.abel.co.uk./~scifi/eafs**
Research material on Fast castle excavation and history of Cramond. This material will be lodged with the National Monuments Record Scotland (NMRS).
(1) Chairman: Kenneth R Murdoch
(2) Secretary: Sandra Fordyce (Tel: 0131 317 8304)
Access: BAO to consult research material.
Leaflets: Publications: Annual Report, Bi-monthly newsletter (on WWW); History of Fast Castle.

**109 Edinburgh Architectural Association**
**15 Rutland Square, Edinburgh EH1 2BE**
*Tel: 0131 229 7545  Fax: 0131 228 2188*
A diverse collection of mainly 19C material covering architecture in Scotland, especially Edinburgh.
(1) Contact : A Anderson
(2) Contact : D Waugh (Tel: 0131 558 1234  Fax: 0131 557 2002)
Access: Tue-Fri 1000-1200. BAO
*W End of Princes St by Caledonian Hotel; Haymarket rail station, bus routes, car park nearby, limited on-street parking.*

**110 Edinburgh City Archives**
**City of Edinburgh Council, City Chambers, High**
**Street, Edinburgh EH1 1YJ**
*Tel: 0131 529 4616  Fax: 0131 529 4957*
The surviving written record relating to the administration of Edinburgh from the 12C to the present, plus former Leith and Queensferry town council records.
(1) City Archivist: Richard Hunter (Tel: 0131 529 4291)
(2) Contact : P McNicol (Tel: 0131 529 4391)
Access: Mon-Thu 0900-1300; 1400-1630. PCA.
*Waverley rail station, St Andrews Sq bus station, parking nearby, on bus routes; limited disabled access.*
Primary sources: Edinburgh Town Council Minutes and associated papers, ledgers etc. 1551-1975 (MS and printed); Dean of Guild court records and plans 1540-1975 (MS); Registers of Burgesses 1487-1975. Other collections of note include: Trinity Hospital, Soutra Hospital, Edinburgh City Police, The Society of High Constables of Edinburgh, The Episcopal congregations of Old St Pauls and St Pauls and St Georges, Edinburgh Police Commissioners, The Incorporation of Hammermen, Leith Shipping Company, Canongate Burgh Court, Voters rolls both local and parliamentary, The

South Bridge Commisioners, Craiglockhart Parochial Board, Edinburgh City Guard, The Convention of Royal Burghs of Scotland, Edinburgh Militia, City Improvement Scheme maps/minutes/memoranda, Stent and Annuity tax rolls, Impost ledgers (ale duty), Portsburgh Barony, Greyfriars, St Cuthberts, Canongate, Edinburgh Southern Cemeteries, The Scottish Modern Art Association, Alex Ferguson Ltd, The Merchant Company of Edinburgh, Canongate Gaol, Edinburgh Police and Burgh Court, Edinburgh Water Trust, West Lothian Police, Leith Sailors Home, Edinburgh Gas Light Company, Incorporation of Bakers of Edinburgh, Miller of Craigentinny, Thistle Golf Club.
Finding aids: In-house lists, catalogues & databases.
Reprographics: R1, photocopies AO-A2 (by arrangement).

## 111 Edinburgh City Corporate Services Library Architectural Services, 154 McDonald Road, Edinburgh EH6 4LA
### Tel: 0131 529 5971  Fax: 0131 554 7780
Collection of drawings of buildings owned by the former Lothian Regional Council (1975-1996) plus local history monographs.
(1) Contact : Maggie Gottier
Access:  BAO
*N of E End of Princes St; Waverley rail station, St Andrews Sq bus station 1 ml, bus routes nearby, parking; disabled access difficult.*
Reprographics: Full chargeable reproduction service.

## 112 Edinburgh City Libraries Edinburgh Room, Central Library, George IV Bridge, Edinburgh EH1 1EG
### Tel: 0131 225 5584 x223  Fax: 0131 225 8783
Extensive collection of printed material on people, places and events, current and historical, associated with the City of Edinburgh, incl. Leith, Portobello and South Queensferry, books, journals, press cuttings, prints, photographs and ephemera, plus books by and about Robert Louis Stevenson, Arthur Conan Doyle and Sir Walter Scott.
(1) Contact : Ann Nix
Access: Mon-Thu 1000-2000; Fri 1000-1700; Sat 0900-1300. PCA.
*In city centre; Waverley rail station nearby, bus station 0.75 ml, on bus routes, parking nearby; disabled access.*
Primary sources: Includes newspapers 1753- (Scotsman 1817- and Evening News 1873-, together with runs of earlier newspapers); maps 16C-; collection of prints, watercolours and plans of buildings; photographic collection (c20000) from 1840s; ephemera includes: Jenners Department Store catalogues and publications, Edinburgh International Festival Programmes and reviews; collection of examples of early printing and publishing in Edinburgh 18/19C. GEN: CEN, OPRs, VR, ER, DIR (1773-1974).
Finding aids: Subject indexes to books, prints, newspaper cuttings; card catalogue for pre 1980 material & computerised catalogue 1980-.

Leaflets: Resource guides.
Reprographics: R1 (b&w, col), R4, R5, computer prints.

## 113 Edinburgh City Libraries: Scottish Library
### Central Library, George IV Bridge, Edinburgh EH1 1EG
*Tel: 0131 225 5584 x237  Fax: 0131 225 8783*

Collection of c70000 books and pamphlets on Scottish life, culture and history; 4000+ prints and photographs from early 20C with a substantial representation of highland life. Scottish maps (late 17C-); videos (150) featuring Scottish culture; press cutting collection and government publications.
(1) Contact : Fiona Myles
Access: Mon-Thu 1000-2000; Fri 1000-1700; Sat 0900-1300. PCA.
*In city centre; Waverley rail station nearby, bus station 0.75 ml, on bus routes, parking nearby; disabled access.*
Primary sources: Glasgow Herald newspaper 1885-; GEN: CEN & OPRs for I5 council areas; VR for Lothians; DIR local and national; ER, IND, MI, IGI, family history books.
Finding aids: Card catalogue pre 1980; on line catalogue 1980-; press cuttings & periodicals index; Glasgow Herald index 1906-84 & CDRom 1994-.
Leaflets: Family history leaflet.
Reprographics: R1, R2, R5

## 114 Edinburgh City Museums: Huntly House & People's Story
### 142 Canongate, Edinburgh EH8 8BN
*Tel: 0131 529 4143(HH)405  Fax: 0131 557 3346*

The collections of Huntly House & People's Story Museum (163 Canongate) contain material from 16C to the present day and features the history of Edinburgh and its people.
(1) Contact : Helen Clark (Tel: 0131 529 4059)
(2) Contact : David Scarratt (Tel: 0131 529 4052)
Access: Mon-Sat 1000-1700. PCA.
*Waverley rail station nearby, St Andrews Sq bus station 0.75 ml, on bus route, parking nearby; limited disabled access.*
Primary sources: Wide ranging records of business and trades include letters, documents, brochures, local regulations, acts and proclamations, advertisements, diplomas, indentures, trade directories; labour records include cards, certificates, rule books, Co-operative Society yearbooks, annuals); Friendly Society and temperance material; 5000+ photographs cover topography, domestic and working life, leisure activities mostly 20C; oral tape archive of 350+ tapes cover many aspects of 20C life in Edinburgh. Special collections include trade union and friendly society banners; the business records etc. of the Holyrood and Norton Park glassworks and Buchans Thistle Pottery; archive material relating to Field Marshall Earl Haig.

Leaflets: Publications list.
Reprographics: R1, R5

## 115 Edinburgh City Museums: Museum of Childhood
## 42 High Street, Edinburgh EH1 1TC
### *Tel: 0131 529 4142/4119  Fax: 0131 558 3103*

Part of the collection incl. toys, games, costumes and items relating to
health, education and pastimes is of Scottish origin. Reference library.
Photographs of children.
(1) The Curators
Access: Mon-Sat 1000-1700; Sun (Edinburgh Festival) 1400-1700. PCA
*In Royal Mile; Waverley rail station, St Andrews Sq bus station nearby, on
bus routes, parking nearby; limited disabled access.*
Leaflets: Museum of Childhood Guide; resource packs; postcards & other
publications & lists.
Reprographics: R1, R5

## 116 Edinburgh City Museums: The Writers' Museum
## Lady Stair's House, Lady Stair's Close, Lawnmarket,
## Edinburgh EH1 2PA
### *Tel: 0131 529 4901  Fax: 0131 220 5057*
### Email: enquiries@writersmuseum.demon.co.uk

The Writers' Museum contains MS books, photographs, portraits, sculpture
and memorabilia relating to Robert Burns, Sir Walter Scott, Robert Louis
Stevenson and George Meikle Kemp (architect of the Scott Monument).
(1) Contact : Elaine Greig (Tel: 0131 529 4064)
Access: Mon-Sat 1000-1700; Sun (Edinburgh Festival) 1400-1700. PCA.
*In Lady Stair's Close, off the Lawnmarket (top of Royal Mile); Waverley rail
station, St Andrews Sq bus station, parking nearby.*
Primary sources: MS poems, songs, correspondence and family papers,
biographies and various editions of works of the three "writers".
Leaflets: Guide books and leaflets availble.
Reprographics: R1, R5

## 117 Edinburgh University Library: Main Library
### George Square, Edinburgh EH8 9LJ
*Tel: 0131 650 3384  Fax: 0131 650 3380*
Email: library@ed.ac.uk
http://www.lib.ed.ac.uk/

Collections in the Main Library & the specialist subject collections in the Faculty libraries are rich in books, periodicals, maps & medieval & modern MS of interest for local & especially historical studies.
(1) Librarian - Special Collections: Murray C T Simpson (Tel: 0131 650 8379 Fax: 0131 650 6863)
(2) University Archivist: Arnott Wilson (Tel: 0131 650 6865  Fax: 0131 650 6863)
(*) Lothian Health Services Archivist: Michael Barfoot (Tel: 0131 650 3392 Fax: 0131 650 6863)
Access: Mon-Thu 0900-2200; Fri-Sat 0900-1700; Sun 1200-1700 (term-time). Mon-Tue, Thu-Fri 0900-1700. Wed 0900-2100 (vacations). Special Collections Dept: Mon-Thu 0900-1800, Fri 0900-1700 (term-time). Mon-Fri 0900-1700 (vacations). PCA; visitors must register as external readers.
Charges: Borrowing on subscription. Charges for genealogical services.
*SW corner of George Sq; buses, parking nearby; disabled access.*
Primary sources: Most of the university's archives (MS & printed). Other material includes ephemeral memorabilia of student life at the university. This collection & the Lothian Health Services Archive form a major resource on the history of medicine in Edinburgh 18-20C. Some parts of these archives are subject to confidential rules. The Laing manuscripts include medieval & modern MS sources on local areas & buildings. The Edinburgh Collection of architectural drawings & plans include those by William Playfair, Sir Rowland Anderson & other notable Edinburgh architects. Older collections of printed books include many 19-20C published local histories. The map collection includes many historical maps of most areas of Scotland.
Finding aids: Printed books: in-house guardbook catalogue & microfiche; on-line catalogue containing all material acquired since 1935 plus retroconverted items. Manuscripts & archives: in-house indexes, handlists & inventories.
Leaflets: Printed guides & lists of publications available.
Reprographics: R1 (plus A2), R4, R5

## 118 Edinburgh University Library: New College Library
### Mound Place, Edinburgh EH1 2LU
*Tel: 0131 650 8957  Fax: 0131 650 3380*
Email: newcoll@srv1.lib.ed.ac.uk
http://www.ed.ac.uk

The library caters for most aspects of the study of the christian religion. It specialises in the Reformed Viewpoint. Holdings include Parish histories and published documents of the Church of Scotland and other Presbyterian Scottish churches; plus the Faculty of Divinity and older New College archives.

(1) Contact : Pamela Gilchrist
(2) Contact : Eileen Dickson
Access: Mon-Thu 0900-2130; Fri 0900-1700; Sat 0900-1230 (term-time).
Mon-Fri 0900-1700 (vacations). PCA.
*In city centre; St Andrews Sq bus station & Waverley rail station, parking nearby; on bus routes; disabled access.*
Primary sources: Manuscript collection mainly 19 & early 20C ministers' papers, notably the Thomas Chalmers papers. Longforgan Free Church Ministers' Library (about 1500 vols); W F Jackson collection of material on the Holy Land (about 1500 vols); Dumfries Presbytery Library (about 1500 vols); large collections printed books (16-18C) and pamphlets (16-19C) of religious controversial nature. James Thin Hymnology Collection (more than 7000 vols).
Finding aids: All holdings after May 1986 are on the public on-line catalogue accessible through JANET on WWW. In-house shelf catalogue.
Leaflets: Guide to New College Library.
Reprographics: R1, R5

## 119  Edinburgh University: Moray House Archive
## Moray House Institute of Education, Holyrood
## Campus, Holyrood Road, Edinburgh EH8 8AQ
### *Tel: 0131 556 8455*

Archives of Moray House Institute of Education & its predecessors 1945-.
(1) University Archivist: Arnott Wilson (Tel: 0131 650 6865  Fax: 0131 650 6863)
Access: Tue 1000-1630. BAO
*E end of Old Town; Waverley rail station, St Andrews Sq bus station 0.75 ml, on bus routes, parking nearby.*
Primary sources: The archive records include: Edinburgh Church of Scotland training college & normal school, Edinburgh United Free Church Training College, Edinburgh Provincial training college, Moray House College of Education, Moray House Demonstration school & its predecessors (1867-1968); records & associated colleges: College of Physical Education, Edinburgh College of Domestic Science, St.Georges training college (1909-1991); Callander Park & Newington Halls of Residence (1916-1997). Access can be arranged to consult the collection of the former Scottish Centre for Physical Education, Movement & Leisure Studies (SCOPEMAL), the former Dunfermline College of Physical Education, Cramond, Edinburgh.
Finding aids: Descriptions & item lists available.
Leaflets: Available.
Reprographics: R1, R5

## 120 Edinburgh University: School of Scottish Studies - Library & Archives
### 27 George Square, Edinburgh EH8 9LD
*Tel: 0131 650 3060  Fax: 0131 650 4163*
### Email: hardcasf@stv1.lib.ed.ac.uk

A substantial library of local and general publications on Scottish history and culture and comparative material from other countries. Card indexes to the contents of numerous relevant publications incl. the old and new statistical accounts. Binders of transcriptions from tapes and box files of newspaper cuttings, pamphlets, questionnaires.

(1) Library: Francesca Hardcastle

(2) Archives: Rhona Talbot (Tel: 0131 650 4159)

Access: Mon-Fri 0900-1230, 1400-1700. PCA.

*W side of George Sq; bus routes, parking nearby; disabled access difficult.*
Primary sources: Sound archive: 10000+ tapes on music and narrative, social history, custom and belief, material culture, history of settlement. Some early cylinder, wire and direct disc recordings. Place Name Survey with 1000000 excerpted names. 500 tapes, photographic, film and video archive: 10000 + negatives; slide collection. A number of film and video tapes. Tale Archive: 6000+ texts and 2000 index cards; The John Levy Collection: c700 tapes, several thousand slides and photographs, some 16mm cine films, 338 discs of music from different countries; The Will Forret Collection: 2000 commercial discs, several hundred cassette recordings. MS and typescripts: Dr R C MacLagan's collections on highland folklore; Lady Evelyn Stewart-Murray's collection of gaelic traditional tales; The Linguistic Survey of Scotland (written and recorded data on Gaelic and lowland Scots dialects and varieties of Scottish English).

Finding aids: Finding aid to archive accessions via WWW, card catalogue to books, printed indexes.

Reprographics: R1, R5

## 121 Fettes College Archives
### Carrington Road, Edinburgh EH4 1QX
*Tel: 0131 332 2281  Fax: 0131 332 3081*

Archives include school records from 1870 plus records of the estate of Redcastle (1808), Arnsheen Denbrae (1825), Gogar Bank (1824-1836); Wamphry (1801-8); Comely Bank (1836); & part of Inverleith (1863).

(1) Archivist: Alexia Lindsay

Access:  BAO

*1.5 ml N of Princes St (W End); bus routes nearby, parking.*
Leaflets: Books on William Fettes & the school - details on request.

## 122 Free Church College Library
### The Mound, Edinburgh EH1 2LS
*Tel: 0131 226 5286  Fax: 0131 220 0597*
### Email: Dmacleod@freescotcoll.ac.uk
Scottish ecclesiastical history, incl. the Highlands and Islands, with Gaelic material.
(1) Contact : Donald MacLeod
(2) Contact : D MacDonald
Access: Mon-Fri 0900-1630. PCA.
*In city centre; Waverley rail station & St Andrews Sq bus station nearby; on bus routes, parking nearby; disabled access.*
Primary sources: Ecclesiastical documents (printed and MS); Victorian pamphlets; biographies; archival material relating mainly to Free Church of Scotland; The Witness newspapers.
Reprographics: R1

## 123 General Register Office for Scotland (GRO)
### New Register House, Princes Street, Edinburgh EH1 3YT
*Tel: 0131 334 0380  Fax: 0131 314 4400*
### Email: nrh.gros@gtnet.gov.uk
### http://www.open.gov.uk/gros/groshome.htm
Scottish birth, death and marriage records (1553-) and decennial census of population returns (1841-1891). WWW site includes statistical tables; Registrar General's annual reports for 1995 and 1996; population estimated and projections); popular surnames and forenames in Scotland (and by region); the Scottish Census (1801-2001); and electorate figures for 1997 and 1996.
(1) Public Counter Supervisor (Tel: 0131 314 4433  Fax: 0131 314 4400)
Access: Mon-Fri 0900-1630. PCA. Advisable to book a seat in advance.
Charges: Search and extracts charges.
*E End of Princes St; Waverley rail station, St Andrews Sq bus station, off-street parking nearby. If informed in advance we can make arrangements for customers with disabilities.*
Primary sources: Main records in the custody of the Registrar General include: Prior to 1855: OPRs covering births, deaths & marriages 1553-1854; Register of neglected entries 1801-1854. Post 1855: Registers of births, deaths and marriages; Adopted children register 1930-; Register of divorces 1984-; Marine register of births and deaths 1855-; Air register of births and deaths 1948-; service records 1881-; War register 1899-; registers of births, deaths and marriages in foreign countries 1860-1965. Also Census enumerators' transcript books 1841-1891. NB. Self-service access in the search rooms to OPRs, Register of neglected entries & census records (microfilm) and Post 1855 records (microfiche).
Finding aids: Computerised indexes to the statutory records of births, deaths & marriages, 1855-; register of divorces 1984-; OPR baptism & marriage entries 1553-1854; & the 1881 census records. Indexes for statutory records

1855-1897; OPR baptism & marriages 1553-1854; & 1881 & 1891 census records available on Internet at www.origins.net.
Leaflets: S1 List of main records in the care of the Register General; S2 Searching by our staff for a particular event; S3 Guidance for general search customers in New Register House. (Updated on 1 April each year).
Reprographics: Official extracts of individual entries in the registers supplied by the organisation. Costs given on leaflets S2 & S3. Microfilm copies of OPR and Census records; microfiche copies of indexes to OPR baptisms and marriages; and the 1891 census index are available from The Microfilm Unit (Tel.0131 314 4425).

## 124 The Grand Lodge of Antient Free & Accepted Masons of Scotland: The Grand Lodge of Scotland Museum & Library
**Freemasons Hall, 96 George Street, Edinburgh EH2 3DH**
*Tel: 0131 225 5304  Fax: 0131 225 3953*

The library houses approx 10000 vols. mostly concerned with freemasonry: history, symbolism, organisation etc; plus a rare collection of 2000 vols., the 'Morison collection' mainly in French.
(1) Curator: Robert LD Cooper
(2) Grand Secretary: C Martin McGibbon
Access: Mon-Fri 0930-1630. BAO
*In city centre; Waverley rail station, St Andrews Sq bus station nearby, on bus routes, parking nearby.*
Primary sources: The Grand Lodge of Scotland founded 1736 is the headquarters of Scottish Freemasonry. Primary source materials comprise the membership record of Scottish Lodges, incomplete 1599-1736 and complete thereafter. Minute books and other records (of Grand Lodge and Lodges), charters & documents.
Finding aids: Card index & Morison collection catalogue.
Leaflets: Lists.
Reprographics: R1

## #125 Heriot-Watt University Archive
**Heriot-Watt University, Riccarton, Edinburgh EH14 4AS**
*Tel: 0131 451 3218  Fax: 0131 451 3164*
**Email: a.e.jones@hw.ac.uk**
**http://www.hw.ac.uk/archive**

The University Archive holds collections relating to the university and its predecessor institutions, the Riccarton Estate, the Currie and Balerno area, and other educational institutions, etc in the Edinburgh area.
(1) University Archivist: Ann Jones
Access: Mon-Fri 0930-1645. BAO

*Archive in the Library/Language building, University 8 ml W of Edinburgh between A70 & A71 roads; bus service to city centre, parking; disabled access.*
Primary sources: Official records of the Edinburgh School of Arts 1821-1854, the Watt Institution and School of Arts 1854-1885, Heriot-Watt College 1885-1966, and Heriot-Watt University 1966-, committee papers, academic records, correspondence, photographs, films, press cuttings, etc; family papers of the Gibson-Craig family, proprietors of Riccarton, incl. estate papers (titles etc) 15-19C, rentals, accounts etc and 19C correspondence; The Tweedie Collection of material (books, papers, photocopies, photographs and artefacts) relating to the history of the Currie and Balerno area; records (official and photographic) of Leith Nautical College 1855-1987; also small reference collection of books, pamphlets etc on Edinburgh educational history and of material relating to James Watt.
Finding aids: In-house lists, indexes, catalogues, summary guides on WWW site.
Leaflets: Available.
Reprographics: R1, R5

## 126 Heriot-Watt University: Edinburgh College of Art
## Lauriston Place, Edinburgh EH3 9DF
### *Tel: 0131 221 6000  Fax: 0131 451 3164*
Collection contains the records of governing body, administration, academic records, photographs and publicity material of the Edinburgh College of Art plus records of the former Trustees Academy and the School of Applied Art.
(1) Secretary: M Wood
Access: Thu 0930-1615. BAO
*Waverley & Haymarket rail stations 0.8 ml; bus station 1 ml; on bus routes; parking nearby; access for disabled persons can be arranged.*
Primary sources: Annual Reports 1908-1991, minutes of governing body 1908-1981, committee minutes and papers 1910-1977, principals papers 1968-77, general administration records 1907-1971, financial records 1908-1982, college building records 1948-1978, staff records 1922-1978, schools of Architecture, Drawing and Painting, Design and Crafts 1940s-1970s; publications and publicity material 1912-1996, photographs 1906-1986.
Trustees Academy School of Art: minute books 1869-1903, student record book 1907-8; The School of Applied Art: minute books 1892-1902, student record book 1892-1904.
Finding aids: Archive lists being developed.
Leaflets: Available.
Reprographics: R1, R5

**127 Historic Scotland Library**
**Room G55, Longmore House, Salisbury Place, Edinburgh EH9 1SH**
*Tel: 0131 668 8651  Fax: 0131 668 8749*
**Email: phill.hs.lh@gtnet.gov.uk**
**http://www.historic-scotland.gov.uk**
Library stock includes reference books; guides to historic buildings and ancient monuments; inventories; official publications; periodicals; Scottish Burgh Surveys; Exploring Scotland's heritage series; Royal Incorporation of Architects of Scotland guides. Subject coverage includes architecture, historic buildings, ancient monuments, archaeology, conservation. Photographs Library has b&w and colour photographs and slides of monuments in care and of listed historic buildings.
(1) Library and Records Manager: Paulette M Hill
Access: Mon-Fri 0900-1630. BAO
*Off Causewayside, 1.25 ml S of Princes St; on bus routes, parking nearby; disabled access.*
Finding aids: Computerised catalogue on WWW.
Leaflets: Publications: Historic Scotland list of and guides to various monuments.
Reprographics: Photocopies A4; photographic slides available from Historic Scotland Photographic Library.

**128 Institute of Chartered Accountants of Scotland**
**27 Queen Street, Edinburgh EH2 1LA**
*Tel: 0131 225 5673  Fax: 0131 225 3813*
**Email: edin.library@icas.org.uk**
**http://www.icas.org.uk**
The library houses a collection of books on accountancy related subjects: the antiquarian collection 1494-1930 maintained by the Institute is on deposit in the NLS; the archives of the three societies which formed the Institute are on deposit with the NAS (SRO). NB. Visitors who wish to consult the antiquarian collection or archives, are advised to contact the Institute prior to visiting in order that they may be directed to the correct source.
(1) Contact : Dorothy Hogg (Tel: 0131 247 4801)
(2) Contact : Bridget Bell (Tel: 0131 247 4801)
Access: Prior contact by phone, fax or email essential.
*In city centre; Waverley rail station, St Andrews Sq bus station, parking near.*
Finding aids: Antiquarian collection catalogues - paper, some on-line.
Reprographics: R1

**129** **Lothian Health Services Archive**
**Special Collections Department, Edinburgh**
**University Library, George Square, Edinburgh EH8**
**9LJ**
*Tel: 0131 650 3392  Fax: 0131 650 6863*
**Email: m.barfoot@ed.ac.uk**
**http://www.lib.ed.ac.uk/speccoll/lhsa.htm**
Records of hospitals and related institutions in Lothian and former counties
1728-. Collection of historical photographs.
(1) Contact : Mike Barfoot (Tel: 0131 650 6863)
(2) Contact : Julie Hutton (Tel: 0131 650 8379)
Access: Mon-Fri 0900-1700. BAO
Charges: Some postal enquiry charges.
*Princes St & Waverley rail station 1 ml, bus routes, parking nearby; disabled
access.*
Primary sources: Royal Infirmary minutes 1728-; Royal Edinburgh Hospital
records early 19C-; records of many of the hospitals in the region (incl. those
recently closed ie Bruntsfield and Elsie Inglis in Edinburgh); papers relating
to notable individuals such as Derek Dunlop & Elsie Stephenson; gifted
records of the Medico Chirurgical Society 1821-1971; records of the
Edinburgh Blood Transfusion Service; collection of clinical cases.
Reprographics: R1

**130** **Meteorological Office**
**Library & Archive, Saughton House, Broomhouse**
**Drive, Edinburgh EH11 3XQ**
*Tel: 0131 244 8368  Fax: 0131 244 8389*
**Email: ekerr@meto.gov.uk**
Meteorological records for Scotland dating back to the late 18C.
(1) Contact : Elizabeth Kerr
(2) Contact : Derek Hancock (Tel: 0131 244 8366)
Access: Mon-Fri 0900-1600. PCA with Moira Taylor.
*3.5 ml W of city centre; on bus routes, parking; disabled access.*
Primary sources: Material collected by the Scottish Meteorological Society in
the period 1855-1920 and by the Meteorological Office 1920-;
meteorological records for Scotland in a variety of MS, charts, tabulation and
autographic records late 18C-1960; similar material 1960- (MS, computer
records and microfilm).
Leaflets: Available.
Reprographics: R1, R3

**131 Museum of Fire**
**Lothian & Borders Fire Brigade, Lauriston Place, Edinburgh EH3 9DG**
*Tel: 0131 228 2401 x267 Fax: 0131 228 6222*
**Email: fas@lothianbordersfb.demon.co.uk**
Museum tells story of the oldest fire brigade in the UK founded 1824. Historic records on fire fighting and the fire brigade incl. collections of photographs and glass slides.
(1) The Librarian
Access: Mon-Fri 0900-1200, 1400-1630. BAO
Charges: Donations to Museum fund.
*At Fire Brigade HQ; on bus routes, parking nearby; disabled access.*
Reprographics: Photocopies (by arrangement).

**132 Napier University Library: Craiglockhart Campus Library**
**219 Colinton Road, Edinburgh EH14 1DJ**
*Tel: 0131 455 4383 Fax: 0131 455 4328*
**Email: c.walker@napier.ac.uk**
**http://www.napier.ac.uk**
The small War Poets Collection, commemorating the work of the WWI poets Wilfred Owen, Siegfried Sassoon (treated at the Craiglockhart War Hospital, now part of the University) and Robert Graves, contains first editions and material on WWI and Dr W Rivers who treated Sassoon.
(1) Campus Library Manager: C Walker
(2) Head of A.R.M.S.: G Forbes (Tel: 0131 455 3558)
Access: Mon-Thu 0845-2100, Fri 8.45-1700, Sat-Sun 1000-1600. PCA.
*2 ml SW of Princes St W End; on bus routes, parking.*
Finding aids: Catalogue & WWW site information.
Reprographics: Photocopies A4.

**133 Napier University Library: Edward Clark Collection**
**Merchiston Campus Library, 10 Colinton Road, Edinburgh EH10 5DT**
*Tel: 0131 455 2582 Fax: 0131 455 3566*
**Email: g.forbes@napier.ac.uk**
**http://www.napier.ac.uk/depts/library/clark/ecchome. html**
The Edward Clark Collection (4500 items) covers printing & book production from I5C (see WWW).
(1) Contact : G S Forbes (Tel: 0131 455 3558)
Access: Mon-Thu 0845-2100 (term-time), 0845-1700 (vacations); Fri 0845-1700; Sat-Sun 1000-1600. BAO

*1 ml S of Princes St W End; Haymarket rail station 1 ml, on bus routes,
parking nearby.*
Finding aids: 2 vol.printed catalogue; library catalogue.

## #134 National Archives of Scotland (NAS) formerly Scottish Record Office (SRO)
### HM General Register House, Princes Street, Edinburgh EH1 3YY
### *Tel: 0131 535 1314  Fax: 0131 535 1360*
### Email: research@sro.gov.uk

The widest ranging archive holdings in Scotland include government & legal records, private & local records with an extensive collection of maps & estate plans. Although holdings date from 12C the bulk date from 16C. There is a small specialised library containing historical, biographical, legal & topographical works which can be consulted by readers.
(1) Historical Search Room (Tel: 0131 535 1334  Fax: 0131 535 1328)
(2) West Search Room (Tel: 0131 535 1413  Fax: 0131 535 1430)
Access: Mon-Fri 0900-1645. Enquiries should be directed to the Keeper of the Records. Visitors should check in advance which Search Room (see below) holds the records they wish to consult; this may be done by telephone unless the enquiry is an involved one.
Charges: Legal enquiries only
*There are two Search Rooms: (1) Historical Search Room at HM General Register House, E end of Princes St; Waverley rail station, bus stations nearby; on bus routes; parking nearby; disabled access. (2) West Search Room at West Register House, W side of Charlotte Sq (W end of Princes St); Haymarket rail station, bus station, car park nearby; disabled access.*
Primary sources: GENERAL REGISTER HOUSE: Records of pre 1700 Scottish governments (Register of the Great Seal 1306-1668 & Privy Seal 1488-1584, Exchequer Rolls 1264-1600, Treasurer's Accounts 1473-1580); public registers (Registers of Deeds (from 1554) & Sasines (from 1599), Retours & Servicing of Heirs from c1545, County Registers of Sasines (c1617-) & for Burghs (c1681-1963); court records pre-1800 (Justiciary & some sheriff commissary courts); local records (Kirk Sessions from mid17C, some independent churches, burgh & county council records to 1975, valuation rolls 1855-, Heritor's records); private archives (over 450 large collections of major landed families, businesses, societies & institutions. The National Register of Archives (Scotland) (NRA(S)) surveys of collections still in private hands are available in both search rooms. WEST REGISTER HOUSE: Scottish Office records 1885-(30 year rule applies); court records 1800-; records of former Nationalised industries (coal, rail, gas, electricity & steel); over 80000 architectural, estate, railway, mining & engineering plans.
Finding aids: Paper catalogue with many collections now searchable on computer with some on microfiche (purchaseable). Indexes to Deeds, Sasines, Testaments(Wills), Confirmations & Inventories, pre-1707 government records.
Leaflets: Publications catalogue & information leaflets.
Reprographics: R1 (incl. A2), R4; photographs supplied by arrangement.

## 135 National Gallery of Scotland: Library
## The Mound, Edinburgh EH2 2EL
### *Tel: 0131 624 6501  Fax: 0131 220 0917*
### Email: paul.shackleton@natgalscot.ac.uk

This is a private working library; access to archival material or books by members of the public is dependant on them not being available in any other library in Edinburgh. Check with the Catalogue of Art Books in Scotland (UCABLIS) in the NLS before contacting the National Gallery of Scotland Library.

(1) Librarian: Paul Shackleton (Tel: 0131 624 6522)
(2) Contact : Valerie Hunter
Access: Mon-Fri 10.30-1230, 1400-1630. PCA. BAO
*Waverley rail station, St Andrews Sq bus station nearby; on bus routes; parking nearby; disabled access & adjacent parking.*
Primary sources: Books, periodicals and exhibition catalogues on Western art, particularly related to the gallery's own collection of paintings; files on the gallery's collection of paintings; photographs of paintings in other collections both private and public; collection of miscellaneaous archival and MS records; press cuttings relating to the galley.
Reprographics: R1

## #136 National Library of Scotland: Main Library
## George IV Bridge, Edinburgh EH1 1EW
### *Tel: 0131 226 4531  Fax: 0131 622 4803*
### Email: enquiries@nls.uk
### http://www.nls.uk

Scotland's largest library with some 6 million printed items, 1.5 million maps & around 100000 volumes of manuscripts. Special emphasis is given to all aspects of Scottish history, life & culture. The library's reading rooms are for reference & research that cannot easily be carried out elsewhere.
Access: Mon-Tue, Thu-Fri 0930-2030; Wed 1000-2030; Sat 0930-1300.
PCA. Admission by ticket only; contact Head of Reference Services.
*City centre location, Waverley rail station, bus station nearby; on bus routes; parking nearby; disabled access.*
Finding aids: Computerised catalogues giving details of some of the library's holdings are available on WWW. Extensive catalogues in reading rooms.
Bibliography of Scotland on CDRom.
Leaflets: Outlines of collections and services.
Reprographics: R1 (b&w, col), R4, R5, photocopies A0-A2

**#137 National Library of Scotland: Manuscripts Division**
**Main Library, George IV Bridge, Edinburgh EH1 1EW**
*Tel: 0131 226 4531  Fax: 0131 220 6662*
**Email: enquiries@nls.uk**
**http://www.nls.uk**

The Manuscript Division houses a very large collection, mostly relating to Scots and Scotland (c30000 vols. fully catalogued, 30000+ less thoroughly listed).
(1) Keeper of Manuscripts (Tel: 0131 226 4531 x2314)
Access: Mon-Tue, Thu-Fri 0930-2030; Wed 1000-2030; Sat 0930-1300. PCA.
Charges: Admission by reader's ticket.
*In city centre; Waverley rail station, bus station nearby, on bus routes, parking nearby; disabled access.*
Primary sources: Papers of a wide variety of individuals, families, estates, organisations relating to many different areas, incl. correspondence, legal, financial and estate papers, maps and plans, photographs, journals.
Finding aids: National Library of Scotland: Catalogue of manuscripts acquired since 1925, vol.1 1938-, further vols in preparation (may be consulted in the library). Inventories of other collections available in the library or in mfiche in the National Inventory of Documentary Sources (UK). Main accessions in the library's Annual Report & in the Historical Mauscripts Commission's on-line list of accessions to repositories. Current cataloguing is on WWW & added retrospectively.
Reprographics: R1 (b&w, col), R4, R5, photocopies A0-A2

**138 National Library of Scotland: Map Library**
**Causewayside Building, 33 Salisbury Place,**
**Edinburgh EH9 1SL**
*Tel: 0131 466 3813  Fax: 0131 466 3812*
**Email: maps@nls.uk**
**http://www.nls.uk**

Map Library is open for research and reference only; users are expected to have tried their local libraries and archives first; no loan of material. Has some 1.6 million cartographic items (inc. maps, charts, plans, atlases, gazetteers and cartographic reference books for all parts of world in both paper, microfiche and CD Rom format. It is particularly strong in maps, charts, plans and atlases with a Scottish association, ie compiled, engraved published or printed in Scotland, but relating to all parts of the world, as well as in foreign-published maps, charts, plans and atlases with particular reference to those parts of the world where Scots have explored, travelled, settled or fought. There is a comprehensive collection of printed maps, charts and plans pertaining to the whole or parts of Scotland 16-20C. There are also some 500 manuscript maps/plans. There are general reference works inc. the Statistical Accounts of Scotland to allow better understanding of the map collection.
(1) Head of Map Library (Tel: 0131 226 4531 x3411)

(2) Depute Map Curator/Map Library Manager (Tel: 0131 226 4531 x3418)
Access: Mon,Tue, Thu,Fri 0930-1700; Wed 1000-1700; Sat 0930-1300. PCA
if pre-1800; digitally scanned imagery or data; or, if a complex range of maps
are to be consulted - contact Assistant Map Curator.
Charges: Handling charges apply for complex or bulk photography orders
and for 'fast-stream' service.
*At junction of Causewayside & Grange/Salisbury Rds (map reference NT
263721), 1 ml due S of Princes St & Waverley rail station; 1.25 ml from St
Andrew Sq bus station, bus routes, limited parking nearby; disabled access
(please telephone in advance).*
Primary sources: Timothy Pont's 38 MS maps (1580s-90s) cover large parts
of Scotland. (Pont Project 1996-2000 is undertaking research and digital
scanning of the MS); Robert & James Gordon's revision of Pont (1630s-40s)
60 MS maps; Blaeu's Atlas Novus 1654 (47 printed maps); some John Adair
county maps and military maps 17/18C; county maps and estate plans
(1750s-1820s); sea charts (1680s-1880s); OS maps (1840s-1940s all
scales) (NB OS maps less than 50 years old can only be copied if
permission has been obtained from the OS).
Finding aids: NLS Manucripts Catalogue (published) incl. maps. See also
The Early Maps of Scotland to 1850, RSGS 1973 & 1983.
Leaflets: Leaflets and guides - essential reading prior to visit.
Reprographics: R1 (b&w, col), R4, photocopies A0-A2, full photographic
service, lamination, reinforcement and digital printouts, all subject to
copyright restrictions

## 139   National Museums of Scotland Library: Royal Museum of Scotland
## Chambers Street, Edinburgh EH1 1JF
*Tel: 0131 247 4137  Fax: 0131 247 4311*
## Email: library@nms.ac.uk
## http://nms.ac.uk

(Note: This library includes the collection formerly located at the Museum of
Antiquities, Queen Street, Edinburgh). Extensive Scottish archaeological
collection; Scottish history and topography, family histories. Key monograph
texts & a good selection of journal publications by county antiquarian &
historical societies. Good coverage of Scottish industrial archaeology &
technology, natural history & geology, incl. biographies of Scottish scientists.
(1) Enquiry Desk
Access: Library open Mon-Thu 1400-1700, Fri 1400-1630 BAO
Charges: Access to library free.
*S of Princes St; Waverley Rail station, bus routes & long stay parking nearby,
short stay parking at door; separate disabled access.*
Primary sources: Acts of Parliament of Scotland; Exchequer Rolls, MS
records of Society of Antiquaries of Scotland; miscellaneous MS. Alexander
Archer drawings (Edinburgh 1834-36); Daniel Wilson scrapbooks, Francis G
Rose scrapbooks. Archival material relating to early history of the museums.
MS letters, notebooks etc belonging to J A Harvie-Brown, William Jardine &
William Bruce, handlists of which were published as RSM information series:
Natural History, nos 7-9.

Finding aids: In-house online catalogue for full stock for consultation only.
Leaflets: Publications leaflet.
Reprographics: R1, R3, R5

## 140 National Museums of Scotland Library: Scottish United Services Museum
## The Castle, Edinburgh EH1 2NG
### Tel: 0131 225 7534 x404

Scottish military history incl. Navy and RAF 1660-; limited biographical information in official Army lists; Scottish regimental histories and journals; print collection of the Department of Armed Forces History. MS relating to regiments incl. some order books; letters and diaries incl. papers of Sir David Baird; Duke of Cumberland's papers.

(1) Custorial Assistant: Edith Philip
Access: Mon-Fri 0930-1230, 1400-1700. Note: Museum closed to Spring 2000. Library facilities will be available. BAO
Charges: Castle admission charges.
*In Edinburgh Castle; Waverley rail station nearby, St Andrews Sq bus station 0.75 ml, bus routes, parking nearby; disabled access by special arrangement.*
Reprographics: R1

## 141 National Museums of Scotland: Scottish Agricultural Museum
## Ingliston, Edinburgh EH28 8NB
### Tel: 0131 333 2674  Fax: 0131 333 2674
### Email: johnshaw@nms.ac.uk

Trade literature archive: manufacturers' catalogues relating to agriculture and rural trades in Scotland.

(1) Curator: John Shaw
(2) Assistant Curator - Collections: Wullie Findlay
(*) Assistant Curator - Public Services: Lesley McEwan
Access: Mon-Fri 1000-1700 (Oct-Mar). Mon-Sun 1000-1700 (Apr-Sep). Previous consultation for group visits only. BAO
*Within the Royal Highland & Agricultural Society Showground; bus services on A8, parking nearby; disabled access.*
Finding aids: Partially catalogued.
Reprographics: R1, R5

## 142 National Museums of Scotland: Scottish Life Archive
### Chambers Street, Edinburgh EH1 1JF
*Tel: 0131 247 4076/4073  Fax: 0131 247 4312*
### Email: dik@nms.ac.uk
### http://www.nms.ac.uk

The Scottish Life Archive, established 1959, records documentary and illustrative evidence of antiquities, country and urban life, industrial and maritime history of Scotland. It covers the period 1880 to the present day.
(1) Contact : Dorothy Kidd
Access: Mon-Fri 0900-1700. Weekend/evening visits may be possible. BAO
Charges: Commercial search charges: no admission charge when visiting archive only.
*Entrance at top of Bristo Port to rear of the Museum of Scotland; Waverley rail station nearby, St Andrew Sq bus station 0.75 ml, bus routes, parking nearby; disabled access can be arranged.*
Primary sources: Photographic collection (c100000 images) includes a number of collections by eminent photographers: William Easton, St Monance 1890-1920; H B Curwin, Foula & Shetland 1901-4; Mary Ethel Muir Donaldson, N W Scotland 1900-30; Alasdair Alpin McGregor, Scotland & Hebrides 1920-60; Scotland's Magazine 1928-75; agriculture practice 1960 (slides); Farm Building Survey 1993-6 (1500 slides). A Miscellaney of 3000 documents; 5000 postcards; scrapbook collection and audio visual collection (100 tapes/films).
Finding aids: Guide & index.
Leaflets: Available.
Reprographics: R1, R5

## #143 The National Trust for Scotland
### 5 Charlotte Square, Edinburgh EH2 4DU
*Tel: 0131 226 5922  Fax: 0131 243 9501*
### http://thenationaltrustforscotland.org.uk

Archives include the Trust's own records from 1931 plus those relating to properties not owned by the Trust but in which it has had an interest.
(1) Archivist: C J Bain (Tel: 0131 243 9524)
Access: Mon-Fri 0930-1630. BAO
*Off Princes St W End; Haymarket rail station nearby; Waverley rail station & St Andrews Sq bus station approx. 0.75 ml, on bus routes, parking nearby.*
Primary sources: MS collections relating to the Trust's properties (central registry, factorial dept, law agent); areas of activity, interest, history & organisation. Historical & archaeological material relating to St.Kilda 19C-. Collections of family & estate papers are held at some properties, notably the Irvine of Drum papers (Drum Castle) & Miss Toward's collection (Tenement House, Glasgow). Properties with book collections include: Barrie's birthplace; the castles at Brodick, Brodie, Drum, Fyvie, Carlyle's birthplace, Haddo House, Hill of Tarvit, Hugh Miller's House and Leith Hall. Contact the Representative in advance of any proposed visit to individual properties, many of which have collections of paintings - details of properties with address/phone/fax contained in each annual guide.

Finding aids: Printed indexes - photocopies available; List of films, slides & videos - can be hired.
Leaflets: Annual guide & publications list.
Reprographics: R1, R5

## 144 The Royal Bank of Scotland Archives
### 36 St Andrew Square, Edinburgh EH2 2YB
*Tel: 0131 523 2055  Fax: 0131 557 1623*
### Email: callachan@rbos.co.uk

The Archives contain the records of the bank from 1727, its associated and incorporated banks and those of smaller local Scottish banks.
(1) Archives Manager: Vicki Wilkinson
(2) Archive Administrator: Margaret Callachan
Access: Mon-Fri 0930-1630. BAO
*In city centre; rail & bus stations, parking nearby; disabled access.*
Primary sources: The Royal Bank of Scotland records from 1727 include Charter, board and committee papers, amalgamation records, ledgers and journals, share, customer, staff, property, note issue, marketing/advertising records; photographs, maps and plans,incl. extensive Darien Company material. The Company of Scotland 1695-1707: Board and committee records, list of subscribers and ship cargo ledgers. The Equivalent Company 1707-1851: Formation documents, debenture registers, share records, directors/partners papers, legal and accounting records, customer accounts, staff lists and remuneration material. Extensive archive material relating to the Commercial Bank of Scotland 1810-1959, National Bank of Scotland 1825-1959 and National Commercial Bank of Scotland 1959-1969, and the constituent banks; Aberdeen Commercial Banking Co, Arbroath Banking Co, Caithness Banking Co, Dundee Banking Co, Greenock Banking Co and Western Bank of Scotland.
Finding aids: Computerised catalogue for some material.
Reprographics: R1

## 145 Royal Botanic Garden Library
### Inverleith Row, Edinburgh EH3 5LR
*Tel: 0131 552 7171  Fax: 0131 248 2901*
### Email: j.hutcheon@rbge.org.uk
### http://www.rbge.org.uk

Historical archives on botany (incl Botanical Society of Scotland), gardening, plant collecting etc, incl. correspondence, diaries, field notebooks, biographical material, photographs (MS).
(1) Contact : Colin Will (Tel: 0131 248 2850/2973)
(2) Contact : Jane Hutcheon (Tel: 0131 248 2850/3)
Access: Mon-Thu 0930-1630; Fri 0930-1600. BAO
*Within Herbarium Building, Inverleith Row; 1.25 ml N of Princes St; on bus routes, parking nearby; disabled access.*
Finding aids: In-house catalogues.
Leaflets: Library information sheet and guide. Publications catalogue.

Reprographics: R1

## #146 Royal College of Nursing Archives
## 42 South Oswald Road, Edinburgh EH9 2HH
### *Tel: 0131 662 1010  Fax: 0131 662 1032*
### Email: archives@rcn.org.uk
### http://www.rcnscotland.org

Collection features the History of Nursing: books, journals, pamphlets, photographs, badges. Records of Royal College of Nursing (est 1916) and other nursing organisations. Oral history collection. NB: This is a UK archive. Approx 10% of the material will be Scottish.
(1) Archivist: Susan McGann
(2) Assistant Archivist: Fiona O'Brien
Access: Mon-Fri 0930-1630. BAO
*2 ml S of Princes St; bus routes nearby, parking; disabled access.*
Primary sources: RCN records: Minutes, reports and files on education, labour relations, international, parliamentary, press and public relations 1916-date. Personal papers of individual nurses, approx 1800-date. NB: the General Nursing Council of Scotland's Register of Nurses 1919-83 is located at the National Archives of Scotland, W Register House.
Finding aids: Catalogues & database.
Leaflets: RCN archives and oral history collection leaflets.
Reprographics: R1

## 147 Royal College of Physicians of Edinburgh
## 9 Queen Street, Edinburgh EH2 1JQ
### *Tel: 0131 225 7324  Fax: 0131 220 3939*
### Email: library@rcpe.ac.uk
### http://www.rcpe.ac.uk

Extensive collection of printed books and MS material 15C- concerning the history of medical science, education and practice, incl. related topics such as botany.
(1) Librarian
Access: Mon-Fri 0900-1700. BAO
*In city centre; Waverley rail station, St Andrews Sq bus station nearby, on bus routes, parking nearby; limited disabled access.*
Primary sources: Archives of the college incl. minutes and correspondence; notes of lectures given by founders of the Edinburgh Medical School case books, correspondence, diaries and other material belonging to medical practitioners; Edinburgh Medical and Surgical Journal 1805- and other periodicals; many portraits and prints of eminent medical men.
Finding aids: Various in-house catalogues, manuscript listing on WWW.
Reprographics: R1, R5

#### #148 Royal College of Surgeons of Edinburgh
#### Nicolson Street, Edinburgh EH8 9DW
*Tel: 0131 527 1630/2  Fax: 0131 557 6406*
#### Email: library@rcsed.ac.uk
#### http://www.rcsed.ac.uk

Archives generated by the College; papers of noted surgeons; printed list of fellows & licentiates of the College 1505-1993 & College Charters.

(1) Librarian

Access: Mon-Fri 0900-1700. PCA.

Charges: Charges at discretion of College.

*Waverley station nearby; St Andrews Sq bus station 0.75 ml, on bus routes; disabled access.*

Primary sources: Papers of Sir James Y Simpson, Sir Henry Wade, Sir John Struthers, Lord Lister, Sir John Bruce, Sir Walter Mercer; Royal Odonto-Chirurgical Society; Playfair's original plans of the College building, 1829-1832, the School of Medicine of the Royal Colleges, Edinburgh; Minutes of the College since 1581.

Finding aids: Summary Listing available plus NRA(S); in-house catalogues; selection of archives on WWW.

Leaflets: Leaflets describing services.

Reprographics: Photocopies & photographs can be supplied.

#### 149 Royal Commission on the Ancient and Historical Monuments of Scotland (RCAHMS)
#### John Sinclair House, 16 Bernard Terrace, Edinburgh EH8 9NX
*Tel: 0131 662 1456  Fax: 0131 662 1477*
#### Email: postmaster@rcahms.gov.uk
#### http://rcahms.gov.uk

Incorporates the **National Monuments Record of Scotland** (NMR(S)) containing an extensive collection of information and material relating to archaeological, architectural and industrial heritage of Scotland, incl. photographs.

(1) Depute Curator: D Murray

(2) Curator of Public Services: L M Ferguson

Access: Mon-Thu 0930-1630; Fri 0930-1600. Appointments needed to consult the Air Photographs Collection; the Royal Incorporation of Architects Collection, and rare material. PCA.

*1 ml S of Princes St & Waverley rail station; on bus routes, parking; disabled access.*

Primary sources: Prints and Drawings Collections incl. office collections of major Scottish architects (William Burn, Basil Spence, Thoms and Wilkie); survey drawings from RCAHMS field surveys, covering archaeology, buildings and industrial archaeology; antiquarian archaeological drawings and modern excavation drawings. Photographs incl. RCAHMS field and aerial surveys; vertical aerial photographs (formerly the Scottish Office Air

Photographs Unit) from the 1940s to the 1990s; archaeological excavation and antiquarian photographs incl. the Rokeby collection of railway photographs. Manuscripts incl. 18C architects contracts; research material compiled for government and other reports (eg Scottish burgh survey, excavation reports to papers on plasterers and decorative woodworkers); Microfilms incl. the OS name book and maps; Books incl. Scottish archaeology, architecture, history and topography; early topographical volumes in rare books collection.
Finding aids: CANMORE (Computer Application for National Monuments Record Enquiries) allows access to NMRS database in-house (on WWW) plus catalogues.
Leaflets: RCAHMS leaflets; User Guide; NMRS Jubilee Guide to the Collections 1991.
Reprographics: R1, R5 plus photo laser copying.

## 150 Royal Highland & Agricultural Society of Scotland: Library
**Royal Highland Centre, Ingliston, Edinburgh EH28 8NF**
*Tel: 0131 335 6227  Fax: 0131 333 5236*
**Email: info@sfacet.org.uk**
**http://www.sfacet.org.uk**

The library has c5000 books on agriculture and related subjects together with an extensive archive collection.
(1) Contact : Dorothy Amyes (Tel: 0131 335 6226)
(2) Contact : Sarah Rose
Access: Mon-Thu 0900-1700; Fri 0900-1530. BAO
*In office building in the showgrounds; bus routes on A8 main road nearby, parking.*
Primary sources: Archival material includes reports and minute books, accounts showing the development of the Society 1784-mid 20C; reports and premium certificates 1785-1831; writs of Old Assembly Hall, Edinburgh 1620-1813; information on shows and competitions mostly latter 19C-mid 20C; correspondence, photographs, printed papers on St Kilda 1859-1920; miscellaneous papers include patents, specifications and diagrams for reaping machines 1799-1852.
Leaflets: Transactions of the Society to 1968.
Reprographics: Photocopies A4.

## 151 Royal Incorporation of Architects in Scotland (RIAS)
### 15 Rutland Square, Edinburgh EH1 2BE
*Tel: 0131 229 7545  Fax: 0131 228 2188*
### Email: library@rias.org.uk
### http://www.rias.org.uk
A book & journal collection (c2000 from 1850s) covering architectural subjects: Scottish architecture & architects; conservation, landscape design, housing and practice matters.
(1) Contact : Eilidh Donaldson
(2) Contact : Helen Leng
Access: Mon-Fri 0900-1700. Postal enquiries preferred. BAO
*In city centre; Haymarket rail station, bus routes nearby; 1 ml from Waverley rail station & St Andrews Sq bus station; parking nearby*
Finding aids: Computer database available late 1999.
Reprographics: R1

## 152 Royal Observatory
### Blackford Hill, Edinburgh EH9 3HJ
*Tel: 0131 668 8397  Fax: 0131 668 8264*
### Email: library@roe.ac.uk
### http://www.roe.ac.uk/library
Extensive collection of astronomical information and data incl. administrative, scientific papers and notebooks of the Astronomical Institution of Edinburgh and the Observatory 1764 -
(1) Librarian
Access: Mon-Fri 0900-1730. BAO
*Approx. 3 ml S of Princes St (E), rail & bus stations, bus routes nearby; parking.*
Primary sources: Papers and correspondence of Astronomers Royal for Scotland and their staffs 1834-, incl. those of Charles Piazzi Smyth (1819-1900) which includes the Royal Society of Edinburgh's Collection; material from the (26th) Earl of Crawford's private observatory at Dunecht, Aberdeenshire, 17-19C; and c3000 photographic plates which include Observatory under construction; Edinburgh from Calton Hill and Isle of May.
Finding aids: NRA(S) 2657.
Reprographics: R1, R5

## 153 Royal Pharmaceutical Society of Great Britain
### 36 York Place, Edinburgh EH1 3HU
*Tel: 0131 556 4386  Fax: 0131 558 8850*
Books and journals covering pharmaceutical subjects; pharmacology; toxicology; chemistry and botany. Historical collection of rare, illustrated botanical works, pharmacopoeias & herbals.
(1) Contact : L C Howden
(2) Contact : C Thomson

Access: Mon-Fri 0900-1300, 1400-1700. Researchers welcome - visitors BAO.
*In city centre; Waverley rail station, St Andrews Sq bus station & parking nearby, on bus routes.*
Reprographics: R1

## 154 The Royal Scots Regimental Museum Library
## The Castle, Edinburgh EH1 2YT
### *Tel: 0131 310 5016  Fax: 0131 310 5019*
Library holds publications, histories, records and archives of The Royal Scots (The Royal Regiment).
(1) Contact : R P Mason
Access: Mon-Fri 0930-1600 (Apr-Oct). Mon-Fri 0930-1500 (Nov-Apr). BAO
Charges: Donation to Museum.
*In Regimental Hq at Castle; Waverley rail station 0.5 ml, bus routes, parking nearby; disabled access.*
Primary sources: Archival material incl. regimental war diaries; rolls of honour (casualties and war graves); regimental record books; copies of training manuals etc.; newspaper cuttings.
Finding aids: NRA(S) list no.2278. In-house index.
Reprographics: R1

## 155 Royal Scottish Academy Library
## The Mound, Edinburgh EH2 2EL
### *Tel: 0131 225 6671  Fax: 0131 225 2349*
Local history/studies material is restricted to material connected with the history and working of the Royal Scottish Academy and with painters, sculptors, architects and engravers working in and around Edinburgh, as well as further afield throughout Scotland.
(1) Assistant Librarian/Keeper: Joanna Soden
Access: Mon-Fri 1000-1300, 1400-1630. PCA & visitors BAO.
Charges: Donation requested.
*Via the rear door of the Academy, located at the mid point of Princes St; Waverley rail station, St Andrews Sq bus station nearby, on bus routes, parking nearby; disabled access.*
Primary sources: Complete set of exhibition catalogues of the Royal Scottish Academy Annual Exhibitions 1827-; collection of other catalogues of various art exhibitions held in Edinburgh c1800-; archives incl. letters written by artists 1827-, documents of art organisations 1729-, and members' files containing photographs, newspapers, cuttings, etc.
Finding aids: In-house: card indices & lists, manual library catalogue.
Reprographics: R1, R5

## 156 Royal Society of Edinburgh
**22-26 George Street, Edinburgh EH2 2PQ**
*Tel: 0131 240 5000  Fax: 0131 240 5024*
**Email: rse@rse.org.uk**
**http://www.ma.hw.ac.uk/RSE/**
The Society has records of its business from its foundation in 1783 and a number of MS collections donated mostly by Fellows. Earlier business records (mainly the involvement of Fellows with the Society) and MS collections are on deposit in the NLS Manuscripts Division, notably the philospher David Hume's (1711-76) collection. The astronomer Piazzi Smyth's (1819-1900) collection is on deposit at the Royal Observatory, Edinburgh.
(1) Publications Officer: Vicki Ingpen
(2) Society Officer: Ian Leslie
Access: Enquiries by post preferred. Visitors BAO.
*E end of George St; Waverley rail station, St Andrews Sq bus station, bus routes, parking nearby; disabled access difficult.*
Finding aids: Card index covers past Fellows, Proceedings & Yearbooks.
Leaflets: Lists.

## 157 The Saltire Society
**The Administrator, 9 Fountain Close, 22 High Street, Edinburgh EH1 1TF**
*Tel: 0131 556 1836  Fax: 0131 557 1675*
**Email: saltire@saltire.org.uk**
**http://www.saltire.org.uk**
Society founded 1936, seeks to encourage everything that might improve quality of life in Scotland & preserve all that is best in Scottish tradition. Interests include history, literature, music, drama, architecture & planning. Publishes books & pamphlets on history & literature topics.
Leaflets: Available; newsletter for members.

## 158 The Scots at War Trust
**Institute for Advanced Studies, University of Edinburgh, 2 Hope Park Square, Edinburgh EH8 9NW**
*Tel: 0131 650 4671  Fax: 0131 668 2252*
**Email: iash@ed.ac.uk**
**http://www-saw.arts.ed.ac.uk**
Information on 20C Scots in the Armed and Civilian Services available on the WWW site only. Enquiry service available on e-mail.
(1) Contact : Diana M Henderson
Access: BAO
Leaflets: Leaflet & newsletter.

**159  Scotsman Publications: Library**
**20 North Bridge, Edinburgh EH1 1YT**
*Tel: 0131 243 3363  Fax: 0131 523 0223*
**Email: mstevenson@scotsman.com**
**http://www.scotsman.com**

A collection of cuttings & electronic record of articles in Scotsman
Publications from 1991. (NB: The Scotsman (1860-), Evening News (1967-)
Scotland on Sunday (1988-) & their predecessors can be seen on microfilm
at Edinburgh' s Central Library, George IV Bridge.
(1) Contact : Moira Stevenson
Access: Enquiries by letter/email only. Visits BAO
Finding aids: Electronic database 1991-
Reprographics: Photographs (Scotsman copyright) can be purchased from
the Photosales Dept.

**160  Scottish Catholic Archives**
**Columba House, 16 Drummond Place, Edinburgh**
**EH3 6PL**
*Tel: 0131 556 3661*

Archive covers five of eight Dioceses of Scotland & the preceding Vicariates;
includes Bishops' papers; Scottish mission c1700-1878 & Diocesan mission
1878-; material on Seminaries in Scotland and abroad. [NB Access to
archives restricted to academic researchers - there is no genealogical
material].
(1) Contact : Christine Johnson
Access: Mon-Fri 0930-1300, 1400-1630. BAO
*In city centre; Waverley rail station & St Andrews Sq bus stations, bus routes
nearby, parking difficult.*
Finding aids: MS catalogues.
Reprographics: R1

**161  Scottish Church History Society**
**c/o Rev Dr Peter H Donald, 1 Denham Green Terrace,**
**Edinburgh EH5 3PG**
*Tel: 0131 552 4059  Fax: 0131 552 4059*

Society founded 1922, promotes study of history of all branches of the
church in Scotland. Papers presented at meetings are published annually in
the Society's journal "Records".
Leaflets: Publications: Records (annual, 1923-).

**162 Scottish Genealogy Society**

**Library & Family History Centre, 15 Victoria Terrace, Edinburgh EH1 2JL**

*Tel: 0131 220 3677  Fax: 070707 13411*

**Email: scotgensoc@sol.co.uk.**

**http://www.scotland.net/scotgensoc/**

Library for the genealogist; family histories, directories, reference works.
(1) Librarian: M A Stewart FSAScot (Tel: 01383 860210)
(2) Honorary Secretary: J P S Ferguson (Tel: 0131 556 3844)
Access: Tue 1030-1730; Wed 1030-2030; Sat 1000-1700.
Charges: Applied to non-members per session.
*Between Johnson Terrace, Lawnmarket & George IV Bridge; Waverley rail station, St Andrews Sq bus station, bus routes, parking nearby.*
Primary sources: OPR index to births & marriages (microfiche), IGI 1992 for the UK (microfiche), collection of Scottish OPRs (microfilm), large collection of graveyard inscriptions, collection of MS family trees.
Finding aids: In-house library catalogue.
Leaflets: Publications: subscription and sales leaflets.
Reprographics: R4, photocopies A4.

**163 Scottish History Society**

**c/o Dr Steve Boardman, Dept of Scottish History, Edinburgh University, 17 Buccleuch Place, Edinburgh EH8 9LN**

*Tel: 0131 650 4035*

**Email: steve.boardman@ed.ac.uk**

Society publishes information on historical sources and records for members of the Society - can be consulted at leading libraries.
Leaflets: Details of back copies can be obtained from the Secretary.

**164 Scottish Museums Council: Information Centre**

**County House, 20-22 Torphichen Street, Edinburgh EH3 8JB**

*Tel: 0131 229 7465  Fax: 0131 229 2728*

**Email: inform@scottishmuseums.org.uk**

**http://www.scottishmuseums.org.uk**

The Centre holds material on all aspects of Scottish museums, incl. examples of their information sheets, educational material and details of their collections, plus, printed books and journals referring to museum collections in Scotland.
(1) Librarian: Sarah Currier
(2) Publications Officer: Lesley Castell
Access: Mon-Fri 0900-1700. BAO
*In W End; Haymarket rail station, bus routes, parking nearby.*

Finding aids: In-house catalogue.
Reprographics: R1

## 165 Scottish National Gallery of Modern Art
### Belford Road, Edinburgh EH4 3DR
*Tel: 0131 624 6312/6351  Fax: 0131 343 2802*
### Email: ann.simpson@natgalscot.ac.uk

The Library and Archive holds material on Scottish arts and artists covering the period from 1900 to the present day; Collection of artist's books by Scottish artists and authors.

(1) Curator, Archive & Library: Ann Simpson (Tel: 0131 624 6312)

(2) Librarian: Elizabeth Ficken (Tel: 0131624 6351)

Access: Mon-Fri 1030-1230, 1330-1630. BAO at least 3 days notice.

*1 ml W of Princes St (W End); Haymarket rail station 0.5 ml, on bus route 13, parking; disabled access.*

Primary sources: Artists' letters, photographs, sketchbooks, slides; major holdings in addtion to the Gallery's own archive include: The Collection of Scottish Artists Books; papers of the 57 and new 57 Gallery, Edinburgh; letters from Robert Colquhoun and Robert MacBryde; the Richard Demarco Archive; the Joan Eardley Archive; letters from J.D. Fergusson; the Ian Hamilton Finlay Archive; the W.O.Hutchison Archive; letterbooks of E.S. Lumsden; the Eduardo Paolozzi Archive; the James Pryde-Derek Hudson Archive; Scottish Arts Council Artists' Files; papers on the Society of Eight; the Scottie Wilson Archive.

Finding aids: In-house card index.

Reprographics: R5

## 166 Scottish National Portrait Gallery
### 1 Queen Street, Edinburgh EH2 1JD
*Tel: 0131 624 2000  Fax: 0131 558 3691*
### Email: helen.watson@natgalscot.ac.uk

Archive of 40000 b&w photographs of portraits c1550- in other collections in Scotland, England and abroad; 14000 portrait engravings; 200 portrait drawings; social history index; artists' biographical materials; c3000 paintings, watercolours, miniatures and medallions representing famous Scots from all localities.

(1) Contact : Helen Watson (Tel: 0131 624 6420)

(2) Contact : Susanna Kerr (Tel: 0131 624 6405)

Access: Portrait Archives: Mon-Fri 1000-1230, 1400-1630 (BAO). Gallery: Mon-Sat 1000-1700, Sun 1400-1700.

*In city centre; Waverley rail station, St Andrews Sq bus station, parking nearby; disabled access.*

Finding aids: Printed concise catalogue of the collections, postcards of some of the paintings.

Leaflets: Available.

Reprographics: R5

**167 Scottish Office Library & Information Service: Saughton House Library**
**Saughton House, Broomhouse Drive, Edinburgh EH11 3XD**
*Tel: 0131 244 8455  Fax: 0131 244 8240*

The library holds official reports etc., produced by the Scottish Office and its predecessors and reports presented to the Secretary of State by local authorities, etc. Main subjects are agriculture and fisheries administration.
(1) Librarian
Access: Mon-Fri 0900-1630. BAO
*3 ml W of city centre; on bus routes; disabled access, parking available.*
Reprographics: R1, R3

**168 Scottish Office Library & Information Service: St Andrew's House Library**
**Regent Road, Edinburgh EH1 3DG**
*Tel: 0131 244 2619  Fax: 0131 244 2619*
**Email: mmacdonald.so.sah@gtnet.gov.uk**
**http://www.scotland.gov.uk**

The library holds official reports etc. produced by the Scottish Office and its predecessors, and reports presented to the Secretary of State by local authorities etc. Main subjects are public administration, public health, social work, police, prisons, housing.
(1) Librarian
Access: Mon-Fri 0900-1630. BAO
*E of Princes St; Waverley rail station, St Andrews Sq bus station, parking nearby; disabled access.*
Reprographics: R1, R4

**169 Scottish Office Library & Information Service: Victoria Quay Library**
**Victoria Quay, Edinburgh EH6 6QQ**
*Tel: 0131 244 7096/7  Fax: 0131 244 7098*
**Email: vq-library@so063.scotoff.gov.uk**
**http://www.scotland.gov.uk**

The Library holds official reports etc, produced by the Scottish Office and its predecessors and reports presented to the Secretary of State by Local Authorities etc. Main subjects: public administration, education, planning, economic affairs, transport.
(1) Librarian
Access: Mon-Thu 0830-1700; Fri 0830-1630. BAO
*2 ml NE of Princes St (E End); bus routes, parking by arrangement; disabled access.*
Finding aids: In-house catalogue.

Leaflets: Library Guide.
Reprographics: R1

## 170 Scottish Working People's History Trust
## c/o Ian MacDougall (Secretary), 21 Liberton Brae,
## Edinburgh EH16 6AQ
### Tel: 0131 664 2436

The Trust searches for, catalogues and encourages permanent preservation of all surviving sources of working people's history in Scotland by their deposit in public repositories throughout Scotland. Source materials sought include minutes, correspondence, photographs, finanical records, membership lists, posters, leaflets etc of individuals, organisations, events & movements 18C-.
Leaflets: Leaflet & Annual Progress Report.

## 171 Signet Library
## Parliament Square, Edinburgh EH1 1RF
### Tel: 0131 225 4923  Fax: 0131 220 4016

The Library contains a Scottish section of c20000 vols that includes many titles relating to local history throughout the country. It does not specialise in a particular area or subject.
(1) Librarian: Audrey Walker
(2) Assistant Librarian: Kate Corbett
Access: Mon-Fri 0930-1600. PCA, in writing.
*Waverley rail station, St Andrews Sq bus station nearby; on bus routes, parking nearby; disabled access to ground floor only.*
Primary sources: Printed source material: Printed Session Papers collection of 700 vols covering 1713-1820, concerning Scottish civil cases heard in the Court of Session, many containing information relating to local disputes, etc., often in some detail (although couched in legal language, they can provide data not available elsewhere; the Papers are indexed by subject, and by the parties involved in the case, making the set unique).
Finding aids: In-house catalogue (printed & card); Session papers indexed by subject & parties.
Reprographics: R1

## 172 The Society of Antiquaries of Scotland
## Fionna Ashmore (Secretary), c/o Royal Museum of
## Scotland, Chambers Street, Edinburgh EH1 1JF
### Tel: 0131 247 4133  Fax: 0131 247 4163

The Society publishes the Proceedings of the Society plus books in its Monograph Series covering a wide range of topics. MS & archival material is located in the Library of the Royal Museum of Scotland.
Leaflets: Publications list.

## 173 Stevenson College: Library
### Bankhead Avenue, Edinburgh EH11 4DE
*Tel: 0131 535 4600 x1258  Fax: 0131 535 4666*
Book collection includes: Robert Stevenson (lighthouse engineer) 1772-1850: life of Robert Stevenson / David Stevenson - Records of a family of engineers / Robert Louis Stevenson - Biographical sketch of the late Robert Stevenson / Alan Stevenson - modern monographs on the history of lighthouses - some aerial photographs & postcards of Stevenson lighthouses - one vol of Robert Stevenson's Journal 1801-1818 (MS) - copies of three letters.
(1) Library Manager (Tel: 0131 535 4691)
Access: Mon, Fri 0845-1645; Tue-Thu 0845-2045 (term-time), Mon-Fri 1000-1600 (vacations). PCA.
*4 ml W of city centre; bus routes nearby, parking; disabled access.*
Reprographics: R1

## Elgin

## 174 Elgin Museum
### 1 High Street, Elgin IV30 1EQ
*Tel: 01343 543675  Fax: 01343 543675*
### http://www.elginmuseum.demon.co.uk
Collection includes archives of museum's history, family & business papers, photographic collection, & papers covering the activities & minutes of the Elgin & Morayshire Association, now the Moray Society.
(1) Contact : Susan Bennett
Access: Mon-Fri 1000-1700, Sat.1400-1700 (Apr-Oct). Library: BAO.
Charges: Admission charges; research free
*In town centre; bus routes, parking nearby; disabled access.*
Primary sources: Photographic collection (c1000) includes early 20C glass negatives and images of the 1920s/30s by local photographers; Hugh Miller's (geologist 1802-56) letters; Watson papers - bills/accounts of local sawmill late 19C; George Gordon (1801-93) collection of scientific letters incl. Darwin, Huxley etc; Sandy papers of the Gordon family.
Finding aids: Watson papers & glass negatives lists; card index local history items.
Leaflets: List.

## 175 The Moray Council: Local Heritage Centre
### Grant Lodge, Cooper Park, Elgin IV30 1HS
*Tel: 01343 544475  Fax: 01343 549050*
Collection covers all aspects of life in Moray past to present. It includes c8000 books, 16000 photographs and slides (1880s-), local authority records, extensive newspapers' collections and archival material.
(1) Contact : Graeme Wilson
Access: Mon, Wed-Fri 1000-1700; Tue 1000-2000; Sat 1000-1200.

Charges: Staff search charges.
*NE of town centre; bus station nearby, parking.*
Primary sources: Newspaper collection (dates include predecessors): Press
& Journal 1747-, Forres Gazette 1837-, Moray, Nairn & Banff Courant 1874-
1967, Northern Scot 1880-, Banffshire Herald 1893-, Banffshire Journal
1845-; the Wittets Ltd and Charles Doig (1854-1918) collection of
architectural plans 1808-1975, c30000 plans cover buildings in the NE
Scotland and beyond with 1880s - WWI a key period; archives of former
town councils (Elgin, Forres & Cullen) 13C-1975; Moray District Council
1975-1996; Moray County Council & Moray and Nairn joint County Council
1930-75; burgh and sheriff court papers 17-19C; school board archive 1873-
1919; kirk session archives 17-20C; business and solicitors' records 16-20C;
GEN: CEN, OPRs, BAP/MAR, VR, MI, IGI.
Finding aids: Catalogue for archives; index for collections & many of the
newspapers.
Leaflets: Tracing Your Roots.
Reprographics: R1, R4, R5

## Ellon

### 176 Aberdeenshire Library & Information Service: Ellon Library
### Station Road, Ellon AB41 9AE
### *Tel: 01358 720865  Fax: 01358 722864*
Books, maps, photographs, newspapers and other material covering Ellon
and district.
(1) Senior Library Assistant
Access: Mon-Fri 1000-1930; Sat 1000-1600. BAO
*In town centre; on bus route, parking; disabled access.*
Primary sources: Newspapers: Ellon and District Advertiser 1957-; Ellon
Times 1991-; Morrison Collection of postcards of local area viewable on
CDRom; OS maps and small collection of photographs; GEN: CEN, OPRs,
IGI(S).
Finding aids: Computerised catalogue.
Reprographics: R1

## Falkirk

### 177 Falkirk Council Library Services: Falkirk Library
### Hope Street, Falkirk FK1 5AU
### *Tel: 01324 503605  Fax: 01324 506801*
### Email: mscott@falkirk-libsuprt.demon.co.uk
Collection includes books, maps, newspapers, pamphlets, ephemera,
photographs and slides.
(1) Contact : Marion Scott (Tel: 01324 506845)
(2) Contact : John Dickson (Tel: 01324 506811)

Access: Mon-Tue, Thu 0930-2000; Wed, Fri-Sat 0930-1700. PCA.
*W of town centre; rail, bus stations, parking nearby; disabled access.*
Primary sources: Newspapers: Falkirk Herald and predecessors 1845-
(gaps); Falkirk Mail 1905-62; plus indexed newspaper clippings collection;
Town Council minutes; Scottish Metalworkers' Union minutes; collection
locally printed books; films and videos of local events 1938 & 1970/80s; OS
maps; 400+ photographs and 1000 slides covering Falkirk area; GEN: CEN,
OPRs.
Leaflets: Publications list.
Reprographics: R1, R2

## #178 Falkirk Museums: History Research Centre
## Callendar House, Callendar Park, Falkirk FK1 1YR
## *Tel: 01324 503779  Fax: 01324 503771*
## Email:
## callendarhouse@falkirkmuseums.demon.co.uk

The collections include local authority records, business records, catalogues
and printed ephemera, archaeological archives, family and personal papers,
records of local organisations, trade unions and professional associations.
Photographic collection of over 26000 images from 1840, incl. local working
life, local places, events, archaeological digs, museum objects and the work
of local photographers. The small reference library has some rare books,
relating to the museum's social and industrial collections.
(1) Museums Archivist: Elspeth Reid (Tel: 01324 503778)
(2) Museums Assistant: Carol Sneddon
Access: Mon-Fri 1000-1230; 1330-1700. PCA.
Charges: Charges for research undertaken by staff. Admission to History
Research Centre only is free
*Located in centre of public park 1 ml E of town centre & rail station; bus
routes nearby, parking; disabled access.*
Primary sources: Burgh records: Falkirk 1803-1975; Grangemouth 1872-
1975; Bo'ness, Denny & Dunipace 1833-1975; some Stirling & West Lothian
County 1930-1975. School Records Falkirk area 1873-1980; VR Burghs
1864-1975 (gaps). NB Stirling County VR & ER held at Stirling archives.
Business records include Grangemouth Dockyard Co 1920s-1970s, P & M
Hurll (Birkhill Clay Mine), 1939-1980, J Baird & Co (Sawmill) 1934-1978,
Grahamston Iron Co 1868-1991, Scottish Tar Distillers 1930-1973. Records
of ironfounding companies incl. Carron Co 1790-1975, Falkirk Iron Co 1864-
1961, Smith & Wellstood 1912-1985. Forbes of Callendar Papers 1530-
1932; MacKay Family (Alloa & Campbeltown shipyards) 1890-1907; Martin
Family, Millfield Dairy, Polmont 1927-1960; Burns Family 1791-1921.
Records of local organisations, trade unions, professional associations, such
as Amalgamated Union of Engineering Workers (Foundry Section) Falkirk
Branch 1879-1974; Falkirk Temperance Café Trust 1919-1991; Falkirk
Women Citizen's Association 1921-1968; Bo'ness United General Seabox
Benificient Society 1613-1897; Westquarter & Polmont Curling Club 1853-
1872; Stirling & District Christian Union 1923-1983.
Finding aids: In-house lists - computer database for collections. Repository
Guide in progress.

Leaflets: Leaflets on aspects of historical research. Guide to the photographic collection.
Reprographics: R1, R4, R5

## Forfar

### 179 Angus Council: Forfar Library
### 50 West High Street, Forfar DD8 2EG
### *Tel: 01307 466071*

Collection includes local newspapers; directories; John C Ewing collection of Scottish material & genealogical information.
(1) Librarian: I K Neil
Access: Mon, Wed 0930-2000; Tue, Fri 0930-1800; Thu, Sat 0930-1730.
*In town centre; bus routes, parking nearby; disabled access.*
Primary sources: The Forfar Dispatch 1912-91; County Year Books 1812, 1829-46, 1855; Forfar Town Directories 1855-1939; Edinburgh Almanac Angus Edition 1833-90; Minutes of Trade Incorporations 17-19C (name indexes); OS maps; GEN: CEN, OPRs, LISTS, IND, IGI.
Reprographics: R1, R2, R5

### 180 Angus Council: The Meffan
### 20 West High Street, Forfar DD8 1DB
### *Tel: 01307 464123*

Small collection of paintings & prints (200), maps & c3000 photographs 1880s- of the Forfar area.
(1) Contact : Margaret H King
Access: Mon-Sat 1000-1700. PCA.
*In town centre; bus routes, parking nearby.*
Reprographics: R1, R5

## Forres

### 181 The Moray Council Museums Service: Falconer Museum
### Tolbooth Street, Forres IV36 0PH
### *Tel: 01309 673701  Fax: 01309 675863*
### Email: 100655.3315@compuserve.com
### http://www.moray.gov.uk/museums/homepage.htm

Photographic collection (000s) covering Moray. Archives of Hugh Falconer (1808-1865) palaeontologist, and Peter F Anson (1889-1975) marine artist and author (paintings within Buckie public library). Medieval MS: part of index to the Chartulary of the Diocese of Moray.
(1) Senior Museums Officer: Alasdair Joyce (Tel: 01309 676688)
(2) Museums Officer: Kris Sangster
Access: Mon-Fri 1000-1700 (Nov-Mar); Mon-Sat 1000-1700 (Apr-Oct). PCA.

*Tolbooth St is off High St; bus route, parking nearby; disabled access to the ground floor only.*
Leaflets: Museum information leaflets.

## Fort William

### 182 Highland Libraries: Fort William Library
### Airds Crossing, Fort William PH33 6EU
*Tel: 01397 703552 Fax: 01397 703538*
Small collection of local history books; Oban Times newspaper 1867-; GEN: OPRs, MI, IGI(S)
(1) Contact : K Finlay
Access: Mon, Thu 1000-2000; Tue, Fri 1000-1800; Wed, Sat 1000-1300. PCA.
*In town centre; rail station, bus route, parking nearby.*
Reprographics: R1

### 183 West Highland Museum
### Cameron Square, Fort William PH33 6AJ
*Tel: 01397 702169 Fax: 01397 702169*
Small varied collection of 18 &19C papers incl. the military occupation and the '45; accounts and minute books of various local committees.
(1) Contact : Fiona C Marwick
Access: Mon-Fri 1000-1600. BAO
*Off High St; rail & bus stations 0.5 ml, parking nearby; disabled access.*

## Fraserburgh

### 184 Aberdeenshire Library & Information Service: Fraserburgh Library
### King Edward Street, Fraserburgh AB43 9PN
*Tel: 01346 518197 Fax: 01346 510528*
Collection of 500 books, 100 photographs 1890s-1950s, OS maps and other material relating to Fraserburgh and district.
(1) Senior Library Assistant: L Noble
(2) Network Librarian: Jan Murdoch (Tel: 01346 515771)
Access: Mon-Wed, Fri 0930-1900; Thu 0930-1700; Sat 1000-1300, 1400-1700. PCA.
*In W end of town; on bus route, parking; disabled access to ground floor.*
Primary sources: Newspapers: Fraserburgh Advertiser 1858-1941 (with gaps); Fraserburgh Herald 1884; GEN: CEN; OPRs, IND B/M, IGI(S).
Finding aids: Part index for Fraserburgh Herald.
Reprographics: R1, R2, R5

## 185 Scotland's Lighthouse Museum: Library & Study Centre
### Kinnaird Head, Fraserburgh AB43 9DU
### *Tel: 01346 511022  Fax: 01346 511033*

Northern Lighthouse Board records, photographs, slide images, books and archives all relevant to lighthouses in Scotland. Collections include lighthouse engineering and technology, social history and art.

(1) Curator of Collections: Sarah Swallow

(2) Museum Director: Richard Townsley

Access: Mon-Fri 1000-1600. Sat BAO.

Charges: Admission charges.

*Near town centre; bus routes nearby, parking; disabled access.*

Primary sources: Northern Lighthouse Board's records for individual lights and buoys (20C - mainly post-war); station records; design plans for lighthouses c12000 images of Scottish and Manx lighthouses and keepers by Keith Allardyce; archival material - documents and photographs from Stevenson family of engineers covering work on the Northern Lighthouses and other engineering projects; reference section of books and journals relating to lighthouses.

Leaflets: Scotland's Lighthouse Museum.

Reprographics: Photographic slides.


## Galashiels

## 186 Galashiels & District Local History Association: Old Gala Club
### c/o Galashiels Public Library, Lawyers Brae, Galashiels TD1 3JQ

Collection of 6000 photographs and slides of Galashiels and district 1900-.

(1) Secretary: Helen Elliot (Tel: 01896 756002)

Access: Wed 1400-1600. BAO

Charges: Search charges.

*In town centre; bus routes nearby, parking; disabled access.*

Reprographics: R1

## 187 Heriot-Watt University: Scottish Borders Campus
**Netherdale, Galashiels TD1 3HF**
*Tel: 01896 753351  Fax: 0131 451 3164*
**Email: a.e.jones@hw.ac.uk**
**http://www.hw.ac.uk**

Records include bound vols., fabrics, loose papers, printed papers, photographs, newspaper cuttings covering the Scottish College of Textiles (SCOT) plus the textile & fashion industry 1921-63.
(1) Contact : Ann Jones (Tel: 0131 451 3638)
Access: BAO
*1 ml SE of town centre; bus route nearby, parking; disabled access.*
Primary sources: Archives include the records of SCOT & its predecessors 1889-1990s; business records of mens & ladies tweed, cloth manufacturers & desingers: (Borders) R&A Sanderson 1852-1956, P&L Anderson 1874-1967, Blenkhorn Richardson 1883-1967, Gibson & Longair 1939-61, Bernat Klein 1960-83, EY Johnston 1965-75, Brown Brothers 1967-71, DB Ballantyne Bros 1960-70, (Kirkcaldy) Robert Stocks 1811-1956, Wm Lumsden 1956-71, plus Hopes of Stow, drapers, 1918-66, Donald Brothers, Dundee, interior furnishings 1896-70s.
Finding aids: Catalogue item lists.
Leaflets: Available.
Reprographics: R1, R5

## Girvan

## 188 Girvan & District Historical Society
**McKechnie Institute, Dalrymple Street, Girvan KA26 9AE**
*Tel: 01465 713643*

Collections relate to Girvan and South Carrick incl. Ailsa Craig.
(1) Contact : Margaret McCance
Access: Tue-Sat 1000-1600.
*In town centre; rail station, parking nearby, on bus route; disabled access.*
Primary sources: Primary source material relates to local history exhibitions since 1982. Includes railway artefacts and records, Ailsa Craig and its lighthouse, Carrick country houses, maps, works by local artists, aerial photographs.
Finding aids: In preparation (1998).
Leaflets: Available.
Reprographics: R1

## Glamis

### 189 Angus Folk Museum
### Kirkwynd Cottages, Glamis DD8 1RT
*Tel: 01307 840288  Fax: 01307 840233*

The Collection contains more than 5000 artefacts. It includes maps and photographs, and a small collection of display books with some data relating to Angus. Forfar children's street rhymes and singing games, some letters from emigrants (manuscript and printed).
(1) Property Manager: Kathleen Ager
Access: Sun-Sat 1100-1700 (end Apr-Sep, Easter). PCA.
Charges: Admission charge.
*Off the square in Glamis; parking nearby; disabled access.*
Leaflets: Publications.

## Glasgow

### 190 602 Squadron Museum
### Queen Elizabeth Avenue, Hillington, Glasgow G52 4TY

Museum commemorates the exploits of 602 (City of Glasgow) Squadron, Royal Auxiliary Air Force from 1925-1957).
(1) Contact : W McConnell (Tel: 01505 612012)
(2) Contact : G Catto (Tel: 01505 862225)
Access: Wed, Fri 1930-2130 (except Jul-Aug). First Sun of month 1400-1700 (Apr-Sep). Other times BAO. Prior consultation in writing advisable to: Chairman, 602 Museum Association, c/o Rolls Royce PLC, Hillington, Glasgow G52 4TY
Charges: Donations appreciated.
*Hillington West rail station & bus routes nearby, parking; disabled access by appointment.*
Primary sources: Photographs, maps, paintings and reference books and video library; "Orde" drawings and Battle of Britain Memorial Book.
Finding aids: Manual records/lists to be computeried.
Leaflets: 602 Squadron Museum Leaflet.

### 191 Archdiocese of Glasgow
### 196 Clyde Street, Glasgow G1 4JY
*Tel: 0141 226 5898 x154  Fax: 0141 225 2600*

Archive of the Bishop's Chancery for the RC Archdiocese of Glagow.
(1) Contact : Mary McHugh
Access: Mon-Fri 0930-1630. BAO
*Beside St Andrew's RC Cathedral; Queen St, Central & underground stations, bus routes nearby; disabled access.*

Primary sources: OPRs prior to 1855; education papers and Catholic Union papers.; Scottish Catholic Directory 1829- and Western Catholic Calendar 1894-.
Reprographics: R1

## 192 Baptist Union of Scotland
## 14 Aytoun Road, Glasgow G41 5RT
### *Tel: 0141 423 6169  Fax: 0141 422 1422*
## Email: buscot@globalnet.co.uk

The Archives Room houses the history of the Baptist Union of Scotland (minute books, year books, etc) plus the archives of several of the churches within the Union.
(1) Contact : Jean Proctor
(2) Contact : Beatrice McLure
Access: BAO
*In Pollockshields 1.5 ml S of city centre; rail stations, bus routes nearby, parking.*

## 193 BBC Resources, Information & Archives Scotland
## Broadcasting House, Queen Margaret Drive, Glasgow G12 8DG
### *Tel: 0141 338 2499  Fax: 0141 338 3640*

BBC Scotland radio, television and written archive. Radio Scotland archive broadcasts mainly 1960s- (some dating to 1930s). BBC Scotland Television broadcasts 1958-. NB Representative archival samples from earlier years, not comprehensive coverage.
(1) Manager - Information & Archives: Noreen Adams
(2) Co-ordinator: Selena Jones (Tel: 0141 338 2880)
Access: Written enquiries only. BAO
Charges: Research and transfer charges.
*Off Great Western Rd at Botanic Gardens; on bus routes, parking nearby.*
Primary sources: Audiotape recordings, DAT recordings and some vinyl recordings. 35mm and 16mm film, 2" videotape, 1" videotape, Beta and Digital Beta recordings. Written archive of scripts and related programme paperwork (microfilm).
Finding aids: In-house catalogues for television, radio, music & written archive holdings.
Reprographics: Playback of audiotape and videotape.

## 194 East Dunbartonshire Libraries: Brookwood Library
## 166 Drymen Road, Bearsden, Glasgow G61 3RJ
### *Tel: 0141 942 6811  Fax: 0141 943 1119*

A local collection of books, pamphlets, folders, maps, photographs, postcards and newspapers. Also holds a small collection compiled by the Milngavie & Bearsden Historical Society.
(1) Contact : Sharon Handyside

Access: Mon-Thu 1000-2000; Fri-Sat 1000-1700. PCA.
*N of Bearsden Cross; rail station, bus routes nearby, parking; disabled access.*
Primary sources: Milngavie & Bearsden Herald from 1901; some Burgh & Town Council minutes; Westerton Garden Suburb Cooperative Society minutes 1915-29; GEN: CEN, OPR, DIR (Glasgow PO 1818-1978).
Finding aids: Milngavie & Bearsden Herald partly indexed.
Leaflets: Leaflets, publications list.
Reprographics: R1

## 195 East Renfrewshire Cultural Services: Local History Collection
### Giffnock Community Library, Station Road, Giffnock, Glasgow G46 6JF
*Tel: 0141 577 4976  Fax: 0141 577 4978*
### Email: giffnockl@eastrenfrewshire.gov.uk

The Local History collection comprises books, over 2000 photographs, over 600 maps, memorabilia, pamphlets and primary material on East Renfrewshire area. Barrhead and Neilston Community Libraries have small collections of books, maps and pamphlets on their own area.
(1) Contact : Maud Devine
(2) Community Librarian, Giffnock
Access: Mon, Wed 1000-2000; Tue, Thu, Sat 1000-1700; Fri 1400-2000. PCA.
*Giffnock rail station, bus routes nearby, parking; disabled access possible.*
Primary sources: Newspapers - Mercury 1972-1990, Extra 1982 - Barrhead News 1957-1980; local authority records 1896 on; ratepayers minutes 1908 on; Crum Memorial Library accounts; memorabilia; letters; documents donated by local people; map collection from 1610 includes County maps and OS from 1863; Ainslie Estate Plans of Eglinton lands end 18C. GEN: CEN, some VR, IGI(S).
Leaflets: Publications (30) leaflet.

## 196 Glasgow & West of Scotland Family History Society
### Unit 15, 22 Mansfield Street, Glasgow G11 5QP
*Tel: 0141 339 8303*
### http://users.colloquium.co.uk/~alistair/gwsfhs/gwsfhs.htm

Mainly Glasgow & W of Scotland material; OS maps 1" to 1ml; 1st edition reprints; transcripts of MIs pre1855 all Scotland; GEN: 1851/81/91 CEN IND; MI; BR; DIR: IGI(BI).
(1) Librarian: June A Willing
(2) Vice-Chairman: Mary Buchanan (Tel: 0141 942 2215)
Access: Tue 1400-1630, 1900-2130; Thu 1000-2130; Sat 1400-1630. BAO
Charges: Charges for non-members.

*Off Dumbarton Rd, Partick, opposite Comet, car access via Hyndland St & Chancellor St; Kelvin Hall underground station, bus routes nearby, limited parking.*
Finding aids: Index to newsletters; Mfiche index; library catalogue; list of microfiche & microfilm holdings.
Leaflets: Publications list & information sheet.
Reprographics: R1, R4, computer prints A4.

## 197 Glasgow Art Gallery & Museum
### Kelvingrove, Argyle Street, Glasgow G3 8AG
### *Tel: 0141 287 2699  Fax: 0141 287 2690*

In addition to an excellent collection of Scottish art 1837-1950, incl. Hornel, Ferguson & Cadell, there is a small collection of local history items (MS & documents) from W of Scotland and the Northern Isles.
(1) Scottish Art: Jean Walsh (Tel: 0141 287 2646)
(2) Scottish Art: Hugh Stevenson (Tel: 0141 287 2632)
(*) Local History: Fiona Hayes (Tel: 0141 554 0223)
Access: Mon-Sat 1000-1700; Sun 1100-1700. PCA.
*W end of Glasgow; underground station nearby, on bus routes, parking; disabled access via Argyle St.*
Leaflets: Publication lists and catalogues.
Reprographics: R1, R5

## 198 Glasgow Caledonian University Library: Special Collections & Archives
### Cowcaddens Road, Glasgow G4 0BA
### *Tel: 0141 331 3920  Fax: 0141 331 3005*
### Email: j.powles@gcal.ac.uk
### http://www.gcal.ac.uk/library/info/specoll.html

Collections mostly cover political, trade union and similar topics plus archives of the University and earlier institutions.
(1) Collection Manager: John Powles
(2) Gallacher Memorial Lib: Audrey Canning (Tel: 0141 331 3028)
(*) Archives: Carole McCallum (Tel: 0141 331 3199)
Access: Mon-Fri 0900-1700. Gallacher Memorial Library Tue-Thu 1200-1600 BAO.
*In city centre; Queen St & underground stations, bus station, parking nearby.*
Primary sources: Norman & Janey Buchanan (1910-70); Scottish & Northern Book Distribution Co-operative Ltd (1960s/70s); Gallacher Memorial Library; Norrie McIntosh Archives: RSSPCC (Children 1st) (1940-76); STUC; Anti-Apartheid Movement in Scotland (1970s-94); University Archive from 1875 - Glasgow School of Cookery and later school/college; Glasgow College of Technology 1971; Glasgow College 1987 & Glasgow Polytechnic 1991.
Leaflets: Available.
Reprographics: R1

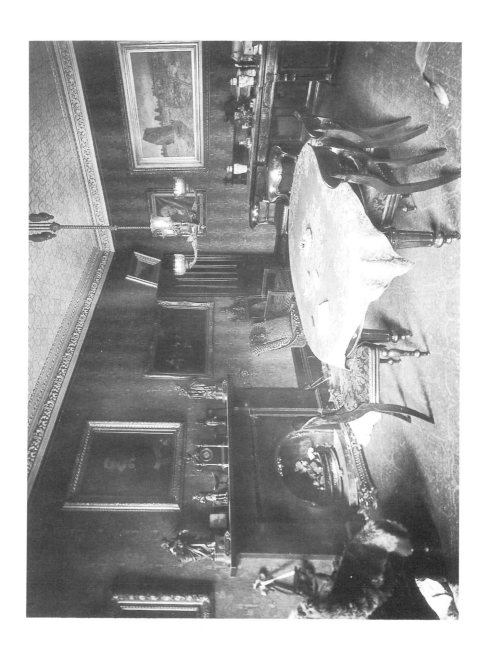

**House room interior - Glasgow 1909 (NAS ref: AD.21/5/3)**

**#199 Glasgow City Archives**
**Mitchell Library, North Street, Glasgow G3 7DN**
*Tel: 0141 287 2913  Fax: 0141 226 8452*
**Email: archives@gcl.glasgow.gov.uk**
**http://www.glasgow.gov.uk/gc1/hom.htm**
The archives, one of the largest in Scotland, house extensive local authority records in the greater Glasgow area together with a wide range of family, estate, solicitors, business & church records, plus maps, plans & photographs.
(1) Searchroom Archivist (Tel: 0141 287 2910  Fax: 0141 226 8652)
Access: Mon-Thu 0930-1645; Fri 0930-1600. Other times BAO. PCA.
Charges: No charge for normal historical enquiries.
*0.75 ml W of city centre beside the motorway; Central & Queen St rail stations, bus station 0.75 ml; Charing X rail station, bus routes nearby, parking difficult; disabled access.*
Primary sources: Archives of the former Glasgow Corporation & the counties of Dunbarton, Lanark, Renfrew & Bute, together with those of Strathclyde Region & City of Glasgow District Council (1975-96); papers of solicitors & surveyors are wide-ranging, from the records of Hutchesons' Hospital (1579-1958) to maps, plans & titles to property in the W of Scotland; family & estate papers include Stirling Maxwell of Pollok (1200-1919), Stirling of Keir (1338-1924), Shaw Stewart of Ardgowan (1540-1958); Business records include: shipbuilders (Fairfields, Connells & Barclay Curle 19/20c), shipowners (Burns & Laird Lines, Thomas Dunlop 19/20C), Scottish Engineering Employers Association 19/20C; church records (Glasgow Presbytery 16-20C, episcopal church 18-20C); customs & excise records; maps 17C- for greater Glasgow area; architectural & Dean of Guild plans; 30000 + photographs 1860s-; Genealogical material is listed in the booklet Tracing Your Ancestors.
Finding aids: Catalogues, calendars & card indexes; databases for genealogical & architectural sources.
Leaflets: General leaflet; education source packs; "Tracing Your Ancestors" booklet.
Reprographics: R1, R5, photocopies A0-A2.

**200  Glasgow City Libraries & Archives: Glasgow Collection**
**The Mitchell Library, North Street, Glasgow G3 7DN**
*Tel: 0141 287 2937  Fax: 0141 287 2815*
**Email: history_and_glasgow@gcl.glasgow.gov.uk.**
**http://www.glasgow.gov.uk/gcl/handg.htm**
The Glasgow Collection comprises 20000 books along with periodicals, maps, plans, newspapers, illustrations, photographs and ephemera covering a wide range of topics relating to the history of the city, its development and current activities. Email enquiries accepted.
(1) Contact : Jack Davis
(2) Contact : Elizabeth Carmichael

Access: Mon-Thu 0900-2000; Fri-Sat 0900-1700.
*Charing Cross local station & bus services nearby; parking difficult; disabled access.*
Primary sources: Glagow Post Office directories 1783-1978; over 1000 vols of newspapers from the Glasgow Journal in 1741 to the Herald today (many on microfilm, Herald on CDRom from October 1993); early maps from 1641, and OS 1860-; 5000+ illustrations of Glasgow people and places incl. some original paintings and lithographs; MS incl. several large collections of family and business papers; North British Locomotive Collection (principally the photographic archive of the North British Locomotive Company and its constituent companies); Wotherspoon & Langmuir Collections (shipping on the Clyde and elsewhere). GEN: ER 1856-; VR 1913-; CEN 1841-91; OPRs; cemetery registers; Family Search (CDRom); IGI 1993 World.
Finding aids: Card catalogue for Glasgow Collection; printed index to Glasgow Herald, 1906-1984; other indexes normally for staff use only.
Leaflets: Tracing your ancestors; The North British Locomotive Company Collection; The Wotherspoon Collection.
Reprographics: R1 (b&w, col), R5

## 201 Glasgow Museums: Museum of Transport
### Kelvin Hall, 1 Bunhouse Road, Glasgow G3 8DP
### *Tel: 0141 287 2623  Fax: 0141 287 2692*
Large collection of archival material relating to public and private transport in the West of Scotland. Plans of Scottish railway locomotives and Glasgow Corporation Transport. Substantial Glasgow and Clyde built ships and shipping records.
(1) Road & Rail Transport: Alastair Smith (Tel: 0141 287 2656)
(2) Shipping & Aviation: Alex Robertson (Tel: 0141 287 2615)
(*) Maritime & Other: Deborah Haase (Tel: 0141 287 2650)
Access: Mon-Sat 1000-1700; Sun 1100-1700. PCA.
*W end of Glasgow off Argyle St; Kelvin Hall underground station, bus routes nearby; parking & disabled access by Old Dumbarton Rd.*
Reprographics: R1, R5

## 202 Glasgow Registration Office
### Strathclyde Area Genealogy Centre, c/o Marriage Suites, 22 Park Circus, Glasgow G3 6BE
### *Tel: 0141 287 8364*
Records for the Strathclyde area include OPRs pre 1855; statutory records (births, marriages and deaths) 1855-1992: CEN 1841-1891 (all microfilm).
Access: Mon-Fri 0930-1600. (Only 12 research places available) BAO
Charges: Search charges.
*Near Woodlands Rd (W city centre); Charing Cross local & St George's Cross underground rail stations, parking near; disabled access & parking by arrangement.*
Finding aids: Lists of census districts.
Leaflets: 'Family Roots' and Centre leaflets.

## 203 Glasgow University Library: Local History Section
**Hillhead Street, Glasgow G12 8QE**
*Tel: 0141 330 6704/5  Fax: 0141 330 4952*
**Email: library@lib.gla.ac.uk**
**http://www.lib.gla.ac.uk/**

Local History Collection contains material on all parts of Scotland with strong representation for Glasgow and W of Scotland with many 19 and early 20C items incl. some periodicals.
(1) History Subject Librarian
(2) Special Collections: Peter Asplin (Tel: 0141 330 5630)
(*) Head of Circulation: Fiona Hall (Tel: 0141 330 4514)
Access: Mon-Fri 0900-2130; Sat 1400-1930; Sun 1400-2130 (term-time). Mon-Fri 0900-1700; Sat 0900-1230 (vacations). PCA.
*Off University Avenue opposite the main University entrance; Hillhead & Kelvinbridge underground stations, parking nearby; on bus routes; disabled access via Hillhead St.*
Primary sources: Collection has almost complete sets of Scottish Historical Club Publications, eg Maitland, Bannatyne, Grampian, Spalding, Scottish Record Society, Scottish Historical Society and Burgh Record Society Publications. The three Statistical Accounts of Scotland, Acts of the Parliaments of Scotland, Scottish Records Office Publications, eg Registers of the Great Seal, Privy Seal, Register of Sasines etc.
Finding aids: Computerised catalogue., available via the Internet. Two earlier catalogues on microfiche.
Leaflets: Directory of Academic Services. Information at www.lib.gla.ac.uk/AboutLibrary/Index.html
Reprographics: R1, R5

## #204 Glasgow University Library: Special Collections Department
**Hillhead Street, Glasgow G12 8QE**
*Tel: 0141 330 6767  Fax: 0141 330 4952*
**Email: library@lib.gla.ac.uk**
**http://www.special.lib.gla.ac.uk/**

Historical collections relating to Glasgow and the West of Scotland. Printed material, ephemera and manuscripts mainly 17-19C. (Catalogue entries for most items available on WWW).
(1) Keeper: David J Weston (Tel: 0141 330 5632)
(2) Contact : Peter W Asplin (Tel: 0141 330 5630)
Access: Mon-Thu 0900-2030 (term-time), 0900-1700 (vacations); Fri 1000-1700; Sat 0900-1230 (except Christmas vacation). PCA.
*Opposite main University entrance; underground stations, bus routes, parking nearby; disabled access.*
Primary sources: Three main collections containing local history material; Euing Collection, the library of William Euing (1788-1874), c17500 vols, includes Scottish history, booksale and library catalogues; Murray

Collection, the library of David Murray (1842-1928), c24000 vols, a superb regional history collection, rich in 17-18C imprints, while 19C strengths include the economic and social development of the West of Scotland - banking, railways, canals & ports - Scottish newspapers, directories, periodicals, chapbooks, printed ephemera, maps and a wide range of manuscripts; Wylie Collection, the library of Robert Wylie (d1921). c1000 volumes on the history and topography of the Glasgow area from 18-early 20C, includes periodicals, directories, chapbooks and ephemera. Bissett Collection of pamphlets by Clydeside socialists; Boyd of Trochrig family documents 1485-c1759; Dougan Collection of mid-19C photographs, mainly by David Octavius Hill & Robert Adamson, based in Edinburgh but covering a wide range of Scottish scenes; Lawson Papers, letters of Christina Hunter Lawson (1876-1963) describing life in Edinburgh; McLagan Collection of c250 Gaelic manuscripts collected or transcribed by James McLagan (1728-1805), minister at Blair Atholl; Henderson Collection of Gaelic manuscripts and transcriptions, assembled by George Henderson; Neilson Papers, Scottish historical documents, 16-20C; Paisley, Glasgow and Ardrossan Canal correspondence, 1808-1846; Trinity College Library Glasgow; **Scottish Theatre Archive** containing a wide range of programmes, playbills, photographs and other material on Scottish theatre history, incl. the archives of the Citizens' Theatre, Glasgow and Scottish Ballet.
Finding aids: Online catalogue at eleanor.lib.gla.ac.uk/search/. Collection descriptions at special.lib.gla.ac.uk/index.html.
Leaflets: Guides to major collections and Scottish Theatre Archive.
Reprographics: R1, R5

## #205 Glasgow University: Archives & Business Records Centre (including Scottish Brewing Archive)
## 13 Thurso Street, Glasgow G11 6PE
*Tel: 0141 330 5515  Fax: 0141 330 4158*
Email: dutyarch@archives.gla.ac.uk
http://www.arts.gla.ac.uk/archives/arcbrc.htm

The administrative records of Glasgow University from 1451, which become more extensive from the 18C. Plus records of staff and student societies, the personal papers of students and professors, businesses throughout Scotland; and the Scottish Brewing Archive.
(1) The Duty Archivist
(2) Scottish Brewing Archive: Alma Topen (Tel: 0141 330 6079)
Access: Mon-Fri 0930-1700. PCA.
Charges: Search charges for postal enquiries possible.
*Off Dumbarton Rd, 2 ml W of city centre opposite Western Infirmary; Kelvin Hall underground station, bus routes nearby, parking difficult; disabled access.*
Primary sources: University of Glasgow, Queen Margaret College, Trinity College, Anderson's College of Medicine and Glasgow Veterinary College records; Jackson Collection of Photographs (14000) mainly topographical (1904-1938); Beith parish documents; Hamilton of Rozelle papers; Royal Scottish Academy of Music and Drama records; Glasgow University records relating to administration, finance, students, staff and teaching. Shipbulding

records: administrative, financial, technical records and photographs relating to the development of shipbuilding on the Clyde 1830's-late 1970's (John Browns, Alexander Stephens, Simons-Lobnitz, Fleming & Ferguson); House of Fraser archive; administrative, financial and promotional records relating to retail stores; James Finlay plc, textile merchants and manufacturers records; North British Locomotive Co. records, incl. technical drawings; Andrew Barclay Sons & Co Ltd., locomotive builders, technical drawings; Anchor Line Ltd. shippers, Glasgow and Edinburgh; J & P Coats Ltd cotton thread manufacturers, Paisley; Scottish Brewing Archive holds records of 50 companies incl. Tennant Caledonian and Scottish & Newcastle. It has a fine library of technical books and periodicals.
Finding aids: Summary guide on WWW. Printed lists available in searchroom & NRA(S) Edinburgh. Computer searchable lists in searchroom.
Leaflets: General plus Source lists for family histories: Renfrewshire; East Dumbartonshire; Highlands and Islands.
Reprographics: R1, R5, plan copying

## 206 Glasgow University: Hunterian Museum: Roman Scotland Archive
### University Avenue, Glasgow G12 8QQ
### Tel: 0141 330 4221  Fax: 0141 330 3617
### http://www.gla.ac.uk/museum

Roman Scotland Archive: documentary coverage of every Roman archaeological site in Scotland, with copies of OS cards; correspondence; excavation reports; site-plans, transparencies, photographs. Small associated library and records of all scattered finds.
(1) Archivist: L J F Keppie (Tel: 0141 330 4402)
Access: BAO
*In main building of Glasgow University, 2 ml W of city centre; Hillhead Underground station nearby, on bus route; disabled access by prior arrangement.*
Finding aids: Database being developed.
Reprographics: Photocopy and photography service on request.

## #207 Greater Glasgow Health Board Archive
### Glasgow University Archives, 77-81 Dumbarton Road, Glasgow G11 6TP
### Tel: 0141 330 5516  Fax: 0141 330 4158
### http://www.arts.gla.ac.uk/archives/gghbhold.htm

Records of Glasgow hospitals since 1787 and Glasgow Health Boards from 1948 (NB. 30 and 75 year closure rules apply).
(1) Archivist: Alistair G Tough
Access: Mon-Fri 0900-1200; 1400-1700. BAO
Charges: Donations welcome.
*2 ml W of city centre, Kelvin Hall underground station, bus routes nearby, parking difficult; disabled access.*

Primary sources: Administrative, financial and clinical records of Glasgow hospitals, dispensaries and clinics from 1787; administrative and financial records of Western Regional Hospital Board and constituent Boards of Management 1948-1974, and of Greater Glasgow Health Board 1974-; papers of various organisations and individuals connected with health care in Scotland.
Leaflets: Guide to Medical Records of Glasgow and Paisley (published book).

## 208 Heatherbank Museum of Social Work
### Glasgow Caledonian University, Park Campus, Park Drive, Glasgow G3 6LP
*Tel: 0141 337 4402  Fax: 0141 337 4500*
Email: a.ramage@gcal.ac.uk
http://lib.gcal.ac.uk/hbank/index.htm

Substantial collection of books (2500), photographs (7000), ephemera, journals & archives on social work/social welfare 1790-, with Glasgow, Edinburgh & Ross & Cromarty strongly represented. (NB: The collection will be located at the City Centre campus from end of 1999).
(1) Contact : A Ramage
(2) Contact : Jo Haythornthwaite (Tel: 0141 331 3860  Fax: 0141 331 3005)
Access: Mon-Fri 0900-1300. BAO
*1 ml W of City centre; Kelvinbridge underground station, bus routes nearby, parking; disabled access by arrangement.*
Primary sources: Archives cover poorhouses, model lodging houses, settlements, childcare, disability, hospitals & prisons and include minutes & some poorhouse registers. There is a significant collection of photographs covering the 1950s.
Finding aids: In-house catalogue - some material on WWW.
Leaflets: Brochure & newsletters.
Reprographics: R1, R5

## 209 The Herald & Evening Times
### 195 Albion Street, Glasgow G1 1QP
*Tel: 0141 552 6255  Fax: 0141 553 2642*
Email: iwatson@cims.co.uk.

Newspaper collection (Glasgow) Herald 1783 - (some gaps); Evening Times 1951-; The Bulletin 1954-1960; Sunday Standard 1981-1983 (microfilm). Photograph archive features Scottish history, industry, sport - especially football.
(1) Information Services Manager: Ian Watson
(2) Contact : Stroma Fraser
Access: Mon-Fri 0900-1700. BAO
Charges: Search charges.
*In city centre (E); Queen St & Central rail stations, parking nearby; disabled access available.*

## 210 Milngavie & Bearsden Historical Society
### c/o E.Dunbartonshire Libraries, Brookwood Library, Bearsden, Glasgow G61 3RJ
*Tel: 0141 942 6811  Fax: 0141 943 1119*

Collection of press cuttings, information & original material on local farms & mills.
(1) Contact : Sharon Handyside
(2) Contact : D S Landale (Tel: 0141 942 1462)
Access: Mon-Thu 1000-2000; Fri,Sat 1000-1700.
*N of Bearsden Cross; rail station, bus routes nearby, parking; disabled access.*

## 211 The National Trust for Scotland: Pollok House
### 2060 Pollokshaws Road, Glasgow G43 1AT
*Tel: 0141 649 7151  Fax: 0141 636 0086*

Estate plans, maps & documentation on Pollok Estate & family history.
(1) The Curator
Access: Mon-Sat 1000-1700; Sun 1100-1700. Archives: Mon-Fri (BAO).
*3 ml S of city centre & 0.75 ml from Pollokshaws Rd entrance to Pollok Country Park; buses to Pollock Country House entrance, thence internal public transport, parking.*
Leaflets: General guide to Pollok House.
Reprographics: R1, R5

## 212 People's Palace
### Glasgow Green, Glasgow G40 1AT
*Tel: 0141 554 0223  Fax: 0141 550 0892*

Small collection of photographs, paintings and prints; some on display, remainder in store.
(1) Curator: Fiona Hayes
Access: Mon-Sat 1000-1700, Sun 1100-1700. PCA.Collections not on display: BAO.
*Located on Glasgow Green; Central & Queen St rail stations approx 1 ml, bus routes nearby, parking; disabled access.*
Leaflets: Publications list incl. People's Palace Book of Glasgow (1998).
Reprographics: Limited photocopying and photographic service.

## 213 Royal College of Physicians & Surgeons of Glasgow
### 232-234 St Vincent Street, Glasgow G2 5RJ
*Tel: 0141 221 6072  Fax: 0141 221 1804*
### Email: james.beaton@rcpsglasg.ac.uk
College records and examination registers.
(1) Librarian: James Beaton (Tel: 0141 227 3204  Fax: 0141 221 1804)
(2) Contact : Carol Parry
Access: Mon-Fri 0900-1700. BAO
*In city centre; Central rail station nearby, Queen St rail station, bus station 0.5 ml, on bus routes, parking difficult.*
Primary sources: Macewen Collection (surgery); Ross Collection (tropical medicine); Transactions of Glasgow Medical Societies.
Finding aids: Card & computerised catalogues for printed books; printed archive catalogue.
Reprographics: Photocopies A4, photographs supplied.

## 214 Royal Faculty of Procurators: Library
### 12 Nelson Mandela Place, Glasgow G2 1BT
*Tel: 0141 332 3593  Fax: 0141 333 9104*
### http://www.scotnet.co.uk/als/
A specialised law library with a collection of 19C and 20C books about Glasgow and archive collections.
(1) Librarian: Alan C McAdams
Access: Mon-Fri 0900-1200, 1400-1700. BAO
*In city centre; Queen St & Central rail stations nearby, on bus routes, parking difficult.*
Primary sources: The archive collection includes those of the Royal Faculty of Procurators 1668-; the Hutcheson-Hill family, 16C- (includes some genealogical MSS): the Dr William Henry Hill (1837-1912) collection (a record of Glagow in the 19C, of sociological interest); Macfarlane Charters and Writs relating to the Clan and its Chiefs 1395-1736; Maps of Glasgow 18C-, and prints.
Finding aids: Catalogue card index to law & Glasgow collections; catalogue card index to Hill collection; printed catalogue of Hill collection (1905); list of defunct Glasgow legal firms 1953-94.
Leaflets: Leaflets, newsletters.
Reprographics: R1

## 215 The Royal Highland Fusiliers Regimental Museum
### 518 Sauchiehall Street, Glasgow G2 3LW
*Tel: 0141 332 0961  Fax: 0141 353 1493*
The library has a comprehensive collection of books, documents, photographs, regimental histories, scrap books and archival material.
(1) Contact : W Shaw MBE
Access: Mon-Fri 0830-1600. Other times BAO. PCA.
*In city centre (NW); Queen St & Central rail stations, bus station 0.75 ml, bus routes, parking nearby; disabled access.*

Primary sources: Archive and regimental records of the Royal Scots Fusiliers and Highland Light Infantry.
Leaflets: Museum leaflet.
Reprographics: R1

## 216 Royal Scottish Geographical Society
## 40 George Street, Glasgow G1 1QE
*Tel: 0141 552 3330  Fax: 0141 552 3331*
## Email: r.s.g.s@strath.ac.uk

A comprehensive range of early and OS maps of Scotland; photographic archive, manuscripts/printed archives relating to Scottish travellers and employers.
(1) Director: David M Munro
(2) Contact : Kerr Jamieson
Access: Mon-Fri 1000-1630. BAO
*Within the University of Strathclyde. Central rail station 0.75 ml; Queen St rail station, bus routes, parking nearby; disabled access.*
Primary sources: Special collections: Archives of Scottish travellers incl. Isobel Wylie Hutchison, Isabella Bird Bishop and Ella Christie; map collection from 17C with important 18 & 19C maps; several thousand Scottish photographic images especial early 20C outer isles; Scottish National Antarctic Expedition 1902-4.
Finding aids: In-house catalogue for early Scottish material.
Leaflets: Available.
Reprographics: R1

## 217 Scotland Street School - Museum of Education
## 225 Scotland Street, Glasgow G5 8QB
*Tel: 0141 429 1202  Fax: 0141 420 3292*

Objects and books relating to education in Scotland from 1872, includes photographs, examples of pupils' work, oral tapes and interactive video. Plans of the building by Charles Rennie Mackintosh
(1) Curator Manager: Dorothy Stewart
Access: Mon-Sat 1000-1700, Sun 1400-1700. PCA.
Charges: Donatons accepted.
*S of city centre; opposite Shields Rd underground station, bus routes, parking nearby.*
Leaflets: Available.

## 218 The Scottish Civic Trust
### The Tobacco Merchant's House, 42 Miller Street, Glasgow G1 1DT
*Tel: 0141 221 1466  Fax: 0141 248 6952*

Collection includes complete set of Scottish Development Dept lists of buildings of architectural and historic interest, technical publications/videos on historic building conservation; some local authority structure and local plans. From 1999 Merchants Room Conservation Centre will have on-line links with Historic Scotland, NMRS, RCHAMS plus a technical library.
(1) Technical Director: John Gerrard
(2) Contact : Leigh Johnston
Access: Mon-Fri 0900-1300, 1400-1700. BAO
*Queen St & Central rail stations, bus station, bus routes, parking nearby.*
Reprographics: R1

## 219 Scottish Daily Record & Sunday Mail Editorial Library
### Anderson Quay, Glasgow G3 8DA
*Tel: 0141 242 3312(3621)  Fax: 0141 242 3527*
### Email: c.macmillan@dailyrecord.co.uk
### http://www.record-mail.co.uk

An in-house reference library with 25m hard copy newspaper cuttings and images. Bound vols. from 1895.
(1) Library Manager: Colin MacMillan
Access:  BAO
Charges: Research/administration charges.
*SW of city centre, N side of river Clyde; Central rail station 0.75 ml, Queen street rail staton 1.25 ml, bus routes, limited parking nearby.*
Finding aids: Printed card indexes of news stories & pictures. Electronic indexes from 1991.
Reprographics: Variety of services - fees on request.

## #220 Scottish Film & Television Archive
### 74 Victoria Crescent Road, Glasgow G12 9JN
*Tel: 0141 302 1742  Fax: 0141 302 1713*
### http://www.scottishscreen.co.uk

The Film Collection (1897-1990s), principally non-fiction includes some 20000 reels comprising documentary, newsreels, shorts, educational, advertising and promotional films, amateur and professional productions, television news material, current affairs and entertainment programmes. The material is largely on 16mm and 35mm with smaller collections of 9.5mm and 8mm film and video-tape. Illustrates local community life, industrial history & the changing nature of leisure. The collection as a whole reflects ways in which Scotland and her people have been portrayed in film more recently the broadcasting sector. The television material represents largely regional output, incl. Gaelic language transmissions.
(1) Film collection enquiries: Anne Docherty (Tel: 0141 302 1742/1700)

(2) MS collection & historical research enquiries: Janet McBain (Tel: 0141 302 1741)
Access: Telephone enquiries: Mon-Fri 1000-1200, 1400-1630. Viewings by appointment Mon-Fri 0930-1230, 1400-1630. Written/fax requests for information to Production Library Administrator. BAO
Charges: Information on request.
*Off Byres Rd, 2 ml NW of city centre; Hillhead underground station, bus routes nearby, parking limited.*
Primary sources: Films of Scotland 1954-84; a special collection of c150 titles reflecting aspects of industrial, cultural & public life. Photographs, ephemera & oral history interviews & ephemera of cinema companies 1897-1980 (various locations); records, publications of organisations 1934-, incl. Scottish Film Council, Scottish Amateur Film Festival, Edinburgh International Film Festival.
Finding aids: Computer database; printed source lists by location & subject areas. General information on WWW.
Leaflets: Leaflets & publications list.
Reprographics: R1, videotapes of films.

## 221 Scottish Industrial Heritage Society
## c/o E T Watt (Publications), 129 Fotheringay Road, Glasgow G41 4LG
### *Tel: 0141 423 1782*
### Email: sihs@aol.com
### http://members.aol.com/sihs/
Society organises conferences, lectures & visits to buildings/sites of importance in the field of industrial archaeology.
Leaflets: A Guide to Scottish Industrial Heritage; Newsletter for members.

## #222 Scottish Jewish Archives Centre
## 127 Hill Street, Glasgow G3 6UB
### *Tel: 0141 332 4911*
Wide range of material relating to history of Jewish community in Scotland, especially Glasgow, Edinburgh, Dundee, Aberdeen, Ayr, Dunfermline, Greenock, Falkirk and Inverness, late 18C-.
(1) Contact : H Kaplan (Tel: 0141 649 4526)
(2) Contact : B Braber (Tel: 0141 956 2973)
(*) Contact : N Cohen (Tel: 0141 332 4911)
Access: Fri 0930-1330. BAO
*In city centre (NW); Queen St & Central rail stations, bus station 0.75 ml; bus routes, parking nearby.*
Primary sources: Minute books of synagogue and communal organisations; newspapers and newspaper cuttings; books; photographs of communal buildings, leaders, activities; papers of communal leaders; financial records & accounts; annual reports; synagogue registers; brochures and magazines; year books.
Leaflets: Leaflet - Archive Centre.

Reprographics: R5.

## 223 Scottish Television Library Services: Film & Videotape Library
### Cowcaddens, Glasgow G2 3PR
### *Tel: 0141 300 3000  Fax: 0141 300 3615*

A working Library holding Regional and Network Programmes and news rushes from 1957.

(1) Head of Library Services: John Rushton (Tel: 0141 300 3615)

(2) Depute Head of Library: Fiona Gunn (Tel: 0141 300 3512)

Access: Bona fide researchers only. BAO

Charges: Standard research charges.

*In city centre; Queen St & Central rail stations, bus station nearby, on bus routes; disabled access.*

Primary sources: Small collection of programme documentation. The primary collections are 16mm film and a variety of videotape and videocassette formats all of which are viewable on the premises.

Finding aids: Bespoke computerised database with STRIX free-text retrieval software. Card catalogues for earlier holdings.

Reprographics: Copies of footage can be purchased, ratecard available on request.

## 224 Springburn Museum
### Atlas Square, Ayr Street, Glasgow G21 4BW
### *Tel: 0141 557 1405  Fax: 0141 557 1405*

Social history and photographic collections include a large section on the railway companies of Springburn; and part of the John Thomas Collection.

(1) Curator: Gilbert T Bell

Access: Tue-Fri 1030-1700, Sat 1000-1630. PCA. Visitors by appointment if specialist information required.

*1.75 ml N of city centre; Springburn rail station adjacent, on bus routes, parking; disabled access.*

Leaflets: Leaflets and books.

Reprographics: R1, R5

## 225 Strathclyde Police Museum
### Police Headquarters, 173 Pitt Street, Glasgow G2 4JS
### *Tel: 0141 532 2000  Fax: 0141 532 2475*

Archives include printed and MS material featuring police work in Glasgow & the W of Scotland, incl. manpower and incident records and 5000+ photographs from end of 19C, incl. groups, inspections etc.

(1) Curator: Jack Skinner (Tel: 0141 532 2483  Fax: 0141 532 2480)

(*) Administration Dept. (Tel: 0141 332 2576  Fax: 0141 532 2475)

Access: Mon-Fri. BAO

*In city centre; rail & bus stations, parking nearby; assisted disabled access.*

**#226 Strathclyde University: Andersonian Library: Special Collections Section**
**Curran Building, 101 St James Road, Glasgow G4 0NS**
*Tel: 0141 552 3701 x4135  Fax: 0141 552 3304*
**Email: librarian@ccsun.strath.ac.uk**
**http://www.lib.strath.ac.uk/**
Selection of secondary, with some primary, material on Glagow and Scottish economic, social and architectural history, with an emphasis on the 19C.
(1) Contact : J M Allan
(2) Contact : F Addis
Access: Mon-Fri 0900-2100 (term-time). Mon-Fri 0900-1700 (vacations). PCA.
Charges: Charges on request.
*Queen St rail station nearby, Central rail station 0.75 ml; Buchanan bus station, bus routes nearby, limited street parking; access for disabled at St James Rd entrance.*
Primary sources: Glasgow Stock Exchange Daily Lists 1847-1963; notebooks of Prof. John Anderson (1726-96), founder of University of Strathclyde (MS); Ludovic Kennedy's papers on the Meehan case (restricted access); publications from Guy A Aldred's presses; Glasgow Dilettante Society Exhibition Books; selection of source material on Glasgow and region in Robertson and other collections.
Finding aids: OPACs accessible via JANET.
Reprographics: R1, R4

**#227 Strathclyde University: Jordanhill Campus Library**
**76 Southbrae Drive, Glasgow G13 1PP**
*Tel: 0141 950 3300  Fax: 0141 950 3150*
**Email: jordanhill.library@strath.ac.uk**
**http://www.lib.strath.ac.uk/Jordanhill**
Jordanhill Archive collection contains documents, photographs etc relating to Jordanhill College of Education and its antecedent institutions, from 1828, on education and teacher training in Scotland generally.
(1) Librarian: Margaret Harrison (Tel: 0141 950 3308)
(2) Senior Library Assistant: Susan Thomson (Tel: 0141 950 3303)
Access: Mon-Thu 0900-2100, Fri-Sat 0900-1700 (term-time). Mon-Fri 0900-1700, Sat 0900-1200 (vacations). PCA.
Charges: Extensive searches chargeable.
*W end of city off Crow Rd; Jordanhill Station 0.5 ml, on bus routes, parking; disabled access.*
Primary sources: Deposits relate to the Glasgow Infant School 1828-34, Glasgow Normal Seminary 1835-45, David Stow collection 1793-1864, Glasgow Church of Scotland Training College 1845-1907, Glasgow Free Church Training College 1845-1907, University of Glasgow Local Committee for the Training of Teachers 1903-6, Jordanhill College of Education 1907-

93, Marjorie Cruickshank papers, Robert Rusk papers, Hamilton College of Education 1966-81 and the records of the Association of Directors of Education in Scotland (ADES). Governing Body minute books, student records, illustrations, student handbooks, magazines and memorabilia, college publications in print and manuscript form.
Finding aids: Printed (2 vol) lists, with general descriptions of the deposits on WWW.
Reprographics: R1, R4, R5

## 228 The Trades House of Glasgow
### 85 Glassford Street, Glasgow G1 1UH
*Tel: 0141 552 2418  Fax: 0141 228 8310*

Collection of c250 books covering history of Glasgow together with records and c500 photographs (1860s-) featuring office bearers, benefactors, people and events connected with the 14 Trade Crafts.
(1) Contact : David McGaffin
(2) Contact : Alex Brewer
Access: Mon-Fri 0900-1700. BAO
*In city centre; rail & bus stations, bus routes, parking nearby.*
Finding aids: In-house catalogue.

## Glenboig

## 229 Scottish Military Historical Society
### Thomas Moles (Hon Secretary), 4 Hillside Cottages, Glenboig ML5 2QY
### http://subnet.virtual-pc.com/~mc546367/homepage.htm

Members undertake research into the history & dress of the Scottish soldier from early times to the present. Results feature in their journal "Dispatch" published three times a year. Enquiries by letter only.

## Glenrothes

## 230 Fife Council: Fife Archaeology Unit: Fife Sites & Monuments Record
### Planning Service, Fife House, Glenrothes KY7 5LT
*Tel: 01592 416153  Fax: 01592 416300*
### Email: fifearch@sol.co.uk

The Fife Sites and Monuments Record is a computer database containing information on 9500+ sites and buildings in Fife, of all periods from the Mesolithic to the present day.
(1) Archaeologist: Peter Yeoman
(2) Contact : Sarah Govan (Tel: 01592 413805)

Access: Mon-Fri 1000-1600. BAO
*In town centre; bus routes nearby, parking; disabled access.*
Primary sources: Written and computerised records of archaeological sites of all periods. Single site reports and surveys, thematic surveys. Large collection of b&w photos and col slides.
Leaflets: Leaflet lists publications.
Reprographics: R1, R5

## Gorebridge

### 231 Gorebridge & District Local History Society
c/o Gorebridge Library, 98 Hunterfield Road, Gorebridge EH23 4TT
*Tel: 01875 820630*

Collections of material covering the Gorebridge district incl. 400 photographs 1850-; 200 slides 1880s-; business papers of 19C local shops; minutes of dramatic society, silver band and mining union 20C.
(1) Chairman: Alasdair Anderson (Tel: 01875 822109)
Access: Mon-Tue, Thu 0930-2015; Wed, Sat 0930-1300; Fri 0930-1700. PCA.
*In village centre; bus routes nearby, parking; disabled access.*
Leaflets: Publications list.
Reprographics: R1, R5

## Grangemouth

### 232 Falkirk Council Library Services: Grangemouth Library
Bo'ness Road, Grangemouth FK3 5AG
*Tel: 01324 504690  Fax: 01324 506801*
Email: mscott@falkirk-libsprt.demon.co.uk

Collection includes books, maps, newspapers, pamphlets and photographs covering Grangemouth.
(1) Contact : Marion Scott (Tel: 01324 506845)
(2) Contact : John Dickson (Tel: 01324 506811)
Access: Mon-Tue, Thu 0930-2000; Wed, Fri-Sat 0930-1700. PCA.
*In town centre; bus routes nearby, parking at rear.*
Primary sources: Grangemouth Advertiser 1902-, indexed from 1930; 250+ photographs 20C; OS maps; some local films and video recordings of local events 1980s-; Grangemouth Town Council minutes; GEN: CEN, OPR.
Leaflets: Publications leaflets.
Reprographics: R1, R2

## 233 HM Customs & Excise
### Custom House, Custom House Quay, Greenock PA15 1EQ
*Tel: 01475 881452  Fax: 01475 881455*

Shipping registers for the Clyde area; plus a wide range of correspondence, reports, government publications affecting the work of the Customs & Excise 1780s-1960s.

(1) Contact : Campbell Dewar (Tel: 01475 881454)

(2) Contact : Jim Docherty (Tel: 01475 881435)

Access: Mon-Fri 1000-1600. PCA.

*In town centre; rail station & bus routes, parking nearby.*

Primary sources: Shipping Registers: Greenock 1785-1894, Port Glasgow 1786-1910, Dumfries 1825-1904, Port Ellen 1900-36, Stranraer/Wigton 1824-1920, Irvine 1837-1937, Ardrossan 1837-48; Greenock Custom House status relating to Customs, Salt Duty etc. 1600-1898; wide collection of C&E letters, records, regulations etc. 1850s-1960s.

Finding aids: Historical records catalogue.

Leaflets: Historical records catalogue.

## 234 McLean Museum and Art Gallery
### 15 Kelly Street, Greenock PA16 8JX
*Tel: 01475 723741  Fax: 01475 731347*

Collection holds c5000 photographs of Clyde paddle steamers.

(1) Assistant Curator: Vincent P Gillen

Access: Mon-Sat 1000-1700. PCA.

*In town centre; Greenock West rail & bus stations, parking nearby; disabled access.*

Finding aids: Computerised catalogue.

Reprographics: R1, R5

## 235 Watt Library
### 9 Union Street, Greenock PA16 8JH
*Tel: 01475 720186*

Comprehensive range of material relating to the Inverclyde district.

(1) Contact : Lesley Couperwaite

Access: Mon, Thu 1400-1700, 1800-2000; Tue, Fri 1000-1300, 1400-1700; Wed, Sat 1000-1300.

*In town centre; Greenock West rail station & bus routes, parking nearby.*

Primary sources: Newspapers - Greenock Advertiser (1802-1884), Greenock Telegraph (1857-), Gourock Times (1915-1980), Port Glasgow Express (1894-1967); Greenock Burgh records pre 1975; collection of photographs 20C; GEN: CEN, OPRs, IND (B.M.D. 1802-1914), BR, DIR.

Reprographics: R1

## Gullane

**236 Gullane & Dirleton History Society**
**c/o Gullane Library, East Links Road, Gullane EH31 2AF**
*Tel: 01620 842073*
Collection comprises maps, photographs, postcards, books and papers depicting life in the two villages.
(1) Secretary by letter
Access: Mon 1400-1700; Tue 1000-1300; Thu 1400-2000; Sat 1000-1200.
BAO
*In centre of village, off Main St; bus route, parking nearby.*
Primary sources: 300+ photographs (125 of Gullane 1910-14); 200 slides; maps 1754-1973; some valuation rolls; material for WWII and Gullane Games exhibitions.
Finding aids: Card index.
Leaflets: Publications list.
Reprographics: R1 (by arrangement).

## Haddington

**237 East Lothian Council Library Service: Local History Centre**
**Haddington Library, Newton Port, Haddington EH41 3NA**
*Tel: 01620 823307  Fax: 01620 822531*
Email: hq@elothlib.demon.co.uk
The Local History Centre houses a comprehensive collection of books on people, places and events in East Lothian plus articles, journals, maps, plans, photographs and ephemera.
(1) Contact : Veronica Wallace
(2) Contact : Chris Roberts
Access: Mon 1400-1800; Tue 1000-1300, 1400-1900; Thu 1400-1900; Fri 1400-1700. PCA.
*In town centre off Market St; bus routes, parking nearby.*
Primary sources: Collection of c6000 books and pamphlets; Register of Sasines: person index 1599-1660, abridgements 1781-1947, and after 1858 includes synopses of deeds of conveyance; Haddingtonshire/East Lothian Courier 1859-, East Lothian News 1971-, Musselburgh News 1889-; 7500 photographs from 1890s; maps end 18C- incl. OS; Hearth Tax return 1691; GEN: CEN, OPRs, IGI(S).
Finding aids: Haddington/East Lothian Courier indexed 1859-90, 1981-, East Lothian News indexed 1981-; indexes/catalogues for books, documents, photographs & maps.
Leaflets: List of local authority records covering Haddingtonshire and East Lothian located at NAS (SRO). Publications list. L.H. Centre leaflet.

Reprographics: R1 (b&w, col), R4, R5

## 238 East Lothian Museums Service
**Libraries & Museums HQ, Dunbar Road, Haddington EH41 3PJ**
*Tel: 01620 828200  Fax: 01620 828201*
**Email: museums@elothlib.demon.co.uk**

Collections include photographs and printed material covering East Lothian's civic life, industry and social history mostly 1880-1960. Refer to WWW at www.scran.ac.uk for 500 East Lothian seaside holiday records, and at muir-birthplace.org for information on John Muir.
(1) Museums Officer: Peter Gray (Tel: 01620 828203)
(2) Resource Assistant: Muriel King (Tel: 01620 828204)
Access: Mon-Fri 0900-1700. BAO
*On E outskirts of town 200 yd from A1; on bus route, parking; disabled access.*
Primary sources: Richardson collection of c300 glass negatives feature North Berwick area end 19C; Spence collection of documents, 200 images, plans and notebooks covers the mining industry c1800-1960; late medieval charters; ephemera (mostly North Berwick).
Finding aids: Computer database.
Leaflets: Leaflet and publications list.
Reprographics: R5, photocopies A4.

## Hamilton

## 239 The Cameronians (Scottish Rifles)
**116 Cadzow Street, Hamilton ML3 7UE**
*Tel: 01698 452163  Fax: 01698 283479*

Collection covers the period 1850s until disbanded in 1968, incl. photographs, paintings, drawings and campaign maps (18C-WWI), war diaries 1914-1952 (limited access 1920 onwards), incl. Field Marshal Wolseley's 1860s-1880s; plus c1000 books on the Regiment and related subjects.
(1) Keeper of Documentation & Information: Terry Mackenzie
(2) Keeper of Collections: Liz Hancock
Access: Museum at 129 Muir St closed for redevelopment until Summer 2000. BAO
Charges: Search charges.
Leaflets: Lists.
Reprographics: R1, R5

## 240 Low Parks Museum
**116 Cadzow Street, Hamilton ML3 7UE**
*Tel: 01698 452163/452165  Fax: 01698 283479*
Collection includes maps (Hamilton estate late 18C plus OS); 2000+
photographs 1850s-; local societies and business papers (include Colliers
Friendly Society 1799- and Keith and Patrick Solicitors 1830-1960).
(1) Keeper of Documentation & Information: Terry Mackenzie
(2) Keeper of Collections: Liz Hancock
Access: Museum at 129 Muir St closed for redevelopment until Summer
2000. BAO
Charges: Search charges.
Finding aids: Computerised catalogues.
Reprographics: R1, R5

## 241 South Lanarkshire Libraries: Local Studies Department
**Hamilton Central Library, Cadzow Street, Hamilton ML3 6HQ**
*Tel: 01698 452403  Fax: 01698 286334*
**Email: hamilton.reference@south.lanarkshire.co.uk**
Collection comprises 8000+ items incl. books, maps, newspapers etc
relating to Lanarkshire and the Hamilton district.
(1) Reference, Local History & Information Librarian: Raymond Cameron
(2) Reference Services Manager: Isabel Walker (Tel: 01698 452402)
Access: Mon-Tue, Thu 0915-1930; Fri 0930-1930; Wed, Sat 0915-1700.
PCA. BAO
Charges: Search charges for mail enquiries.
*In town centre; rail & bus stations, off-street parking nearby; disabled access
difficult (prior contact advised).*
Primary sources: Burgh of Hamilton: Council minutes 1701-1975, Abstract of
Accounts 1879-1975, Police Commissioners Minutes 1857-1901, Water
Works Commissioners Minutes 1854-1901, Road Trustees Minutes 1808-
1865, Hamilton Combination Poor House (later Hamilton Home) Minutes
1864-1975. Hamilton District: Council Minutes 1975-1996, Abstract of
Accounts 1975-1996. Lanark County Council: Council Minutes 1890-1975
(incomplete). Newspapers: Hamilton Advertiser 1856 to date and Hamilton
Herald 1888-1925. For others see newspaper list. Hamilton Estates: Small
collection of 18/19C rentals and accounts incl. inventories of Hamilton
Palace. GEN: CEN, OPRs, ER(1851-), DIR(1847-1909), IGI(SI).
Finding aids: Library catalogues; indexes for some material.
Leaflets: Genealogical, newspaper and publications lists.
Reprographics: R1, R4

## 242 Hawick Archaeological Society: Historical Collection c/o Public Library, North Bridge Street, Hawick TD9 9QT
*Tel: 01450 372637*

Local history collection comprises books and material covering Hawick and district incl. incorporated trades MS. NB. Some earlier books and material are at the Hawick Museum whilst other Hawick material is at the Scottish Borders Archive and Local History Centre.
(1) Area Librarian: Gillian McNay
(2) Secretary: Ian Landles (Tel: 01450 375546)
Access: Mon, Wed, Fri 0930-1700; Tue, Thu 0930-1900; Sat 0900-1230.PCA.
*In town centre; on bus route, parking.*
Leaflets: Annual transactions.

## 243 Scottish Borders Council Museums & Galleries: Hawick Museum & Gallery
## Wilton Lodge Park, Hawick TD9 7JL
*Tel: 01450 373457  Fax: 01450 378506*

The library collection donated by the Hawick Archaeological Society includes 500 books, journals and articles, newspapers, guide books and ephemera. An extensive archival collection includes maps, plans and photographs.
(1) Curator: Fiona Colton
Access: Mon-Fri 1000-1230, 1330-1700; Sat-Sun 1400-1700 (Apr-Oct). Mon-Fri 1330-1700; Sun 1400-1600 (Nov-Mar). PCA.
Charges: Admission charges; staff search charges.
*0.75 ml from the town centre; parking nearby; access for disabled limited to ground floor.*
Primary sources: c8000 photographs 1850s- plus 600+ glass negatives and slides 1880s-1907; knitwear/hosiery records include local businesses: Lyle & Scott, Pringles and Elliotts; 600 maps and plans include 16C MS pertaining to Mary Queen of Scots, mostly end 18-19C with OS; estate and farming papers include inventories and land transfers mid 19C- 1920; motor vehicle licencing record and MI for Roxburghshire; photographic archive of archaeological excavations; Hawick Common Riding MS; family history and genealogical papers; newspapers: Hawick Advertiser and Roxburghshire Gazette 1855-1914; Hawick News and Border Chronicle 1882-91, 1906-8.
Finding aids: Card indexes, lists.
Reprographics: R1, R5

# Huntly

## 244 Aberdeenshire Library & Information Service: Brander Library
### The Square, Huntly AB54 9SN
*Tel: 01466 792179*
Books & materials relating to the history of Huntly and surrounding area, incl. the George Macdonald (1845-1905) collection of books; Huntly Express newspaper (1864-). GEN: CEN,OPRs, IGI(S).
(1) Librarian
Access: Mon, Thu 1430-1700; Tue, Fri 1430-1930; Wed 1030-1230, 1430-1930; Sat 1030-1230, 1400-1600. PCA.
*In town square; rail station 0.75 ml; bus routes, parking nearby.*

# Inverbervie

## 245 Aberdeenshire Library & Information Service: Inverbervie Library
### Church Street, Inverbervie DD10 0RU
*Tel: 01561 361690*
Small collection of books and other material relating to Inverbervie and district, incl. GEN: CEN, OPRs, IGI(S).
(1) Senior Library Assistant: Joan Anderson
(2) Network Librarian: Pearl Murray (Tel: 01569 762071)
Access: Mon, Wed 1800-2000; Tue, Thu 1400-1630; Sat 1030-1230, 1400-1530. BAO
*In village centre; bus route nearby, parking; disabled access.*
Finding aids: Computerised catalogue.

# Inverness

## #246 Highland Council Archive Service
### Inverness Library, Farraline Park, Inverness IV1 1NH
*Tel: 01463 220330  Fax: 01463 711128*
Archives of the former counties of Inverness, Ross & Cromarty, Sutherland & Caithness and Inverness Burgh, court records, Highland farm and estate records 1780-1940, records of businesses, societies and institutions 18-20C.
(1) Archivist: Robert Steward
(2) Archive Assistant: Fiona Macleod
Access: Mon-Thu 1000-1300, 1400-1700. BAO
Charges: Written search charges.
*In town centre, off Academy St; bus station at the Library, rail station, parking nearby; disabled access.*
Primary sources: Minutes of former counties early 18C-1975 plus VRs from 1870, parochial and school board records, school log books; Inverness

Burgh records 1556-1975, include VRs, register of sasines, court records, trades guild records; Inverness-shire Sheriff Court records 1700-1900; access to the records of the 8 District Councils 1975-1996 can be arranged: Badenoch & Strathspey, Caithness, Inverness, Lochaber, Nairn, Ross & Cromarty, Skye & Lochalsh and Sutherland; Highland Constabulary records 1860-1960; registers of shipping and fishing boats: Inverness, Fort William, Mallaig 1789-1970; Nairn Fishermen's Society records 1767-1979; Caledonian Canal plans and papers 1803-1963; Inverness Liberal Association records 1898-1986; Baillie of Dunain, Inverness, family and estate papers 18-19C; Northern Meeting records 1788-1957 (social gathering of leading families of Highlands); Inverness, Loch Ness and Nairn Tourist Board records 1948-1989; Tartan archive papers 1830-1990; Harris Tweed Association records; AI Welders, Inverness, records 1872-1992; MacTavish Camanachd Association records (shinty); Alexander Fraser & Co. timber merchants, Inverness 1775-1850; MacDonald and Fraser, solicitors, Portree, Skye, estate management and business papers, incl. crofting disturbances, Skye Farming and Agricultural Societies records 19-20C.
GEN: CEN; OPRs; IND; MI; VI; IGI(UK).
Finding aids: Archive Guide.
Leaflets: Highland Council Archives and Family History Guides.
Reprographics: R1, R4

## 247 Highland Council Museum Service: The Whyte Photographic Collection
### Inverness Service Point, 23 Church Street, Inverness IV1 1DY
*Tel: 01463 703912  Fax: 01463 703918*

The collection of 140000 images came from the photographic business established by David Whyte in 1860 & which continued until 1985. Strong on family groups, weddings & shooting parties but with significant number of shop front & displays & some topographical. Day books, card indexes & appointment diaries from 1920s.
(1) Contact : Lesley Junor
Access: Mon-Fri 0900-1700 BAO
*In town centre; rail & bus stations, parking nearby; disabled access*
Leaflets: Available.
Reprographics: R1, R5

**248 Highland Health Board Archives**
**Highland Health Sciences Library, Stirling University - Highland Campus, Old Perth Road, Inverness IV2 3FG**
*Tel: 01463 705269 Fax: 01463 713471*

The Health Board's archives contain the records of many of the hospitals and health authorities which once existed or still exist in the Highland area. These date mainly from the mid/late 19C although some of the records of the (Royal) Northern Infirmary date from c1800.
(1) Information Officer: Rob Polson
(2) Area Librarian: Rebecca Higgins
Access: Mon-Fri 0900-1700. BAO
*Situated within Highland College of Nursing/Postgraduate Medical Centre 1.5 ml E of town centre; rail station 1.5 ml, bus services nearby, parking; disabled access.*
Primary sources: Minutes, financial records, patient and staff registers, case notes, nurse training records, annual records and some plans and photographs from most of the hospitals in the north of Scotland; administrative records of the Northern Regional Hospital Board and its constituent boards of management set up under NHS (Scotland) Act 1947; also some material from local authority health departments incl. annual reports of the Medical Officers of Health and Registers of Notification of Infectious Disease.
Reprographics: R1

**249 Highland Libraries: Inverness Public Library**
**Farraline Park, Inverness IV1 1NH**
*Tel: 01463 236463 Fax: 01463 237001*

Reference and local history collection (30000+ items) include: Charles Fraser-Mackintosh collection (5300 vols of mainly 19C Highland history and culture); library of the Gaelic Society of Inverness (2500 vols) and the Inverness Kirk Session Library, an early Burgh Library (founded c1705, 3400 vols); newspaper collection.
(1) Contact : Norman S Newton
(2) Reference Librarian
Access: Mon, Fri 0900-1930; Tue, Thu 0900-1830; Wed, Sat 0900-1700. PCA.
*In town centre; bus station adjacent; rail station, parking nearby; disabled access.*
Primary sources: Newspaper collection (dates include predecessors): Inverness Journal 1807-48; Inverness Courier 1817-; Inverness Advertiser 1849-85; Northern Chronicle 1881-1969; Highland News 1883-; Scottish Highlander 1885-98; Ross-shire Journal 1877-. (NB. Genealogical material is kept in the Highland Archive).
Finding aids: Computer database plus card catalogues for special collections.
Leaflets: Leaflets and book lists.
Reprographics: R1, R4

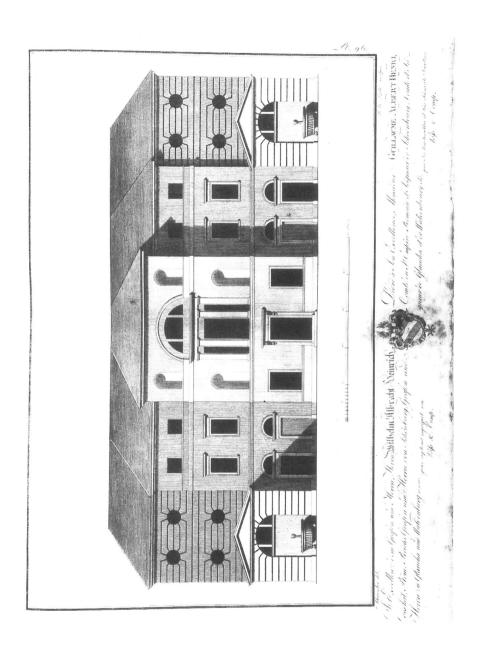

**Elevation of Bellville House, Inverness 1800 (NAS ref: RHP. 43968/F.96)**

151

## 250 Inverness Museum and Art Gallery
Castle Wynd, Inverness IV2 3EB
*Tel: 01463 237114  Fax: 01463 225293*

A small library of books and pamphlets relating to Inverness and district plus an extensive photograph collection (40000 1890s-1950s) covering Inverness and the Highlands; and map collection (300 18C-1979) incl. estate plans, town maps, thematic maps, OS Maps.
(1) Assistant Curator - Social History: Lorna MacKenzie
(2) Assistant Curator - Archaeology (Maps): Patricia Weeks
Access: Mon-Fri 0900-1700.
*In town centre; rail station, parking nearby, on bus route; disabled access.*
Finding aids: Map catalogue.
Reprographics: R1, R5

### Inverurie

## 251 Aberdeenshire Library & Information Service: Inverurie Library
Town Hall, Market Place, Inverurie AB51 3SN
*Tel: 01467 621619  Fax: 01467 621619*

Small collection of materials relating to Inverurie and district, incl. Inverurie & District Advertiser 1959-; GEN: CEN, OPRs, IGI(S).
(1) Senior Library Assistant
Access: Mon, Wed-Fri 1000-2000; Tue 1000-1700; Sat 1000-1600. BAO
*In town centre; rail station, bus route, parking nearby; disabled access.*
Finding aids: Computerised catalogue.
Reprographics: R1

### Irvine

## 252 Scottish Maritime Museum: Laird Forge
Gottries Road, Irvine KA12 8QE
*Tel: 01294 278283  Fax: 01294 313211*

Small collection of business records re ship & boat building & shipping lines. Archives re seamen's lives & passenger transport. Specialist maritime library.
(1) Documentation Officer: James Grant
(2) Curator: Veronica Hartwich
Access: Mon-Fri 1000-1600. BAO
Charges: Search charges.
*By Irvine harbourside; rail station, bus routes & parking nearby; disabled access possible with assistance.*
Primary sources: Business records 1900-1980's: Wm Fyfe & Sons and Fairlie Yacht Ship Co., Fairlie, North Ayrshire, yacht builders & designers; Ayrshire Dockyard Co Ltd, Irvine. Limited information on Ayr & Irvine Harbours and vessel movements. Library comprises 2700+ books and

periodicals: Nautical Magazine 1833-1902, Lloyds Registers 1900-1990, runs of Lloyds Yacht Register, Sea Breezes, Ships Monthly, TIESS, TINA, etc.
Finding aids: In-house archival and library catalogues. Photocopies available of former.
Reprographics: R1 (b&w, col), R5

## Isle of Arran

### 253 Isle of Arran Heritage Museum
### Rosaburn, Brodick, Isle of Arran KA27 8DP
### *Tel: 01770 302636*
### Email: tom.k.macleod@btinternet.com

A large collection of material relating to life on Arran includes papers, letters, journals and photographs; an oral tape collection covering islanders describing life in their youth, plus music and poetry.
(1) Archivist: Stuart Gough (Tel: 01770 302670)
(2) Secretary: Tom MacLeod (Tel: 01770 302185)
Access: Mon-Sat (Apr,May, Sep,Oct) 1100-1600; (Jun-Aug) 1000-1700; Sunday (Easter-Oct) 1100-1600. BAO
Charges: Admission charges.
*1 ml N of Brodick pier; on bus route, parking; disabled access.*
Primary sources: Photographic collection features farming, fishing, housing and family groups 1870-; papers, journals and correspondence covering genealogy, land tenure, clearances and emigration, geology, archaeology, island life; oral history, music and poetry tapes by islanders.
Finding aids: Fiche Reader.
Leaflets: Museum leaflet.
Reprographics: Photocopies A4.

## Isle of Barra

### 254 Comann Eachdraidh Bharraigh Agus Bhatarsaidh - Barra & Vatersay Historical Society
### Dualchas, Barra Heritage & Cultural Centre, Castlebay, Isle of Barra HS9 5XD
### *Tel: 01871 810413 Fax: 01871 810413*

Centre holds a collection of 2000+ photographs from late 19C covering the social history of Barra.
(1) Secretary: R Thomson (Tel: 01871 890394 Fax: 01871 890394)
(2) Treasurer: R Campbell (Tel: 01871 810507)
Access: Mon-Fri 1100-1700 (Apr-Sep). BAO
Charges: Admission charge to centre.
*On main road 0.5 ml from town of Castlebay; parking; disabled access.*

**255 Comhairle Nan Eilean Siar (formerly Western Isles Council): Community Library**
**Castlebay Community School, Castlebay, Isle of Barra HS9 5XD**
*Tel: 01871 810471  Fax: 01871 810650*
A small gaelic and local history collection of books, articles, maps and periodicals, incl. some of An Comnan Gaidhealach collection of gaelic literature and highland history and school log books.
(1) Contact : Linda MacKinnon
Access: Mon, Wed 0900-1630; Tue, Thu 0900-1630, 1800-2000; Fri 0900-1530; Sat 1000-1230. PCA.
*5 mins from ferry, 20 mins from airport, parking; disabled access.*
Finding aids: Catalogue.
Leaflets: Gaelic and local history user guides.
Reprographics: Photocopies A4.

## Isle of Benbecula

**256 Comhairle Nan Eilean Siar (formerly Western Isles Council): Community Library**
**Sgoil Lionalleit, Liniclate, Isle of Benbecula HS7 5PJ**
*Tel: 01870 602211  Fax: 01870 602817*
Gaelic and local history collection of books, articles, periodicals and maps, incl. much of An Comnan collection of Gaelic literature and Highland history. Archive material includes some Uist school log books, CEN & OPRs for Uist & Barra, Lawsons Croft histories.
(1) Contact : Janet Keith
Access: Mon, Thu 0900-1600; Tue, Fri 0900-2000; Wed 0900-1230, 1330-1600; Sat 1100-1300, 1400-1600. PCA. Mark fax: fao Community Library
*Air & Ferry links; limited bus service, parking; disabled access.*
Finding aids: Card catalogue.
Leaflets: Gaelic and local history user guides.
Reprographics: R1

## Isle of Islay

### 257  Museum of Islay Life
### Port Charlotte, Isle of Islay PA48 7UA
### Tel: 01496 850358

Collection includes over 1400 books covering all aspect of Islay life; c4000 photographs 1870s-; document and records of past life on Islay incl. distilleries.
(1) Curator: Margot Perrons
Access: Mon-Sat 1000-1700, Sun 1400-1700 (Easter-Oct). Other times BAO. PCA.
*In village centre; ferry 25 ml, parking nearby.*
Finding aids: Books & photographs on computer database.
Leaflets: Publications list.
Reprographics: Photocopies A4.

## Isle of Lewis

### 258  Bernera Local History Society
### Bernera Museum, Bernera, Isle of Lewis HS2 9LT
### Tel: 01851 612331  Fax: 01851 612331

Collection includes reports/information on archaeological digs: 600+ photographs 1860s-; Seaforth muniments rent roll 1760-1820; local family genealogy 18C-; local boat survey/register 1869-; 15+ audio interviews 1990s; GEN: CEN.
(1) Contact : Noreen Maciver (Tel: 01851 612285)
Access: Mon-Sat 1100-1700 (May-Sep). Other times BAO.
Charges: Admission charge..
*Within Bernera Community Centre; limited bus service, parking; disabled access.*
Finding aids: Card index boat catalogue; computerised catalogue.
Reprographics: R5, photocopies A4.

### 259  North Lochs Historical Society
### 31 Ranish, Lochs, Isle of Lewis HS2 9NN

NB: the new Community Hall will become available from late 1999.
Collection of information on archaeological sites, history of the North Lochs area incl. genealogical material & oral tapes of local people recorded 1995-.
(1) Chairman: John MacDonald (Tel: 01851 860432)
(2) Secretary: Jean Macleod (Tel: 01851 860431)
Access: BAO.
*10 ml S of Stornoway; bus service nearby, parking; disabled access.*
Finding aids: Information on database from late 1999.
Leaflets: Quarterly newsletter.
Reprographics: R1

## 260 Pairc Historical Society
**Ravenspoint Centre, Kershader, South Lochs, Isle of Lewis HS2 9QB**
*Tel: 01851 880225 Fax: 01851 880386*
**Email: donnie@sol.co.uk**
**http://www.hebrides.com**

Collection includes 800+ photographs 1880s-; school attendance and log books; croft history covering the ten villages in the Pairc area of South Lochs.
(1) Contact : Donnie Morrison
(2) Contact : Maureen MacMillan (Tel: 01851 880200)
Access: Mon-Sun 1400-1630 (Jun-Aug). Other times BAO.
Charges: Donations welcomed.
*27 ml S of Stornoway on B8060 road; limited bus service, parking adjacent; disabled access.*
Finding aids: Photographs indexed.
Leaflets: Quarterly newsletter, photographic collection on CDRom.
Reprographics: Photographs printed from CDRom.

## 261 Uig Heritage Centre
**Crowlista, Uig, Isle of Lewis HS2 9JE**
*Tel: 01851 672456*

Collection of 800 photographs 1880-1940, mostly of people with 1930s topographical; small folklore archive. GEN: CEN.
(1) Contact : C Murray (Tel: 01851 672363)
(2) Contact : M Gillies (Tel: 01851 672419)
Access: Mon-Sat 1200-1700 (mid Jun-mid Sep). Other times BAO.
Charges: Admission Charge
*Off the B8011 Garynahine to Timsgarry road beside Uig School; limited bus service nearby, parking; disabled access.*
Finding aids: Index of Archives.
Reprographics: R1, computer scanner.

## Isle of Mull

## 262 Isle of Mull Museum (Library & Archive)
**Columba Buildings, Main Street, Tobermory, Isle of Mull PA75 6NY**

The Museum houses a small collection of books relating to Mull, Coll, Tiree & Morven; a photographic collection (1000+, 1860s-) & MS Collection
(1) Librarian: B B Whittaker (Tel: 01688 302171)
Access: Mon-Fri 1030-1630, Sat 1030-1330 (Easter-mid Oct). BAO
Charges: Admission charges. Search charges possible
*Bus services Craignure (ferry terminal) to Tobermory, parking.*

Primary sources: British Fisheries Society Estate, Tobermory descriptive rentals 1825-1844; Lochbuie Trust folio 1862-73 (470pp); Solicitors letter books folio mid & late 19C; tradesmen's account books & ledgers mid & late 19C; 19C legal documents concerning many Mull & Morven prominent persons; Allans of Aros papers (Allan shipping line); HMS Western Isles records - Atlantic convoy duty WWII.
Finding aids: Library & maps card indexes.
Reprographics: R1 (by arrangement), R5

## Isle of Skye

### #263 Clan Donald Centre Library
### Armadale, Ardvasar, Isle of Skye IV45 8RS
### *Tel: 01471 844389  Fax: 01471 844275*
### Email: library@cland.demon.co.uk

A comprehensive collection of 7000 books covering Scottish history, literature & culture with emphasis on the Highlands & Islands plus archive material for Skye.
(1) Contact : Maggie Macdonald
(2) Contact : Ann Mackinnon
Access: Mon-Sun 0930-1730 (Easter-Oct). Mon-Fri 0930-1700 (by appointment Nov-Easter). PCA.
Charges: Admission charges & search fees for postal enquiries.
*1 ml from Armadale pier, at rear of Centre's gardens; parking; limited disabled access.*
Primary sources: c4000 photographs from 1854 but with majority 1978-; a collection of maps - some from 17C, estate maps 19C & OS; prints & drawings, topographical/people 19C; Macdonald estate papers for Skye & N Uist 18/19C; Glenaladale business papers early 19C; GEN: CEN & OPRs (Inverness-shire, Argyll & mainland Ross & Cromarty).
Finding aids: Catalogues, card indexes, handlists; microfiche catalogue of Macdonald estate papers available through NRA(S), survey no.3273.
Reprographics: R1

## Kemnay

### 264 Aberdeenshire Library & Information Service: Kemnay Library
### Kendal Road, Kemnay AB51 5RN
### *Tel: 01467 643906*

Small collection of books and other materials relating to Kemnay and district, incl. GEN: CEN, OPRs, IGI(S).
(1) Senior Library Assistant: Margaret Moir
(2) Network Librarian: David Leggatt (Tel: 01467 643535)
Access: Mon, Fri 1500-1700, 1800-2000; Tue 1000-1200, 1500-1700; Wed 1000-1200, 1800-2000; Sat 1000-1200. BAO

*In town centre; parking; disabled access.*
Finding aids: Computerised catalogue.
Reprographics: R1

## Kilbarchan

**265  Scottish Natural History Library
Foremount House, Kilbarchan PA10 2EZ
*Tel: 01505 702419***
Largest separate collection of Scottish natural history books and journals in
existence, natural history bibliographical service.
(1) Director: J A Gibson
Access: Available for special research by prior arrangement.
*5 ml W of Paisley; bus routes, parking.*
Primary sources: 120000 vols of monographs and journals covering all
aspects of natural history of Scotland; publications of local Scottish
societies.
Leaflets: The Scottish Naturalist (founded 1871, 3 times a year).
Reprographics: R1

## Kilmarnock

**266  East Ayrshire Council Library Service: Ayrshire
Collection
Dick Institute, Elmbank Avenue, Kilmarnock KA1 3BU
*Tel: 01563 526401  Fax: 01563 529661*
Email: dick_institute@compuserve.com**

*554*

*310*

Ayrshire collection includes extensive range of books, newspapers,
pamphlets, magazines on Ayrshire.
(1) Contact : Anne Geddes (Tel: 01290 421701  Fax: 01290 421701)
(2) Weekday mornings only: Archie Connell
Access: Mon-Tue, Thu-Fri 0900-2000; Wed, Sat 0900-1700. PCA.
Charges: Staff search charges.
*In town centre off London Rd; rail station, bus station nearby, parking;
disabled access at rear.*
Primary sources: Local newspapers (1830-) include: Kilmarnock Herald &
Ayrshire Gazette (1880-1955), Kilmarnock Standard (1863-); Kilmarnock
Midwife's Register (1777-1829); Kilmarnock Mortality Register (1728-63);
GEN: CEN, OPRs, MI(pre 1855), DIR, IGI(S).
Finding aids: Index for some books, pamphlets & newspapers.
Leaflets: Publications list.
Reprographics: R1, R4, R5

*Cemetery records with Registrar*

**Postcard showing the Post Office at Craighouse, Isle of Jura c1900**
**(NAS ref: GD.64/1/361/19)**

## Kilmartin

### 267 Kilmartin House Centre for Archaeology & Landscape Interpretation
**Kilmartin House Trust, Kilmartin PA31 8RQ**
*Tel: 01546 510278  Fax: 01546 510330*
**Email: museum@khouse.demon.co.uk**
**http://www.kht.org.uk**

Proceedings of the Society of Antiquaries of Scotland 1871-; RCAHMS Argyll Vols 1-7; Natural History & Antiquarian Society of mid Argyll: reports etc by members on local archaeological finds and excavations (some featured in Society's publication list); c10000 colour slides with aerial views of landscape & sites plus artifacts, flora & fauna in Argyll.
(1) Curator: Rachel Clough
(2) Marketing Officer: D J Adams McGilp
Charges: Admission charges.
*Museum in former Manse, 9 ml N of Lochgilphead; parking, disabled access.*
Finding aids: In-house catalogues.
Reprographics: R5

## Kinghorn

### 268 Costume Society of Scotland
**c/o Fiona Leslie (Secretary), 48 Pettycur Road, Kinghorn KY3 0RL**
*Tel: 01592 870524*

Members interests include the development of costume in Scotland. Members' research essays are featured in the "Annual Bulletin".

## Kingussie

### 269 Highland Folk Museum
**Duke Street, Kingussie PH21 1JG**
*Tel: 01540 661307  Fax: 01540 661361*

The library contains material covering the social history of the highlands and islands of Scotland.
(1) Contact : Rachel Chisholm
Access: Mon-Fri 0900-1700. PCA.
*Rail station, bus route nearby; parking.*
Primary sources: Collection of 2500+ books; 3000+ photographs and 6000 slides from 1870s; papers of the founder of the museum Dr I F Grant incl. research notes, accounts, photographs covering Iona (1920s) and Kingussie (1944-1970s); Dalcross farm papers 1750-1800; 19C family papers: Ross of Pitcalnie and Mackintosh of Farr (related to I F Grant); minutes of Kingussie

Parochial Board 1873-94; Kingussie tradesmen's catalogues; papers of J S
Macpherson, builder early 20C; Badenoch Field Club minutes and notes
1930s-60s.
Finding aids: Library classification list.
Reprographics: R5

## Kirkcaldy

## 270 Fife Council Central Area Libraries: Local History Collection
**Central Library, War Memorial Grounds, Kirkcaldy KY1 1YG**
*Tel: 01592 412879  Fax: 01592 412750*

The collection covers towns and villages of Central Fife and includes books,
newspapers, maps, photographs and genealogical material.
(1) Contact : Sheila Campbell
(2) Contact : Janet Klak (Tel: 01592 412939  Fax: 01592 412941)
Access: Mon-Thu 1000-1900; Fri,Sat 1000-1700. BAO
*In town centre; rail station adjacent, bus routes, parking nearby; disabled
access.*
Primary sources: Newspapers: Fife Free Press 1871-; Fifeshire Advertiser
1845-1965; Leven Advertiser & Wemyss Gazette 1906-39; Leven Advertiser,
Buckhaven & Methil News 1897-1905; collection of mostly OS maps;
photographs 9000 images from 1880s, plus a collection of books (10000)
covering Fife and mid Fife in particular. GEN: CEN, OPRs, VR, DIR, IND, MI,
IGI(SEI).
Finding aids: Computerised & card catalogue; many photographs on
photofile; index to Fifeshire Advertiser 1846-66; press cuttings index.
Leaflets: Family History sources and book list.
Reprographics: R1, R4

## 271 Kirkcaldy Museum & Art Gallery
**War Memorial Gardens, Kirkcaldy KY1 1YG**
*Tel: 01592 412860  Fax: 01592 412870*

Miscellaneous records and photographs relating to social & industrial history
of central Fife, with printed ephemera & secondary material.
(1) Curator: Dallas Mechan
(2) Assistant Curator: Gavin Grant
Access: Mon-Sat 10.30-1700; Sun 1400-1700; Curatorial staff not available
Sat-Sun. BAO
*In town centre; rail station adjacent, bus station nearby, limited parking;
disabled access.*
Primary sources: Miscellanaeous records (incomplete) of local industries (eg
Burntisland shipyard, Kirkcaldy linoleum manufacturers, Douglas & Grant
Engineers); Burgess Tickets relating to Burntisland; misc. archive and MS
records; small map collection from 18C; 15000 photographs & 10000
transparencies 1870s- (eg local architecture, local mining, linoleum

manufacture); lantern slides and glass negatives (large group of 1930s East Wemyss).
Finding aids: Printed index of archives.
Reprographics: R1, R5

## Kirkcudbright

### 272 The National Trust for Scotland: E A Hornel Art Gallery & Library
### Broughton House, 12 High Street, Kirkcudbright DG6 4JX
*Tel: 01557 330437*

The Hornel Library is a large collection (25000+ items) of mainly local history material covering Dumfries & Galloway. It includes works relating to Scottish art and a fine MS Collection. The general library includes books written by local authors; Robert Burns (2500+ items), Thomas Carlyle, JM Barrie, SR Crockett & the Covenanters.
(1) Librarian: James Allan
Access: Mon-Fri 1030-1230; 1330-1630. BAO
Charges: Charges on application.
*In town centre; bus route, parking nearby.*
Primary sources: Archives include Hornel's letters, CK Sharpe material, Macmath & Childe correspondence, border ballads; map collection includes Blaeu's Atlas of Scotland (1654) & other early atlases, estate & railway maps and OS maps; Sasines from 1515; small collection of photographs 20C; minutes & account books of societies include: Stewartry Agricultural Society 19C, curling societies & Friendly Societies 1770-20C; estate valuation documents 18/19C; many scrapbooks (most indexed); GEN: VR ER.
Finding aids: Catalogues & indexes.
Reprographics: R1

### 273 The Stewartry Museum
### St Mary Street, Kirkcudbright DG6 4AQ
*Tel: 01557 331 643  Fax: 01557 331643*
**Email: daviddevereaux@dumgal.gov.uk**

The museum holds a general library relating to the history of Galloway and the Stewartry plus archive and photographic collections covering the Stewartry.
(1) Museum Curator: David Deveraux
Access: Mon-Fri 0900-1300, 1400-1700. BAO
Charges: Staff research charges.
*In town centre; bus routes nearby, parking; disabled access possible with assistance.*
Primary sources: Kirkcudbright Town Council minutes 1576-1870 and miscellaneous burgh archives 1680- include Treasurer's accounts early 18 & 19C; miscellaneous burgh archives from Castle Douglas, Gatehouse-of-Fleet, New Galloway 1785-; papers of Kirkcudbright Gentlemen and

Yeomanry Cavalry 1804-36, and Independent Kirkcudbright Troop of Yeomanry Cavalry 1831-36; Burgh Court records; 150 maps from end 16C incl. estate maps, sea charts; c5000 photographs and 500 postcards from 1880s; GEN: CEN, OPRs, VR.
Finding aids: Catalogues & database.
Reprographics: R1, R5

## Kirkintilloch

## 274 East Dunbartonshire Libraries: Reference & Local Studies Library
**The William Patrick Library, 2 West High Street, Kirkintilloch G66 1AD**
*Tel: 0141 776 8090  Fax: 0141 776 0408*
Local studies collection has 3000+ books & pamphlets (covering East Dunbartonshire & adjacent areas), maps, photographs, newspapers and genealogical material.
(1) Reference & Information Librarian: Don Martin
(2) Reference Librarian: Christine Miller
Access: Mon-Thu 1000-2000; Fri-Sat 1000-1700. PCA.
*At Kirkintilloch Cross; bus routes nearby, parking; disabled access.*
Primary sources: Archives include those of the Burghs of Bishopbriggs and Kirkintilloch; Strathkelvin District Council (1975-1996); papers of Provost James Peter of Kirkintilloch (supplements official archives); Kirkintilloch Gazette 1898-1938 plus short runs of other newspapers. Records of local societies & community groups; family papers of Cleland family of Chryston; paper of: local historian John Cameron (Campsie & Kirkintilloch); Peter Mackenzie (Glasgow political historian 18&19C); the McEwan (1906-91) Scottish transport collection; archives of the Lion Foundry, Kirkintilloch (catalogues, drawings, photographs) plus other industrial firms, railways, Forth & Clyde Canal. 30000+ photographs, mostly with negatives & 25000 transparencies from 1860; newspapers Kirkintilloch Herald 1886-, Kirkintilloch Gazette 1898-1938, plus short runs of other newspapers; GEN: CEN, OPR, VR, MI, BR, IGI.
Finding aids: Catalogue of Collection of Scottish Transport History. Card Index Kirkintilloch Herald 1886-1975.
Leaflets: Publications list.
Reprographics: R1, R4, R5

## 275 East Dunbartonshire Museums: Auld Kirk Museum
### The Cross, Kirkintilloch G66 1AB
### *Tel: 0141 578 0144  Fax: 0141 578 0140*
Collection of records and photographs of local industries.
(1) Contact : Cecilia McDaid
Access: Tue-Sat 1000-1300, 1400-1700. PCA.
*In town centre, bus routes nearby, parking; disabled access.*
Primary sources: Records of iron foundry works principally Lion Foundry
(catalogues, pattern books, photographs) 1860s-1984; canal boat & puffer
builder J&J Hay late 19C-1950s; 500+ photographs also include coalmining
in addition; 300+ postcards of towns & villages in vicinity.
Leaflets: Available.
Reprographics: R1

## Kirkliston

## 276 Kirkliston Local History Archive Trust
### 19 Station Road, Kirkliston EH29 9BB
### *Tel: 0131 333 3157*
Collection includes OS maps (a few earlier), 1000+ photographs 1870s-;
graveyard inscriptions, lair ownership and gravediggers records; minute
books of societies; Kirkliston Nursing Association 1904-54,Kirkliston
Community Association 1967-80, Kirkliston Community Council 1980-.
(1) Contact : Colin Davies
(2) Contact : Ina Morris (Tel: 0131 333 3210)
Access:  BAO
Charges: Donations welcomed.
*In village centre; on bus route, parking.*
Finding aids: Catalogue & card index.
Leaflets: Publications.
Reprographics: R1, R5

## Kirkwall

## #277 Orkney Library & Archive Service
### The Orkney Library, Laing Street, Kirkwall KW15 1NW
### *Tel: 01856 873166  Fax: 01856 875260*
Local collection of c3000 books and 1200 pamphlets in Orkney Room. The
extensive archives include a photographic and sound archive.
(1) Local History: Robert Leslie
(2) Archives: Alison Fraser
Access: Library: Mon-Fri 0900-2000; Sat 0900-1700. Archive: Mon-Fri 0900-
1300, 1400-1645. Archives BAO.
*In town centre; parking nearby; disabled access to Archives only.*
Primary sources: Local authority archives from the Commissioners of Supply
1660s to the present Council; extensive Sheriff & Justice of the Peace

Courts (1561-1970); Customs & Excise records (1790-1950); Newspapers: Orcadian (1854-), Orkney Herald (1861-1961); photographic archive 25000 images 1870-; sound archives of 1000+ recordings (1980s-) of people and music; GEN: CEN, OPRs, MI, VR, ER, DIR, IND, LISTS, IGI(S).
Finding aids: Archives on disk; local history books mostly on database.
Reprographics: R1, R5 (limited).

## Lanark

### 278 New Lanark Conservation Trust Library
### Robert Owen's House, New Lanark Mills, Lanark ML11 9DB
### *Tel: 01555 661345  Fax: 01555 665738*
### Email: education@newlanarkmills.demon.co.uk
### http://www.newlanark.org

Reference library of books feature the work and life of Robert Owen 1771-1858 and the causes with which he was associated. These can only be consulted by bona fide researchers.
(1) Education Officer: Lorna Davidson
Access: Mon-Fri 1100-1700. PCA.
Charges: Admission charges.
*Near New Lanark village; parking.*
Primary sources: 1000+ photographs from 1880s; plans, incl. site plans, and maps incl. OS 1851-1911. GEN (New Lanark): CEN, B.M.D. reg 1818-55, MI IND (these records can be consulted in the Reading Room).
Finding aids: Book catalogue, lists.
Leaflets: Publications, information sheets lists.
Reprographics: Reprographic services can be arranged.

### 279 Royal Burgh of Lanark Museum Trust: Lanark Museum
### 8 West Port, Lanark ML11 9HD
### *Tel: 01555 666680*
### http://www.biggar-net.co.uk/lanarkmuseum/

Local history material includes books, plans, maps, photographs, diaries and ephemera covering the Royal Burgh of Lanark.
(1) Contact : A B H Wilson
(2) Contact : Paul Archibald
Access: Museum: Fri-Sat 1030-1630 (Apr-Sep). Archives: by appointment only - all year.
*In town centre, rail station, parking nearby, on bus route.*
Primary sources: Morrison & Marr collection of plans and maps of roads, railways and buildings (c1813-50); Lanimar brochures and ephemera; 3000 photographs 19-20C; 1st Scottish International Aviation Meeting 1910-photographs, brochure and ephemera; papers of Caledonian Mineral Oil Co (1891-1906); minutes of Lanark Gas Consumers Co (1906-14), Lanark Boat

Club (1882-1900). Lanark Female Society (1948-92) Lanark Toastmasters Club (1951-86).
Finding aids: Some archive material on database.
Leaflets: Book: A Brown & Co - Fancy Box Makers (1866-1907).
Reprographics: Photocopies and photographic reproductions by arrangement.

## 280 South Lanarkshire Libraries: Lanark Library: Reference & Local Studies Dept.
## Lindsay Institute, 16 Hope Street, Lanark ML11 7LZ
## *Tel: 01555 661144 Fax: 01555 665884*

Collection comprises 7500+ items, incl. books, documents, scrapbooks; 160+ maps & plans 1850-; 300 photographs & 600 postcards from end 19C.
(1) Library Supervisor: Paul Archibald
(2) Library Supervisor: Iain McIver
Access: Mon,Tue, Thu 0915-1930, Wed, Sat 0915-1700, Fri 0930-1930. PCA
Charges: Search charges for mail enquiries.
*In town centre; rail & bus stations, parking nearby; disabled access.*
Primary sources: Local Authority records: The Royal Burgh of Lanark 1469-1975; Biggar Town Council 1863-1970; Lanark/Clydesdale District Council 1975-1995; Lanark County Council - County Medical Officers Reports 1896-1973, miscellaneous minutes and papers, Minutes of the Upperward District Councils 1930-1975 (incomplete); Register of Sasines (abridgements) for County of Lanark 1781-1947; Newspapers: Hamilton Advertiser 1862-1899, Lanark & Carluke Advertiser 1982-, Carluke & Lanark Gazette 1906-1953, Clydesdale Journal 1856, Lanarkshire Upperward Examiner 1863; Special Collections: William Smellie Library: 400 books, 50% medical, mainly mid 18C; Robert Owen Collection: 100+ books/pamphlets etc. mainly by and about Owen; Local posters: over 200 subjects. GEN: CEN, OPRs, VR IGI(BI).
Finding aids: Library catalogues, indexes for some material.
Leaflets: Genealogical & publications list.
Reprographics: R1, R4

## Langbank

### 281 Clan MacMillan Centre
**Finlaystone, Langbank PA14 6TJ**
*Tel: 01475 540713  Fax: 01475 540285*
**Email: macmillan_centre@compuserve.com**

Clan MacMillan archives, library and extensive genealogical collection relating to MacMillans. Correspondence of modern chiefs. Papers of late clan historian, Rev Somerled MacMillan, includes some non-MacMillan matters.

(1) Curator & Clan Genealogist: Graeme Mackenzie

(*) Chief Ranger at Finlaystone (to see Archive Room): Alastair Stewart (Tel: 01475 540505)

Access: Public exhibition: Mon-Sun 1100-1700 (summer). Sat-Sun 1100-1700 (winter). Archive Room; BAO.

Charges: Admission charge.

*On the A8 nearby Langbank Village; parking, no public transport nearby.*

Reprographics: R1

## Largs

### 282 Largs & District Historical Society
**c/o Largs Museum, Kirkgate House, Manse Court, Largs KA30 8AW**
*Tel: 01475 687081*

A reference library of c1000 books covering mainly the history of both the Largs area & N.Ayrshire plus 1000+ photographs 1890- & the Largs & Millport Weekly News 1877-1996.

(1) Curator: Kay McCreadie

(2) President: J D Easton

Access: Mon-Sat & most Sun 1400-1700 (end May-early Sep). Other times BAO.

*Off Main St; rail station, bus routes, parking nearby; disabled access.*

Leaflets: Publications list.

## Leadhills

### 283 Leadhills Miners Library & Reading Institute: Allan Ramsay Library
**Leadhills Miners Reading Institute, Main Street, Leadhills ML12 6XP**
*Tel: 01659 74216 Fax: 01659 74459*
Over 3000 books incl. biography, geography, history and theology. Special collection covering mining records, mining tools and minutes from mid 18C.
(1) Honorary Secretary: S M Egginton
Access: Wed, Sat, Sun 1400-1600 (May-Sep) BAO
Charges: Donations welcome.
*In village centre; parking nearby.*
Primary sources: Book collection, catalogued, incl. much of the original stock (copies of the catalogue are in the NLS, Edinburgh and the Mitchell Library, Glasgow); MS: Library Society minutes 1821- (MS); Curling Club minutes 1784-1864 (MS); Water Committee records 1940-61 (4 books) (MS); Friendly Society a/c Book 1908-15 (MS); two hand written catalogues (no date); Gibson Letters 1834-45 and journals and Bargain Books of the Scots Mines Company 1740-1854 (on microfilm in NAS (SRO)); 4 boxes of micellaneous papers (part hand listed); 2 folders of press cuttings etc; 4 albums of photographs c1880s- (unlisted).

## Lerwick

### #284 Shetland Archives
**44 King Harald Street, Lerwick ZE1 0EQ**
*Tel: 01595 696247*
**Email: shetland.archives@zetnet.co.uk**
Archives contain local authority, court, customs & estate records; printed local author & history collections; oral history collection.
(1) Contact : Brian Smith
(2) Contact : Angus Johnson
Access: Mon-Thu 0900-1300, 1400-1700; Fri 0900-1300, 1400-1600. BAO
*In town centre; parking; disabled access.*
Primary sources: Comprehensive local authority records 18C-1980; court testaments, customs records some 16C-; registers of sasines to 1781, abridgements thereafter; collection of works by Shetland authors. GEN: CEN, OPRs, IGI.
Finding aids: Computerised catalogue.
Reprographics: R1

### 285 Shetland Family History Society
**6 Hillhead, Lerwick ZE1 0EJ**

Comprehensive genealogical material: GEN; CEN; OPR's, MI, ER Lists (Estate, whaling, navy, court), IGI(S) plus some newspapers; library of genealogical books & exchange journals.
(1) General Secretary: Elizabeth Angus (Tel: 01595 692276)
Access: Mon-Sat 1400-1600, Mon, Thu 1900-2100. Other times BAO.
Charges: Donations plus postal search charges.
*In town centre near Library; parking difficult; disabled access.*
Finding aids: Genealogical lists & indexes.
Leaflets: Publications list.
Reprographics: Photocopies A4.

### 286 Shetland Library
**Library Headquarters, Lower Hillhead, Lerwick ZE1 0EL**
*Tel: 01595 693868  Fax: 01595 694430*
Email: info@shetland-library.gov.uk
http://www.shetland-library.gov.uk

Collection of Shetlandiana incl. Gilbert Goudie and E S Reid Tait Collections of monographs (c300), books, pamphlets, postcards, thesis collection, and newspapers: Shetland News 1885-1962 & Shetland Times 1872-.
(1) Chief Librarian: J G Hunter ALA
(2) Contact : D Garden MA ALA
Access: Mon, Wed, Fri 1000-1900; Tue, Thu, Sat 1000-1700. PCA.
*In town centre near Town Hall; parking (disabled spaces available); disabled access.*
Finding aids: Database catalogue of most items but limited catalogue on WWW; small percentage of newspapers indexed.
Reprographics: R1

### 287 Shetland Museum
**Lower Hillhead, Lerwick ZE1 0EL**
*Tel: 01595 695057  Fax: 01595 696729*
Email: shetland.museum@zetnet.co.uk
http://www.zetnet.co/sigs.shetland-museum

Large Shetland photographic collection 80000 images from 1860.
(1) Curator: Tommy Watt
Access: Mon, Wed, Fri 1000-1900; Tue, Thu, Sat 1000-1700.
*In town centre near Town Hall; on-street parking; disabled access possible.*
Finding aids: Computerised catalogue.
Reprographics: R1, R5

## Linlithgow

### 288 The Linlithgow Story Museum
### Annet House, 143 High Street, Linlithgow EH49
*Tel: 01506 670677*

Small collection of books and items covering Linlithgow and district.
(1) Contact : Alan Young (Tel: 01506 843859)
(2) Contact : Catherine Laduss (Tel: 01506 670697)
Access: Mon, Wed-Sat 1000-1700; Sun 1300-1600 (Easter-Oct). Other times BAO.
*300 yd W of Linlithgow Cross; rail station, parking nearby, on bus routes.*
Primary sources: Archive material includes some W Lothian County Council minutes; c100 early 20C photographs; 19C maps; legal documents incl. land transactions, poor law rates etc late 17-early 20C; society records include papers and minutes of Linlithgow Rowing Association early 20C.

### 289 West Lothian History & Amenity Society Library
### c/o Linlithgow Library, The Vennel, Linlithgow EH49 7EX
*Tel: 01506 775490*

Books about West Lothian topography, geology and industrial history, plus small collection of postcards, pamphlets etc.
(1) Contact : Sybil Cavanagh (Tel: 01506 776331)
Access: Mon, Fri 0930-1730; Tue, Thu 0930-2000; Wed 1000-1730; Sat 0900-1300. BAO
*In town centre; bus routes, parking nearby; disabled access.*
Finding aids: Library catalogue

## Lismore

### 290 Comann Eachdraidh Lios Mor - Lismore Heritage Society
### Achnacroish, Lismore PA34 5UG
*Tel: 01631 760346  Fax: 01631 760346*

Collection includes 300 photographs 1890s-; information on WWII convoy mustering and defence installations; 250 placename register from oral tradition; GEN: CEN, OPRs plus Bap/Mar 1836-56.
(1) Contact : Donald M Black (Tel: 01631 760257)
(2) Contact : Margaret MacDonald (Tel: 01631 760285)
(*) Contact : Catherine Carmichael (Tel: 01631 760235)
Access: Mon-Sat 1000-1700 (May-Sep). Other times BAO. PCA.
Charges: Admission charges.
*Near Oban Ferry terminal.*
Leaflets: Available.

Reprographics: Photocopies A4.

## Loanhead

## #291 Midlothian Council Libraries: Local Studies Centre Libraries Headquarters, 2 Clerk Street, Loanhead EH20 9DR
*Tel: 0131 271 3980  Fax: 0131 440 4635*
Email: mc_libhq_blossoming@compuserve.com
http://www.earl.org.uk/earl/members/midlothian

Collection of books includes those by & about local people and 19C directories plus maps, plans, photographs, prints, newspapers, pamphlets, printed records and ephemera.
(1) Local Studies Officer: Marion M T Richardson
(2) Records Officer: Ruth Calvert
Access: Mon 0900-1700, 1800-2000; Tue-Thu 0900-1700; Fri 0900-1545.
*In town centre; on bus route, parking nearby; disabled access.*
Primary sources: Local authority archives include minute books etc of former Burghs of: Bonnyrigg and Lasswade, Dalkeith, Loanhead and Penicuik; pre 1975 District Councils of Galawater, Lasswade, Newbattle and Penicuik; Midlothian District Council 1975-1996; School Board and Education Committee records 1870-1919; School Log Books 1870s-mid 20C; Parochial Board and Parish Council Minutes plus miscellaneous welfare and public health records; private archives include: Lucas family of Dalkeith; Wauchope of Edmonstone late 18/19C; Black of Penicuik; national printed records: Privy Council, Privy Seal, Great Seal etc; newspapers: Dalkeith Advertiser 1869-, South Midlothian Advertiser 1932-52 and 1960-73, Midlothian Journal 1884-1932; c100 estate plans include Clerk of Penicuik, Melville estates; 500+ maps 18C - incl. OS; 4000+ photographs, incl. glass negatives and prints; GEN: CEN, OPRs, VR, IGI(S).
Finding aids: Books card index.
Leaflets: Leaflet, publications list.
Reprographics: R1, R4

## Lochgilphead

## 292 Argyll & Bute Archives Kilmory, Manse Brae, Lochgilphead PA31 8RT
*Tel: 01546 604120  Fax: 01546 606897*

Local Authority records and deposited records from businesses and families. Small reference library.
(1) Archivist: Murdo MacDonald
(2) Archives Assistant: Louise Logue
Access: Tue-Fri 1000-1300, 1400-1630. BAO
*Within Council Offices; bus routes nearby, parking; disabled access.*

Primary sources: Commissioners of Supply records Argyll 1744- & Bute 1678-; County Council records Argyll & Bute 1890-1975; Argyll & Bute District Council records 1975-1996; Burgh records of Campbeltown, Cove & Kilcreggan, Dunoon, Helensburgh, Inveraray, Lochgilphead, Oban, Rothesay, Tobermory varying dates from end 17/19C-1975; Newspapers: The Argyllshire Herald 1867-1917; The Campbeltown Courier 1873-1917, 1925-1988; The Argyllshire Leader 1929-34. Family & estate papers of Campbell of Kilberry, MacTavish of Dunardry, Malcolm of Poltalloch, Duncan Colville (Kintyre) and John Blain (Bute), Campbell of Craignish (charters 16C–, Sproat & Cameron letters (Mull 19C). OS maps. Business records: Thomas Corson & Co., Oban (livestock auctioneers); Campbeltown Coal Co; Sproat & Cameron, Tobermory (Solicitors) & Campbeltown Whisky Distilleries. Records of Episcopal Diocese of Argyll & the Isles mid 19-20C. Some records of clubs and societies (sport, recreation, music, gaelic). GEN: family history notes, VR (Argyll from 1858, Bute from 1927). ER (Argyll from 1889) MI.
Finding aids: Catalogues & indexes.
Reprographics: R1

## 293 Lochgilphead Registrar's Office
### Dalriada House, Lochnell Street, Lochgilphead PA31 8ST
*Tel: 01546 604511  Fax: 01546 604530*
GEN: CEN, OPRs (Argyll & Bute) some MI. There is a computer link to the General Register Office, Edinburgh.
(1) Registration Staff Duty Officer
Access: Mon-Fri 1000-1200, 1400-1600. BAO
Charges: Search and computer link charges.
*Bus route, parking nearby.*


## Lossiemouth

## 294 Lossiemouth Fisheries & Community Museum
### 2 Pitgaveny Quay, Lossiemouth IV31 6TW
*Tel: 01343 813772*
A small museum with 100+ photographs 1890s- of fishing vessels & fisher people; paintings, Stotfield disaster records late 19C.
(1) Chairman: John W C Thomson (Tel: 01343 813219)
(2) Secretary: John S Scott (Tel: 01343 543221)
Access: Mon-Fri 1000-1700, Sat 1000-1400, (May-Sep). BAO
Charges: Admission charges.
*In East Basin Harbour area. Limited parking.*
Leaflets: Available.

## Macduff

### 295 Aberdeenshire Library & Information Service: Macduff Library
### 17 High Street, Macduff AB44 1LR
*Tel: 01261 833289*

Small collection of books and other material of relevance to Macduff and district, incl. Banffshire Journal 1845-; Banffshire Reporter 1869-1920; GEN: CEN, OPRs, IGI(S).
(1) Senior Library Assistant: Marjory Nicholson
(2) Network Librarian: Isobel Turner (Tel: 01261 812591/812723)
Access: Tue 1500-2000; Wed 1500-1700; Thu 1000-1200, 1800-2000; Fri 1500-2000; Sat 1000-1600. BAO
*In town centre; bus route nearby, parking; disabled access.*
Finding aids: Computerised catalogue.
Reprographics: Photocopies A4.

## Mallaig

### 296 Mallaig Heritage Centre
### Station Road, Mallaig PH41 4PY
*Tel: 01687 462085  Fax: 01687 462085*
### Email: MallaigHeritage@compuserve.com
### http://visitweb.com/mallaig-heritage-centre

Local history collection and genealogical material of the area.
(1) Contact : Malcolm Poole
Access: Sat 1300-1600 (Nov-Mar). Mon-Sat 1100-1600 (Apr-Oct). PCA.
Charges: Admission charges.
*Beside Mallaig rail station; parking nearby; disabled access.*
Primary sources: c1500 photographs covering people, places, railway and steamer interest from 1895. Maps of area from 1834, plans of Mallaig from 1901, Transport information from 1965. 'Westward' newspaper 1995-. GEN: CEN; MAR/BR 19C; MI.
Leaflets: Publications: Knoydart 1750-1894: North Morar.
Reprographics: R1

## Markinch

### 297 Fife Council: Law & Administration Archive Records Centre
**Carleton House, Balgownie Road, Markinch KY7 6AQ**
*Tel: 01592 413256 Fax: 01592 414142*

An extensive collection of local authority records in Fife with some trade and trust papers.

(1) Contact : Lisa Wood
(2) Contact : Alison Baillie (Tel: 01592 416601)
Access: Mon-Fri 0900-1700. BAO
*In town centre; rail station, bus routes nearby, parking adjacent; disabled access.*
Primary sources: Minutes and other records of Commissioners of Supply 1709-20C; Fife County Council to 1975 incl. Highway and Education Committees; Fife Burgh and Town Councils mainly 19/20C but some 17/18C; Fife Regional and District Councils (NE Fife, Kirkcaldy, Dunfermline) 1975-1996; Fife Council 1996-; Parochial Boards/Parish Council 1845-1930; School Board minutes 1873-1919; extensive material covering Glenrothes Development Corporation 1948-96 includes plans, maps, promotional literature, photographs (c5000), minutes etc.
Finding aids: Indexes for different collections.
Reprographics: Photocopies A4.

## Methil

### 298 Fife Family History Society: Family History Room
**Methil Library, Wellesley Road, Methil KY8 3QR**
*Tel: 01333 592470 Fax: 01333 592415*

Genealogical material includes: CEN, OPR, MI (pre1955 Fife), BR, IGI (1988S). Lists - Fife: newspaper deaths 1822-54 and abroad 1855-1900; Shopkeepers/Trades 1820-70; Apprentices/Freemen 1524-1899.
(1) Contact : A J Campbell (Tel: 01592 712805)
Access: Mon-Thu 1000-1900; Fri-Sat 1000-1700.
*In town centre; on bus routes, parking; disabled access.*
Finding aids: Indexes: Fife Baptism Registers; Wills 1824-92; Sheriff Court/Burgh Court/Commissary Court records.
Leaflets: List available.
Reprographics: R1, R2

**Men at the coalface in the Westwood Pit, West Calder 1929
(NAS ref: GD.367/1/No5)**

## Moffat

### 299 Moffat Museum
### The Neuk, Church Gate, Moffat DG10 9EG
### *Tel: 01683 220868*

A history of Moffat covering geology, spa town, railway, religion, farming, local crafts, Moffat family, local pastimes, education. Baptisms, printed marriages & deaths: Moffat 1709-1854; Journals of convict ships (1833-8); Cash book of Burnie, the Draper, Moffat, 1825; Information on local families.
(1) Contact : John B Murray (Tel: 01683 220980)
(2) Contact : Jane I Boyd (Tel: 01683 221330)
Access: Mon-Tue, Thu-Sat 1030-1300, 1430-1700; Sun 1430-1700 (Easter weekend, Whitsun-Sep). PCA.
Charges: Admission charges
*In town centre; parking nearby*
Leaflets: Publications list.

## Monifeith

### 300 Angus Council: Monifeith Library
### 48/50 High Street, Monifeith DD5 4AE
### *Tel: 01382 533819*

Comprehensive collection of printed material about Monifeith plus OS maps. GEN: IGI.
(1) Contact : Dorothy Milne
Access: Mon-Fri 0930-1930, Tue 0900-1700, Wed 1000-1930 Thu, Sat 0930-1300.
*Central location; bus routes, parking nearby; disabled access.*
Reprographics: R1

## Montrose

### #301 Angus Council Archives
### Montrose Public Library, 214 High Street, Montrose DD10 8PH
### *Tel: 01674 671415  Fax: 01674 671810*
### Email: anguscularch@sol.uk
### http://www.angus.gov.uk/history

The archives contain the burgh and trade records of Arbroath, Brechin, Forfar and Montrose plus the burgh records of Carnoustie and Kirriemuir, plus the minute books, plans, legal documents etc covering the 'Angus heritage'. The miscellaneous collection covers a wide range of subjects and people, and includes diaries, newspaper clippings, society records, sermons.
(1) Contact : Fiona Scharlau

Access: Mon-Fri 0930-1700. BAO
Charges: Genealogical in-depth research charges.
*In town centre; street parking nearby; disabled access.*
Primary sources: Burgh records: minute books; protocol books, service of
heirs, decreets etc. court books; chartularies, charities. Trade records:
Arbroath: glovers 1653-1938, hammermen 1844-1938, shoemakers 1741-
1937; Brechin: Bakers 1622-1880, tailors 1660-1675, shoemakers 1660-
1849, weavers 1685-1878; Forfar: tailors 1648-1898, shoemakers 1649-
1898, weavers 1685-1878; Montrose: apprentice hammermen 1725-1762.
Miscellaneous collection includes diaries of Margaret Forrest Mill 1910-
1914; Tarry Mills (Arbroath) Cash Book 1803-1823; Brechin Infant School
1835-1858; Weddermain of Pearsie Farm accounts 1833-1856. GEN: CEN,
OPR, BR/MAR/D. IGI(S) 1988; Collection of typescript and MS tabulations of
family genealogies, incl. Burns and Coull.
Finding aids: Full list and subject indexes, transcripts. Family tree index on
database.
Reprographics: R5, photocopies A4.

## 302 Angus Council: Montrose Library
## 214 High Street, Montrose DD10 8PH
### *Tel: 01674 673256*

Montrose Year books; local photographs plus maps and newspaper
collections & genealogical records.
(1) Librarian: J Doherty
Access: Mon, Wed 0930-2000; Tue, Thu 0930-1800; Fri-Sat 0930-1700.
*In town centre; parking nearby; disabled access.*
Primary sources: A small collection of local photographs; newspapers:
Garden City News (Montrose) 9/5/1935-5/3/1936, Montrose, Arbroath &
Brechin Review 17/4/1818-18/10/1839, 1844-47, 1849-75, 1884-1988,
Montrose Chronicle 1895-98, Penny Press (Montrose) 1865-67, Scottish
Nation (Montrose) 8/5/1923-14/12/1923, Montrose Standard 1844-1970;
Montrose Year books 1888-1979; OS maps, GEN: CEN, OPR, VR, some
ER, IGI(S)
Reprographics: R1, R2, R5

## 303 Angus Council: Montrose Museum and Art Gallery
## Panmure Place, Montrose DD10 8HE
### *Tel: 01674 673232*

Collection of maps, prints, drawings, photographs, portraits and a range of
Montrose records and local history files.
Access: Mon-Sat 1000-1700. PCA.
*In town centre; parking nearby; disabled access.*
Primary sources: Angus Craftsmen, arranged by town; Montrose building
and property index, based on 1926 Valuation Roll; Montrose Burgh records,
alphabetical index by subject and name; Montrose Chamber Chest, based
on J G Low's Inventory; Montrose industry and commerce index, based on
the Montrose Yearbooks; Montrose Kirkyards; Montrose obituaries 1884-
1930, based on the Montrose Yearbooks; Montrose Old Kirkyard gravestone

inscriptions; Montrose shipping index; Wood's map of Montrose 1822; Burgh Court claims 1707-1820, 1824-1856; Montrose Harbour records 1937-1967.
Reprographics: R1, R2, R5

## 304 Montrose Air Station Museum (Trust)
### Waldron Road, Montrose DD10 9BD
### Email: 106212.152@compuserve.com
### http://ourworld.compuserve.com/homepages/airspeednews

Museum archives include: station history, photographs, reminiscences, memorabilia and manuals.
(1) Contact : Peter Davies (Tel: 01674 674210)
(2) Contact : Graham McIntosh (Tel: 01674 673107)
Access: Sun 1200-1700. PCA.
Charges: Admission charges.
*Off A92 N of town centre; bus routes nearby; parking.*
Finding aids: In house list & WWW.
Leaflets: Available.
Reprographics: R5

## Motherwell

## 305 North Lanarkshire Council: Motherwell Heritage Centre
### High Road, Motherwell ML1 3HU
### *Tel: 01698 25100  Fax: 01698 253433*

Collection comprises books (1000), maps, photographs (3000+), videos, oral history tapes and ephemeral information covering the Motherwell area.
(1) Local History Librarian: Margaret McGarry
Access: Mon-Wed, Fri-Sat 1000-1700; Thu 1000-1900; Sun 1200-1700. PCA.
Charges: Genealogical search charges.
*In town centre; rail & bus routes nearby, parking; disabled access.*
Primary sources: Minute books of Burgh of Motherwell and Wishaw, and local co-operative and other societies; Lord Hamilton of Dalzell collection of books (3000) plus family documents 17-19C; Hurst Nelson & Co collection of photographs of railway rolling stock, trams etc. Newspapers: Motherwell Times 1883- ; The Wishaw Press 1873- ; Bellshill Speaker 1898-; Hamilton Advertiser 1862-1899; GEN: CEN, OPRs, some VR/ER, IGI(UK)
Finding aids: Newspaper, photograph & slide indexes. Lists of videos & oral history tapes.
Leaflets: Available.
Reprographics: R1, R2, R5

## Nairn

### 306 Nairn Literary Institute Library
### Viewfield House, Nairn IV12 4EE
### *Tel: 01667 456791*

Extensive collection of historical books with most published in 19/early 20C incl. Spalding Club publications, covering the Church in Scotland, social history, travel in Scotland, biography and genealogy, northern and north central Scotland.

(1) Curator: A Fergusson
(2) Honorary Libraran: A McGowan
Access: Mon-Sat 1030-1630. PCA. BAO
*Off King St in town centre; rail station, bus station nearby; parking.*
Finding aids: Card indexes.
Leaflets: Publications; Teens and Twenties (reminiscences of Nairn).

## Newcastleton

### 307 Liddesdale Heritage Centre
### Liddesdale Heritage Association, Townfoot Kirk, Newcastleton TD9 0QT

Miscellaneous collection of local artefacts, photographs and printed historical data. GEN: CEN, OPRs, MI.

(1) Contact : Frank Rutherford (Tel: 013873 75283)
Access: Wed-Mon 1330-1630 (Easter-end Sep). PCA.
Charges: Admission & search charges.
*In former Congregational Church; limited bus service, parking nearby.*
Leaflets: Available.

## Newton Stewart

### 308 Newton Stewart Museum
### York Road, Newton Stewart DG8 6HH

Museum holds a collection of photographs (1000+ 1890s-) & postcards (100 1890-1950); 19C OS & some earlier maps; business records include: drapery shop accounts etc., chemist's prescription books & co-operative society's minutes & accounts book, all early 20C.

(1) Contact : James McLay (Tel: 01671 402472)
Access: Mon-Sat 1400-1700 (Easter-Oct); Sun 1400-1700 (Jul-Sep); Mon-Fri 1000-1230 (Jul-Aug). Other times BAO. PCA.
Charges: Admission charges.
*In town centre; bus route nearby, parking; disabled access.*

## Newtongrange

### 309 Scottish Mining Museum
**Lady Victoria Colliery, Newtongrange EH22 4QN**
*Tel: 0131 663 7519  Fax: 0131 654 1618*
The Museum library holds 15000+ books, periodicals, trade publications and
catalogues, maps and associated archive material covering the
technological, social and economic history of coal, coal minng and the use of
coal in Scotland; collections of photographs, slides and films; and a limited
ephemera collection.
(1) Curator: Kirsty Lingstadt
(2) Contact : George Archibald
Access: Library: Mon-Fri 1000-1600. BAO
*In Visitor Centre of Museum, on A7 10 ml S of Edinburgh; on bus routes,
parking; disabled access difficult (contact in advance).*
Primary sources: National Coal Board/British Coal corporation publications
incl. Coal Magazine/Coal News, annual reports and accounts, technical
specifications, 1947-; National Union of Mineworkers (Scottish Area)
McDonald Memorial Collection incl. MFGB/NUM annual reports & Minutes
1900-, Scottish executive committee minutes 1945-, closure consultation
minutes 1950-70; Royal Commissions on the coal industry 1842-1940;
annual reports of the Mines Inspectors (national and divisional) 1900-,
Inspectors' incident reports 1920-; reports and publications of the Safety in
Mines Research Board 1923-49; reports of the Fuel Research Board 1917-
31; Guide to the coalfields 1948-; Colliery Guardian 1949-; Journal of the
Institute of Mining Engineers (Federated) 1890-; Colliery Engineering 1924-
68; National Association of Colliery Managers Transactions 1909-42;
records of the Lothian Coal Company 1890-1947.
Finding aids: Library guide
Leaflets: Educational booklets list.
Reprographics: R1, R5

## Oban

### 310 Easdale Island Folk Museum
**Easdale Island, Oban PA34 4TB**
*Tel: 01852 300370  Fax: 01852 300370*
Museum contain documents covering the slate industry, societies together
with a photographic collection.
(1) Curator: Jean Adams
(2) Assistant Curator: Mary Withall (Tel: 01852 300449  Fax: 01852 300473)
Access: Mon-Sun 1030-1730 (Apr-Oct).
Charges: Admission charge
*Approx. 10 ml S of Oban off Seil Island; foot passengers via ferry operating
on demand from Seil Island, parking on pier.*
Primary sources: Photographic collection (600 1890s) feature the slate
quarries, volunteers, domestic scenes and ferry boats. Archives include

records of Argyll & Bute Volunteers (1860-1911); records of Friendly Societies; minutes and membership of Easdale Technical Institute; Census material 1841-; public health records of district (1895-1912); records of industrial buildings now ruined; Easdale quarries map.
Finding aids: Volunteers material listed.
Leaflets: Publications list.
Reprographics: R5, cameras can be used in museum.

## 311 Lorn Archaeological & Historical Society
### c/o John Campbell-Kease (Secy), 8 Ferryfield Road, Connel, Oban PA37 1SR
*Tel: 01631 710517*
Society publishes "Historic Argyll" annually featuring historic & archaeological information in the Lorn area of Argyll.
Leaflets: Publications by members - list available.


## Oldmeldrum

## 312 Aberdeenshire Library & Information Service: Local Studies Department
### Meldrum Meg Way, Meadows Industrial Estate, Oldmeldrum AB51 0GN
*Tel: 01651 872707  Fax: 01651 872142*
Collection of 15000 books covering counties of Banff, Moray and Kincardine, plus maps, photographs, postcards, newspapers and genealogical material.
(1) Local Studies Librarian: David Catto (Tel: 01651 871220)
(2) Senior Library Assistant: Dorothy Dewar (Tel: 01651 871219)
Access: Mon-Fri 0900-1700. BAO
*On outskirts of village on B9170 Inverurie road; bus route nearby, parking; disabled access.*
Primary sources: 1000+ photographs 1860s-; 3000 postcards 1890s-; estate plans and maps from 19C with OS; 150 videos; newspapers include: Mearns Leader 1913-, Stonehaven Journal and Kincardineshire Advertiser 1848-1917 (gaps), Aberdeen Journal/Weekly Journal 1748-1922, Banffshire Journal 1876-; Strichen Estate Papers 18-20C. George MacDonald (1824-1905 novelist) collection; GEN: CEN, OPRs, IND, IGI(S).
Finding aids: Computerised catalogue.
Leaflets: Leaflets and facsimile early 19C maps.
Reprographics: R1 (b&w, col), R4

## Paisley

### 313 Paisley University: Local/Special Collection
**High Street, Paisley PA1 2BE**
*Tel: 0141 848 3759  Fax: 0141 887 0812*

Local collection of c1000 titles relating to the history of Paisley, Renfrewshire and the West of Scotland.

(1) The Librarian (Tel: 0141 848 3750)

(2) Deputy Librarian (Technical Services) (Tel: 0141 848 3763)

Access: Mon-Thu 0900-2100; Fri-Sat 0900-1700 (term-time). Mon-Fri 0900-1700 (vacation). PCA.

*Library is in Storie St in town centre; rail station, bus routes nearby, parking & disabled access by prior arrangement.*

Primary sources: Collection of Railway maps; notebooks of L F Richardson FRS, Quaker, Physicist, pacifist and climatologist; political papers of Norman Buchan MP; papers and materials relating to the history of Paisley Technical School, Paisley College and the University of Paisley; newspapers: Paisley and Renfrewshire Standard (1869-71), Paisley Advertiser (1824-27, 1842-44), Renfrewshire Advertiser (1848-50).

Finding aids: Calendar of railway documents & of L F Richardson papers.

Reprographics: R1

### 314 Renfrewshire Council Library Service: Local Studies Library
**Central Library, High Street, Paisley PA1 2BB**
*Tel: 0141 887 2360  Fax: 0141 887 6468*
**Email: renlib4@cqm.co.uk**

A large collection of books, manuscripts, cuttings, maps, local newspapers, local authority records, postcards, films and video and ephemera, genealogical material and the Paisley Burns Club Collection.

(1) Contact : Tricia Burke

(2) Contact : David Weir

Access: Mon-Fri 0900-2000; Sat 0900-1700. PCA.

*Opposite University of Paisley; rail station, bus routes, parking nearby; disabled access by prior arrangement.*

Primary sources: Over 30 newspapers 1824-, with longest runs of Paisley and Renfrewshire Gazette and predecessors 1883-, Paisley Daily Express 1874-; Paisley Poor Law records 1839-1948 (some still closed); Burgess Rolls 1682-1822; Poll Tax rolls 1695; Cairn of Lochwinnoch 45 vol 1827-45 papers; Incorporation of Old Weavers of Paisley; pamphlets and ephemera 1739-1893; 500+ postcards; extensive coverage of Paisley shawl and other industries; local authorities Paisley and Renfrewshire mostly from 19C; GEN: CEN, OPR, MIpre1855, BR, some ER, DIR (1810-1938), IGI.

Finding aids: Catalogues, card & printed indexes & guides (IGI on CDRom).

Leaflets: Family historians leaflet and newspapers' list.

Reprographics: R1, R4

## 315 Renfrewshire Council Museum Service: Paisley Museum
### High Street, Paisley PA1 2BA
### *Tel: 0141 889 3151  Fax: 0141 889 9240*

Photographic, archival and family history collections relating to Paisley and Renfrewshire. NB. Archive and Family History collections are joint responsibility of the Museum and Paisley Central Library. See the latter's entry for 'GEN' sources.

(1) Keeper - Archives & Historical Photographs: David A Roberts
Access: Tue-Sat 1000-1700. Curatorial staff available Mon-Fri only. PCA.
*Opposite University of Paisley; rail station, bus routes, parking nearby; disabled access by prior arrangement.*

Primary sources: Large photographic archive (c20000 images) c1850-1980, covering Paisley and Renfrewshire incl. topography, thread and shipbuilding industries in a variety of formats. Archive record include J & P Coats (thread industry), Dean of Guild Court architectural plans and other local government records.

Finding aids: Indexes for photographic collection; lists for J & P Coats & local government records; shipbuilding lists 1879-98.
Reprographics: R1, R5

## Peebles

## 316 Tweeddale Museum
### Chambers Institute, High Street, Peebles EH45 8AP
### *Tel: 01721 724820  Fax: 01721 724424*

Newspaper cuttings; legal & business documents relating to Peebles; 200+ photographs, mostly early 20C; portraits/information on local people, incl. John Buchan (1875-1900) & William Chambers (1800-83).

(1) Contact : Rosemary Hannay
(2) Contact : Chris Sawers
Access: Mon-Fri 1000-1200, 1400-1700; Sat 1000-1300, 1400-1600 (Easter-Oct). Mon-Fri 1000-1200, 1400-1700 (Nov-Easter). BAO
Charges: Research charges.
*In town centre; on bus routes, parking nearby; disabled access difficult.*
Reprographics: R1, R5

## 317 Black Watch Regimental Museum
### Balhousie Castle, Hay Street, Perth PH1 5HR
*Tel: 01738 621281 x8530  Fax: 01738 643245*

Collection contains material relating to the history of The Black Watch 1725-, incl. 42nd, 73rd and allied Commonwealth Regiments, with a Photographic Archive 1860s-.

(1) Curator
(2) Archivist

Access: Museum: Mon-Sat 1000-1630 (May-Sep); Mon-Fri 1000-1530 (Oct-Apr). Archive: By appointment only.
Charges: Search charges by arrangement.
*N of city centre; rail station approx. 1 ml; bus routes, parking nearby.*
Reprographics: R5, photocopies A4.

## #318 Perth & Kinross Council Archive
### A K Bell Library, 2-8 York Place, Perth PH2 8EP
*Tel: 01738 477022  Fax: 01738 477010*
### Email: library@pkc.gov.uk

Archives hold local authority and deposited private records for the Perth & Kinross areas 12C-.

(1) Contact : Steve Connelly (Tel: 01738 477012)
(2) Contact : Jo Peattie (Tel: 01738 477022)

Access: Mon-Wed, Fri 0930-1700; Thu 0930-2000. BAO for Thu evenings.
Charges: Search charges.
*In city centre; rail & bus stations nearby, parking nearby; disabled access.*
Primary sources: Records of the City & Royal Burgh of Perth 1210-1975; Perth & Kinross counties 1650-1975, and small Burghs c1708-1975 (Aberfeldy, Abernethy, Alyth, Auchterarder, Rattray, Blairgowrie, Coupar Angus, Crieff, Kinross & Pitlochry) and Perth & Kinross District Council 1975-1996; Justice of the Peace records for Perth & Kinross mostly 18-19C, Perth County Constabulary and Perth Burgh Police records 19-20C; records of Perth Trades Council 1897-1969, 1980-94, various local trade union branches (AEU, ASW, ASLEF, NUR etc), various Conservative & Unionist Associations c1892-1975 (Perth, Bridge of Earn, Crieff etc), Drummond of Comrie papers c1446-1786, Ferguson of Baledmund 1328-1900, Barons Kinaird of Inchture 1172-1930, Drummond-Hay of Seggieden 1704-1972, Richardson of Pitfour 1695-1890, Stewart-Meiklejohn of Edradynate 1460-1893. Extensive business records include Alexander & Brown, seed merchant 1897-1981, Burt Marshall, bleachers 1889-1939, David Gorrie & Son engineers 1900-45, McEwan's of Perth, department store 1868-1993. Miscellaneous records include some church records, literary papers, local societies records, Harry Hynd MP's scrapbooks.
Finding aids: Summary of holdings lists.
Reprographics: R1

## 319  Perth & Kinross Libraries: Local Studies Section
### A K Bell Library, 2-8 York Place, Perth PH2 8EP
*Tel: 01738 477062  Fax: 01738 477010*
### Email: library@pkc.gov.uk
### http://www.pkc.uk/library.htm

Collection has 50000+ items: 9000 books, 3000 pamphlets, directories, newspapers, photographs, postcards, posters, maps etc. Special collections include the Soutar Collection (William Soutar 1898-1943, Poet); Atholl Collection (early Scottish fiddle music) and Mackintosh Collection (Donald Mackintosh 1743-1808, episcopal priest).

(1) Contact : Jeremy Duncan

(2) Contact : Lorna Mitchell

Access: Mon, Wed 0930-1700; Tue, Thu-Fri 0930-2000; Sat 0930-1600. PCA.

Charges: Postal enquiries/research and use of microfilm reader by non council area residents chargeable.

*W side of town centre; rail & bus stations nearby, parking; disabled access.*

Primary sources: Extensive map collection includes: James Stobie's - Perth & Clackmannan 1783, 50 early maps Perthshire & Perth 1715-1900, general and specialist OS maps 1860s-, road, railway and estate maps; 4500 photographs Perth & Kinross mostly 1960s-; plus aerial photographs of main towns and villages and 1990s colour views of central Perth; 6600 postcards mostly early 20C; newspapers: Perthshire Courier 1809-1929, Perthshire Advertiser 1833-, Perthshire Constitutional 1835-1951, Blairgowrie Advertiser 1861-, Strathearn Herald 1856-, Kinross-shire Advertiser 1847-1970 (gaps), (Dundee) Courier & Advertiser 1934-42, 1958-72, 1978-; GEN: CEN, OPRs, MI, VR, ER, DIR (1837-1939), Registers non conformist congregations, IGI(UK).

Finding aids: Computerised catalogue; pamphlets & photographs via card catalogue; limited index for two newspapers.

Leaflets: Standard grade and family history leaflets.

Reprographics: R1, R4, R5

## 320  Perth Museum & Art Gallery
### George Street, Perth PH1 5LB
*Tel: 01738 632488  Fax: 01738 443505*
### Email: museum@pkc.co.uk

Social history, archives, photographs, numismatics, archaeology, fine and applied art and natural sciences. In the main these cover the history of Perth and Kinross District.

(1) Principal Officer Human History: Susan Payne

Access: Mon-Sat 1000-1700. PCA.

*Near Perth bridge; rail & bus station nearby, parking adjacent; disabled access.*

Primary sources: c200000 negatives with views of Perth and Perthshire c1860-; archives relating to the history of Perth Museum, the Perthshire Society for Natural Science and the Literary and Antiquarian Society of Perth; some local trades material (eg Wrights Incorporation c1680-1921)

(mostly MS); small collection of maps and plans; topographical views of the district; portraits of local people and works by local artists etc.
Finding aids: In-house card & computerised indexes. Archives on NRA(S) lists; negatives 1860-1930 on NMRS lists.
Leaflets: Catalogue of the permanent collection of paintings and drawings.
Reprographics: R1, R5

## 321 Scottish Society of the History of Medicine
### Dr J D Macgregor (Hon Secretary), 74 Glasgow Road, Perth PH2 0PG
*Tel: 01738 624493  Fax: 01738 624493*
### Email: JDMac74@aol.com
Many of the subjects discussed at meetings of the Society (1948-97) have been published in "Medical History" or the Society's "Report of Proceedings". Some earlier papers deposited with the University of St Andrews Archives.
Leaflets: List available of the wide ranging subjects discussed by Speakers to the Society 1948-1997.

## 322 Scottish Urban Archaeological Trust (SUAT)
### 65 South Methven Street, Perth PH1 5NX
*Tel: 01738 622393  Fax: 01738 631626*
### Email: director@suat.demon.co.uk
### http://www.suat.demon.co.uk
The Trust carries out, mainly medieval urban assessments, evaluations & research assignments throughout Scotland. Some research assignments published in academic journals.

## Peterhead

## 323 Aberdeenshire Heritage: Arbuthnot Museum
### St Peter Street, Peterhead AB42 1QD
*Tel: 01779 477778*
### Email: general@abheritage.demon.co.uk
### http://aberdeenshire.gov.uk/ahc.htm
Large photographic collection of NE Scotland (1859-); Peterhead Harbour shipping records (1865-90); records and material on whaling, George Macdonald (Victorian author), James Ferguson (18C astronomer), David Scott (19C printer); Peterhead Sentinel (1865-95).
(1) Curator of Local History: David M Bertie
Access: Mon-Tue, Thu-Sat 1030-1330, 1430-1700; Wed 1030-1300. No curatorial staff on Sat. PCA.
*In town centre; bus routes, parking nearby.*
Finding aids: In-house catalogue.

Leaflets: Publication: Literary families.
Reprographics: R1, R5

## 324 Aberdeenshire Library & Information Service: Peterhead Library
### St Peter Street, Peterhead AB42 1QD
*Tel: 01779 472554  Fax: 01779 480414*

Small collection of books (c300) and other material relating to Peterhead and district incl. newspapers: Peterhead Sentinel 1856-1914, Buchan Obersver 1863-, Selector 1817, Banner of Buchan 1864, Buchan Journal 1865-6 GEN: CEN, OPRs, IGI(S).
(1) Senior Library Assistant
Access: Mon-Tue, Thu-Fri 0930-2000; Wed, Sat 0930-1700. BAO
*In town centre; bus station nearby; parking; disabled access.*
Finding aids: Computerised catalogue.
Reprographics: R1, R4

## Pitlochry

## 325 Clan Donnachaidh Museum
### Bruar, Pitlochry PH18 5TW
*Tel: 01796 483264  Fax: 01796 483338*
### Email: 106030,156@compuserve.com

Collection of books, journals (original and reprints) covering clan and Scottish history. Clan annuals since 1951. Extensive files covering family genealogy of clan members.
(1) Contact : Ronald B Greer
(2) Contact : James Taylor
Access: Mon-Sat 1000-1700, Sun 1100-1700 (Apr-May, Sep-Oct). Closes 1730 Jun-Aug. PCA.
Charges: Admission charge.
*4 ml W of Blair Atholl off A9; local bus service, parking; disabled access.*
Finding aids: Card index & associated entry files.
Leaflets: Available.
Reprographics: Photocopies A4.

## Portree

### 326 Skye & Lochalsh Area Museum Service: Dualchas Tigh na Sgire, Park Road, Portree IV51 9GP
*Tel: 01478 613857  Fax: 01478 613751*

Library of c2000 books covering Skye and Lochalsh; 100 paintings and prints; c4000 photographs - some 1860s, 1890s-; early and OS maps; some estate and business papers, incl. Strathearn estate and solicitors' papers; NMR(S) indexes of archaeological/buildings.
(1) Contact : Mary Carmichael
Access: Mon-Fri 1000-1700. BAO
*In town centre; bus routes, parking nearby; limited disabled access.*
Leaflets: Book catalogue.
Reprographics: R1

## Rothesay

### 327 Bute Museum, Buteshire Natural History Society Stuart Street, Rothesay PA2 0BR
*Tel: 01700 505067*

Local History archives contain books on the history & natural history of Bute; maps of area 18c-; postcards (500 from 1890s); photographs (c800 1860s-); newspaper cuttings, plans and pamphlets.
(1) Contact : K Clegg (Tel: 01700 502033 (Home))
Access: 1030-1630, Sun 1430-1630 (summer). Tue-Sat 1430-1630 (winter). Archives: Wed 1430-1630. BAO
Charges: Donations welcomed; Genealogy search charges.
*0.25 ml from Rothesay pier opposite Rothesay Castle; limited parking; disabled access.*
Primary sources: Examination Rolls for Rothesay Parish for 1775, 1776, 1814 & 1815; marriage records Nov 1798-Apr 1804, Jan 1811-Dec 1815, Jan 1816-Jan.1822, Apr 1822-Jul 1823; baptismal records Aug 1815-Jun 1822, 1832-1835, plus Kincorth 1821; deeds & papers relating to Parish of Kingarth 1504-1745; deeds & papers relating to Ascog Estate 1507-1752; MS of sermons in Gaelic & English by Rev. Archibald McLea 1765-1824, and sermons by Rev. J Buchanan, Kinsgarth 1818-1819; MS & reports relating to Robert Thom, water engineer 1827-47.
Finding aids: Archivist service only.

## Ruthwell

### 328 Savings Bank Museum
### Ruthwell DG1 4NN
### Tel: 01387 870640

Museum is devoted to work & times of Henry Duncan (1774-1846) founder of the Savings Bank movement. Material includes papers & records of the first savings bank & those established at Annan, Hawick, Jedburgh, Glasgow etc, plus records fo the Ruthwell Friendly Society from 1780s.
(1) Curator: Rene Anderson
(2) Contact : Elizabeth Hill
Access: Mon-Sun 1000-1300, 1400-1700 (Easter-Oct). Tue-Sat 1000-1300, 1400-1700 (winter). BAO.
*In village, bus route nearby, parking; disabled access possible.*

## Saltcoats

### 329 North Ayrshire Museum
### Manse Street, Saltcoats KA21 5AA
### Tel: 01294 464174  Fax: 01294 464234

Collection of material covering the Saltcoats, Stevenston & Ardrossan areas.
(1) Contact : Mark Strachan
(2) Contact : Martin Bellamy
Access: Mon-Tue, Thu, Sat 1000-1300; 1400-1700. PCA.
*In town centre; rail station, bus routes, parking nearby; disabled access.*
Primary sources: Photograph collection 1880s- (8000); glass lantern slides & negatives1890-1910 (400 each); maps from 17C include canal surveys, Eglinton estate books, OS; original Burgh Charter of Saltcoats 1528; original ensigns armorial of N Ayrshire Burghs; Society of Six landscape/seascape paintings end 19-early 20C.
Reprographics: R1 (b&w, col).

## Selkirk

### #330 Scottish Borders Archive & Local History Centre
### Library Headquarters, St.Mary's Mill, Selkirk TD7 5EW
### Tel: 01750 20842  Fax: 01750 22875
### Email: libary1@netcomuk.co.uk

A large collection of printed material covering the history and way of life in the Scottish Borders; books by and about local authors incl. Sir Walter Scott, Andrew Lang & James Hogg; runs of local newspapers, postcards & maps.
(1) Archive & Local History Centre (Tel: 01750 20842 x26)
Access: Mon-Thu 0900-1300, 1400-1700; Fri 0900-1300, 1400-1530.
Appointment required for use of microfilm reader.

*On North Riverside Industrial Area (turn off A7 at Selkirk Glass Visitors Centre); parking; disabled access; bus routes nearby.*
Primary sources: Pre-1975 records of the County Councils of Berwick, Peebles, Roxburgh and Selkirk, include County Council minutes, abstracts of accounts, collection of local business records, local society records etc.
GEN: CEN, OPRs, MI, VR, IND, IGI(BI).
Finding aids: Card catalogue for books; lists for archives.
Leaflets: Available.
Reprographics: R1, R4, CDRom copies.


## South Queensferry


## 331 Edinburgh City Museums: Queensferry Museum
## 53 High Street, South Queensferry EH30 9HN
*Tel: 0131 331 5545  Fax: 0131 557 3346*
The museum contains material relating to the history of the former Royal Burgh of Queensferry and its people from the 16C to the present day, incl. the Forth road and rail bridges and a photographic collection (500) from 1880s.
(1) Contact : Denise Brace (Tel: 0131 529 4139)
(2) Contact : Helen Clark (Tel: 0131 529 4059)
Access: Mon, Thu-Sat 1000-1300, 1415-1700; Sun 1200-1700. PCA.
*In town centre, 8 ml W of Edinburgh; on bus route, parking nearby.*
Finding aids: Accessions Register; card indexes.
Leaflets: Available.
Reprographics: R1, R5


## 332 South Queensferry History Group
## c/o Council Offices, 53 High Street, South
## Queensferry EH30 9HN
Collection includes c2000 photographs 1890s-; 150 transcripts of interviews 1990s; records of Ferry Fairs include Annuals 1930s-; drawings/histories of High Street buildings.
(1) Secretary: Len Saunders (Tel: 0131 331 3620)
(2) Chairperson: Mary Anderson (Tel: 0131 331 3395)
Access: Thu 1930-2130. Other times BAO.
*In town centre, bus route, parking nearby.*
Leaflets: Publications.
Reprographics: R5

## Spean Bridge

### 333 Clan Cameron Museum
### Achnacarry, Spean Bridge PH34 4EU
### *Tel: 01397 712480*
A growing collection of material on the Clan Cameron, the Commandos who trained at Achnacarry in WWII, and some estate records.
(1) Curator: Denis Muir
Access: 13.30-1700 (Easter-mid Oct). 1100-1700 (Jul,Aug). Other times BAO.
Charges: Admission charges.
*6 ml from Spean Bridge off B8005 road; parking; disabled access.*
Leaflets: Publications: Museum & Clan Cameron books.
Reprographics: Photocopies can be obtained with prior notice.

## St Andrews

### 334 British Golf Museum
### Bruce Embankment, St Andrews KY16 9AB
### *Tel: 01334 478880  Fax: 01334 473306*
Collections for consultation by bonafide researchers only, contains material relating to the development & history of golf.
Charges: Admission charge to museum.
*W end of town; R & A Golf Club House & car park adjacent; bus routes nearby; disabled access.*
Primary sources: Royal & Ancient Golf Club archives include minutes 1754-, secretary's correspondence 1890s & records of the Open Championship 1860-; extensive photographic, press cuttings & film collections.
Finding aids: Computerised catalogue.
Reprographics: R1

### 335 The Hay Fleming Reference Library
### St Andrews Library, Church Square, St Andrews KY16 9NN
### *Tel: 01334 412685*
### Email: st.andrews@fife.ac.uk
The Hay Fleming (1849-1931) Reference Library comprises c13000 vols. incl. pamphlets, periodicals, early photographs, maps, prints & press cuttings about St Andrews. 250+ works on Mary, Queen of Scots; publications of 19C history clubs & periodicals, church history.
(1) Community Librarian
Access: Mon-Wed, Fri 1000-1900; Thu, Sat 1000-1700.
*In town centre, off South St; bus station, parking nearby.*
Primary sources: Local history material includes congregational rolls of local churches; records of local trades (wrights, tailors, weavers); St Andrew

Citizen newspaper (1873-1997); notebooks & correspondence of David Hay Fleming.
Finding aids: Card catologue.
Leaflets: Available.
Reprographics: R1, R5

## 336 The St Andrews Preservation Trust Museum
## 12 North Street, St Andrews KY16 9PW
### Tel: 01334 477629

Local history collection of books, photographs, local authority and business records, with newspaper cuttings from 1850s.
(1) Curator: Matthew Jarron
Access: Mon-Sun 0900-1700 (Easter-end Sep). Other times BAO.
*In city centre; bus routes nearby; parking with voucher; disabled access difficult.*
Primary sources: The 200+ books of local interest date from 18C; c8000 photographs 1840s-; 500 postcards mostly 1890s- WWI; 18/19C Burgh Council minutes, accounts etc; business records of shops 19C-; 50 oral history tapes 1960s-; GEN: CEN, VR.
Leaflets: Publications lists.
Reprographics: R5

## #337 St Andrews University Library: Special Collections Department
## North Street, St Andrews KY16 9TR
### Tel: 01334 462280  Fax: 01334 462282
### Email: library@st-andrews.ac.uk
### http://www-library.st-and.ac.uk

The Special Collection of printed materials has a particular emphasis on works about the town and University. The general collection of printed books contains many works of interest to the local historian both of Fife and elsewhere in Scotland. An extensive collection of manuscripts, archives and photographs has consideralbe north-Fife interest, as well as material of national and international significance.
(1) Manuscripts: Norman H Reid (Tel: 01334 462324)
(2) Printed material: Christine M Gascoigne (Tel: 01334 462325)
(*) Photographic: Cilla Jackson (Tel: 01334 462326)
Access: Mon-Fri 0900-1700, Sat 0900-1215 (term-time only). PCA.
Charges: No charges for "reasonable" searches.
*1 block W of St Salvators College tower; bus station nearby, Leuchars rail station 4 ml (bus or taxi); parking; disabled access from The Scores.*
Primary sources: Estate and family papers, business records, maps and archictural plans, etc., mainly concerning NE Fife; St.Andrews University's own records, incl. extensive property administration papers from medieval times onwards; burgh records of NE Fife (Anstruther, Auchtermuchty, Crail, Cupar, Earlsferry, Elie, Falkland, Kilrenny, Ladybank, Newburgh, Newport, Pittenweem, St Andrews, St Monance and Tayport); church records of

congregations in the former presbyteries of Cupar and St Andrews and of the presbyteries themselves; photogrpahic collections incl. Valentine and Sons Ltd., covering the whole of the British Isles and beyond, George Cowie covering NE Fife; Robert M Adam covering Scottish topography (especially the Highlands), and some dozen other smaller collections, altogether totalling c300000 images.

Finding aids: General description of holdings access etc. & photographic image base on WWW; typescript finding aids & slip indices to most collections; detailed database catalogue of manuscripts & muniments in preparation, will be accessible from WWW. Printed books online public access catalogue is accessible from WWW.

Leaflets: Special collections, Manuscripts and Rare Books leaflets.

Reprographics: R1 (b&w, col), R4, R5, computer prints A4, slides 35mm.

## Stewarton

## 338 Stewarton & District Museum
### East Ayrshire Council Office, Avenue Square, Stewarton KA3 5AP

A small library of reference books; tape interviews; old photographs and bonnet making industry records.

(1) Trustees Chairman: Ian H Macdonald (Tel: 01563 524748 (eve))
(2) Contact : Gillian Barclay (Tel: 01560 483836)
Access: BAO
*In town centre; rail station nearby, on bus routes, parking.*
Primary sources: 30+ interviews with local people; 12 boxes of photographs of Stewarton past & present; heritors' minutes; school rolls; WWI soldiers' records. GEN: CEN, BR.

## Stirling

## 339 Argyll & Sutherland Highlands Regimental Museum
### The Castle, Stirling FK8 1EH
### *Tel: 01786 475165  Fax: 01786 446038*

Collection includes printed Regimental histories: WWII diaries of 10 Battalions; nominal rolls and miscellaneous regimental material 1794-.

(1) Contact : A W Scott-Elliot
(2) Contact : R MacKenzie
Access: Museum: Mon-Sat 1000-1745; Sun 1100-1645 (Easter-Sep). Mon-Sun 1000-1615 (Oct-Easter). Archive: BAO.
Charges: Castle admission charges; entry to museum free. Research charges possible.
*Within Stirling Castle; rail & bus stations 0.75 ml, parking.*

## 340  Forth Naturalist & Historian
**c/o L Corbett, Hon Editor/Secy, University of Stirling, Stirling FK9 4LA**
*Tel: 01259 215091*
**Email: lindsay.corbett@stir.ac.uk**
**http://www.stir.ac.uk/theuni/forthnat/**
FNH, a Stirling University informal enterprise, provides a focus for interests & publications of environmental, heritage & historic studies for the mid Scotland area.
Leaflets: The FNH Annual from 1976, books, pamphlets plus Godfrey 1890 OS maps - lists available.

## 341  Smith Art Gallery & Museum
**Dumbarton Road, Stirling FK8 2RQ**
*Tel: 01786 471917  Fax: 01786 449523*
**Email: museum@smithartgallery.demon.co.uk**
Collection includes paintings, prints & photographs (300+) relating to the history of Stirling & Stirlingshire.
(1) Contact : Elma Lindsay
(2) Contact : Elspeth King
Access: Tue-Sat 1030-1700, Sun 1400-1700. BAO
*On Dumbarton Rd, 0.25 ml W of Tourist Information Centre; rail & bus stations nearby; assisted disabled access.*
Finding aids: Catalogued on computer & available via SCRAN.
Leaflets: Publications list.
Reprographics: R1, R5

## #342  Stirling Council Archives Services
**Unit 6, Burghmuir Ind. Estate, Stirling FK7 7PY**
The Archives' main holdings are local authority records for, or inherited by, Stirling Council; local church, Justice of the Peace, Customs and Excise records and over 100 collections of privately deposited records; two long and one short runs of local newspapers (bound print or mfilm).
(1) Council Archivist: John Brims (Tel: 01786 450745)
(2) Archivist: Peter Clapham (Tel: 01786 450745)
Access: Wed-Fri 1000-1230, 1330-1630. PCA.
Charges: Staff search charges.
*100 yd S of Craigs roundabout (A9) in S central Stirling; rail station, bus routes & parking nearby; disabled access.*
Primary sources: Stirling Royal Burgh records 1360-1975; Police Burgh records for the other towns in the Stirling area 1860s/1890s-1970s; Commissioners of Supply minutes for Stirlingshire 1693-1930, County Council minutes and accounts 1890-1975 (some gaps) and for Central Region 1975-95, several hundred large-scale maps, incl. OS 1858-1970s and smaller-scale maps c1590-1850; School Board minutes 1873-1919; various business, trades union, association, and family (esp MacGregor of

Macgregor c1314-1921, and Murray of Polmaise 14-19C) records; church records of Stirling Presbytery and constituent Kirk Sessions 1580s-1980s; Register of Deeds, Stirling 1620s-1860s; index to burgess admissions Stirling 1700-1938; some burial registers and registers of lairs 1760s-20C; Stirling Guildry and Incorporated Trades records 15-20C; testaments: indexes to the pre 1801 Registers of Testaments, Commissariat of Stirling and Dunblane; sasines abridgements for Stirlingshire 1781-1986, indexed by person from 1869, by place from 1872; MI pre 1855, for East and West Stirlingshire, and SW Perthshire; assorted trade, commercial and county directories; 19-20C gazetteers; local histories; landownership directory for Scotland c1770; collection of miscellaneous 19 & 20C photographs; OPRs; St Ninians Parish, MAR 1688-1854, BAP 1820-1854, Kippen Parish, BAP & MAR 1700-1854, BR1783-93; 1841 and 1851 CEN for various parishes, Stirling Observer 1836-1980, 1986-.
Finding aids: Catalogue - 16 vols.
Reprographics: R1

## 343 Stirling Council Library Service: Local History Collection
### Central Reference Library, Corn Exchange Road, Stirling FK8 2HX
### *Tel: 01786 432106  Fax: 01786 473094*
Collection includes books, pamphlets, newspapers, maps, postcards, ephemera and genealogical materials.
(1) Local History Officer: Elma Lindsay (Tel: 01786 432394)
(2) Reference Librarian: Steve Dolman
Access: Mon, Wed, Fri 0930-1730; Tue, Thu 0930-1900; Sat 0930-1700. PCA.
Charges: Staff search charges.
*In town centre; rail & bus stations nearby, parking.*
Primary sources: Newspapers: Stirling Journal and Advertiser 1820-1970, Stirling Observer 1970-, Stirling Sentinal 1889-1961 (gaps), Bridge of Allan Gazette 1884-1971, Callander Advertiser 1884-1971; Scottish Record Society publications; Commissariot Record & Register of Testaments - Stirling 1607-1800, Dunblane 1539-1900; 2000 postcards mainly pre 1920s; GEN: CEN, OPRs, IGI(GB) (latter also available at the Bridge of Allan and Dunblane libraries).
Leaflets: Library service information pack.
Reprographics: R1 (b&w, col), R4

**344** **Stirling University Library**
**Stirling FK9 4LA**
*Tel: 01786 467235   Fax: 01786 466866*
**http://www.stir.ac.uk/inforserv/library/**
Printed books of local history are in the general history collection. The special collections contain MS and printed material, incl. newspapers; the Drummond Collection, the Tait Collection and the Leighton Library - 4000 vols.16-19C founded by Archbishop Robert Leighton (1611-1684).
(1) Grierson Archive: Carolyn Rowlinson (Tel: 01786 467228)
(2) Other Collections: Gordon Willis (Tel: 01786 467236)
Access: Mon-Thu 0900-2200; Fri 0900-1900; Sat 1100-1600; Sun 1200-1800 (term-time). Mon-Fri 0900-1700, Wed.0900-1900 (vacations). Special collections: Mon-Fri 0900-1700 (BAO). NB: 3 working days notice required if requiring to consult a Leighton Library book.
*On the A9 road, on outskirts of Bridge of Allan; bus service to library entrance from Stirling bus & rail stations & Bridge of Allan rail station, parking; disabled access.*
Primary sources: Grierson Archive: correspondence & papers of John Grierson (1898-1972), founder of the documentary film movement; letterbooks, accounts etc. of Howietoun Fishery 1873-1978; MS records, incl. registers of borrowings, of the Leighton Library, Dunblane (founded 1687); Tait Collection (socialist material) incl. correspondence, minute books, etc., of left-wing political parties mainly in Edinburgh 1883-1943; Drummond collection of publications of the Drummond Press/Stirling Tract Enterprise 1848-1980; Stirling Journal & Advertiser 1820-1970; Stirling Observer 1970-77, 1986-; Devon Valley Tribune 1899-1967.
Finding aids: Library's online catalogue accessible by Telnet; older material in card catalogue; list of contents for Grierson archive; Stirling Journal & Advertiser local index 1820-1970; lists etc for collection; Leighton Library MS catalogue & contents list.
Leaflets: Special collections leaflet
Reprographics: R1, R4


## Stonehaven


**345** **Aberdeenshire Library & Information Service:**
**Stonehaven Library**
**Evan Street, Stonehaven AB3 2ET**
*Tel: 01569 762136   Fax: 01569 765483*
Collection of books (800) and other material covering the history of the NE Scotland and the Stonehaven area.
(1) Senior Library Assistant
Access: Mon-Tue, Thu-Fri 1000-2000; Wed 1000-1700; Sat 1000-1600. BAO
*In town centre; rail station nearby, on bus route, parking.*
Primary sources: Newspapers: Stonehaven News 1904-1906
Kincardineshire Observer 1907-, Mearns Leader 1913-, Stonehaven Journal

1840-1917, minutes of local authorities include Kincardineshire County Council, Kincardine and Deeside District Council 1975-96, Aberdeenshire Council 1996-; Minutes of Water and Hospital Boards; GEN: CEN, OPRs, IGI(S). ,
Finding aids: Computerised catalogue.
Reprographics: R1, R2

## Stonehouse

## 346 Stonehouse Heritage Group
### c/o Stonehouse Library, 4/5 The Cross, Stonehouse ML9 3LQ
### Tel: 01698 793984

Records relate to Stonehouse only. They include schools 1877-1890; WWI & II; poor relief 1851-1900; miner fatality 1882-1914; rent records 1874; photographs late 19C. GEN: CEN, OPR, B/CH/MAR, BR, IGI.
(1) Contact : Lindsay D Greenock (Tel: 01698 793134)
(2) Contact : Harry Carty (Tel: 01698 791381)
Access: Thu 1700-1930, Sat 0900-1300. Other times BAO.
Charges: Donations appreciated and search charges possible.
*Above Stonehouse Library; bus route nearby, parking.*
Finding aids: All records on computerised database.
Reprographics: R5

## Stornoway

## 347 Comhairle Nan Eilean Siar (formerly Western Isles Council): Stornoway Library
### Keith Street, Stornoway HS1 2QG
### Tel: 01851 703064  Fax: 01851 705657

The Gaelic and Local History Reference Room has a comprehensive collection of books, articles, newspapers, periodicals, maps (18C- incl. OS), photographs (1890s-), c1000 postcards (mostly 1890s-1960s), audio visual and archive material. It incorporates much of the An Comnan Gaidhealach Collection of Gaelic literature and highland history.
(1) Chief Librarian: Robert Eaves
(2) Senior Librarian Adult Services: David Fowler
Access: Mon-Thu 1000-1700; Fri 1000-1900; Sat 1000-1300.
*Close to town centre; bus station, ferry terminal & parking.*
Primary sources: Minutes of former Town Council and Comhairle Nan Eilean 1974-; School Board minute books 1870s-1930s (gaps); school log books 1870s-1980s (gaps); estate rentals 1800s-1930s (gaps); some croft histories; unique collection of estate and town maps; aircraft movement log books 1957-92 and air traffic control watch logs 1963-94 for Stornoway and Benbecula; miscellaneous collection of MS papers of local authors;

newspapers: Stornoway Gazette 1917-, West Highland Free Press 1972-;
GEN: CEN, OPRs, VR, IGI(S).
Finding aids: Card catalogue & Gaelic resource database.
Leaflets: Available.
Reprographics: R1, R4

## Stranraer

### 348 Stranraer Museum
### Old Town Hall, 55 George Street, Stranraer DG9 7JP
### *Tel: 01776 705088  Fax: 01776 704420*
### Email: john_pickin@dumgal.gov.uk
Archives include Wigtownshire Burgh records from late 16C; local paper
ephemera and historical photographs.
(1) Contact : John Pickin
(2) Contact : Nicola Goldsworthy
Access: Archives: BAO.
*In town centre; on bus routes, parking nearby; disabled access.*
Primary sources: Archives cover the former burghs of Stranraer, Newtown
Stewart, Whithorn and Wigtown and Wigtown county; Records of the
Commissioners of Police; treasurers accounts and the workings of the Rhins
and Machars Councils; business records incl. protocol books of the early
17C; Original photographs and many copy negatives.
Finding aids: In-house catalogues & card indexes .
Leaflets: Information on request.
Reprographics: Limited A4 photocopying; other services on request.

## Strichen

### 349 Aberdeenshire Library & Information Service:
### Strichen Library
### 59a Water Street, Strichen AB4 6ST
### *Tel: 01771 637347*
Local history collection contains books, photographs and other materials on
Strichen and surrounding area incl. Strichen Estate papers. GEN: CEN,
OPRs, IGI(S).
(1) Contact : Sheila Maclean (Tel: 01771 637294)
Access: Mon, Wed, Fri 1700-1900; Thu 1400-1700; Sat 1000-1200. PCA.
*In village centre; on bus routes, parking.*
Reprographics: R1

ROYAL COMMISSION (HIGHLANDS AND ISLANDS)

# RETURN RESPECTING COTTARS

on the Estate of North Uist ___ the Property of Sir John Campbell Orde Bart as at the 1st day of January 1883.

No. 1
Knocknatorran

| No. | NAME | Residence, whether on a Croft, or not on a Croft. | | Rent, if any. | | | Occupation or Means of Subsistence. |
|---|---|---|---|---|---|---|---|
| | | On a Croft. | Not on a Croft. | Amount. £ s. d. | To whom paid. Proprietor or Tenant. | | |
| 1 | Angus Laing | Not on a croft. | | 10 | Payable to Proprietor | | Labourer Fields |
| 2 | Don McDougald | " | | 10 | " | | do |
| 3 | Angus McDougald | " | | 10 | " | | do |
| 4 | Finlay McDougald | " | | 10 | " | | do |
| 5 | Flora McDonald | on a croft. | | 5 | " | | Work |
| 6 | John MacBain | | Not on a croft. | | | | Labourer Fields |
| 7 | Marion McLeanB | | " | | | | Work |
| 8 | Catherine Matheson | on a croft | | | | | Weavers |
| 9 | Angus Ferguson | | | | | | Supported by family |
| 10 | Christy Matheson | | Not on a croft. | | | | Servant. |

Signed ___
Address ___
Date ___

## Thurso

**350 Highland Libraries: Thurso Library**
**Davidson's Lane, Thurso KW14 7AF**
*Tel: 01847 893237 Fax: 01847 896114*
Book collection (c500) includes those donated by the Glasgow Caithness Society; periodical collection; Caithness Courier 1866-; GEN: OPRs, MI, IGI(S).
(1) Area Libraries Officer: Joyce Brown
Access: Mon, Wed 1000-1800; Tue, Fri 1000-2000; Thu, Sat 1000-1300. PCA.
*In town centre; rail station, bus route, parking nearby.*
Reprographics: R1

## Ullapool

**351 Ullapool Museum & Visitor Centre**
**7/8 West Argyle Street, Ullapool IV26 2TY**
*Tel: 01854 612987 Fax: 01854 612987*
Social history books, archives, photographs & genealogical material relating to the Parish of Lochbroom.
(1) Contact : Juliet Rees
(2) Contact : Frances Ross
Access: Mon-Sat 0930-1730 (Easter- Jun,Sep); 0930-2000 (Jul-Aug); 1100-1530 (Oct-Easter). BAO
Charges: Admission charges; search charges possible.
*In town centre, limited bus service, parking nearby; disabled access.*
Primary sources: Archive & copied material includes: minutes of Railway Committee 1918; local occupations (fishing & carding); minutes of School Board; school Log Books; Crofters & Cottars Condition Report 1882; Roy & OS maps; c1000 photographs, GEN, CEN, OPR, IND, VR.
Reprographics: R1

## Wanlockhead

**352 Museum of Lead Mining (formerly Scottish Lead Mining Museum)**
**Wanlockhead ML12 6UT**
*Tel: 01659 74387 Fax: 01659 74481*
**Email: wanlockhead@dial.pipex.com**
The miners' library houses a collection of 3000 books bought by the miners 1754-, largely theologically based; plus archives & village society minute books, mining records & plans.
(1) Curator/Manager: Veronica Travers
(2) Contact : Carole Davies (Tel: 01659 74551)

Access: 1100-1630 (Apr-Jun, Sep). 1000-1700 (Jul-Aug). BAO (Oct-Mar). PCA.
Charges: Admission charges.
*In village centre; minimal bus service, parking; disabled access.*
Primary sources: Mining company records; maps & plans of mines; minute books for village band; curling, quoiting societies; library minutes books; photographs & village memorabilia; village history documented in diaries; Free Church of Scotland records; miners bargain records; census returns.
Finding aids: Book collection catalogued.
Reprographics: R1

## West Kilbride

## 353 West Kilbride Museum Trust
## 1 Arthur Street, West Kilbride KA23 9EN

Small collection (50+) of books relating to the area from 1620, include church "text books"; photographs 1880s-(200+) & early OS maps (Ayrshire).
(1) Contact : E A W Scott (Tel: 01294 822102)
(2) Contact : L Clark (Tel: 01294 822308)
Access: Tue, Thu, Sat 1030-1230, 1400-1600. BAO
*On upper floor of public hall; bus route, parking nearby.*
Reprographics: Photocopies A4 (on request).

## West Linton

## 354 West Linton Historical Association
## The Village Centre, Raemartin Square, West Linton EH46 7ED

Collection comprises 1500+ photographs, 800+ slides, maps, project files (railway, gas works, shops, trades, houses) and secondary source material covering the social and economic life of the Lynedale area of Tweeddale.
(1) Archivist: I Paterson (Tel: 01968 660346)
Access: BAO
*In village centre ; bus route nearby, parking; disabled access.*
Finding aids: Photographs catalogued.
Reprographics: Photocopies and photography by arrangement.

## Westray

### 355 Westray Heritage Centre
### Pierowall, Westray KW17 2BZ

Collection of photographs (400+); people, families, events. Some Westray family histories.
(1) Contact : Cathy Rendall (Tel: 01857 677354)
(2) Contact : Nancy Scott (Tel: 01857 677231)
Access: Mon-Sun 1400-1700 (May-Sep). Other times BAO. PCA.
Charges: Admission charges.
*In village centre; public transport from ferry, parking; disabled access.*
Leaflets: Local and dialect publications.
Reprographics: R1

## Wick

### 356 Highland Libraries: Wick Library
### Sinclair Terrace, Wick KW1 5AB
### *Tel: 01955 602864  Fax: 01955 603000*

Collection of 2000+ books mainly covering Caithness includes Neil Gunn (1891-1973) collection (60 books) and items by Sir John Sinclair (1754-1835) plus large end 18/19C pamphlet collection and Old Caithness local history collection 19C-; Newspapers: John O'Groat Journal 1836- and Northern Ensign 1850-1926 (gaps); GEN: OPRs, IGI(S).
(1) Contact : Jenny Shanks
Access: Mon, Thu 1000-1800; Wed, Sat 1000-1300; Tue, Fri 1000-2000. PCA.
*In town centre; rail station, bus route nearby, parking.*
Reprographics: R1

### 357 North Highland Archive
### Wick Library Building, Sinclair Terrace, Wick KW1 5AB
### *Tel: 01955 606432  Fax: 01955 603000*

Archives hold records of local authorities, public bodies, private records, maps and plans, newspapers and genealogical material.
(1) Archival Material: Brenda Lees
(2) Local History : Genealogy: Trudi Mann
Access: Mon-Tue, Thu-Fri 1000-1300, 1400-1730; Wed 1000-1300. BAO
Charges: Archival and genealogical search charges.
*In town centre; rail station, bus routes nearby, parking.*
Primary sources: Minute books of Wick (1660-1975) and Thurso Burghs (1904-65); Thurso Police Commissioners (1841-1904); Caithness County records include: Commissioners of Supply 1720-1929; County Council minutes 1890-1975, Road Trustees (1815-1915), Parochial Boards 1845-1930, various school records 1873-1974; Wick Harbour Trust papers, incl.

arrivals and sailings 1851-1980 and fish landings 1889-1974; Wick and Pulteneytown District Nursing Association 1893-1946; legal family Keith of Thurso papers 1887-1965; maps and plans include OS and valuation maps; newspapers: John O'Groats Journal 1836-, Northern Ensign 1850-1922; GEN: CEN, OPRs, IGI(S).
Finding aids: Guide to the Highland Council Archive.
Leaflets: Guide and leaflet.
Reprographics: R1, R2

## 358 Borders Family History Society

Members undertake research into their family histories covering former counties of Berwick, Roxburgh, Selkirk & Peebles.
(1) Hon Secretary: Carol Trotter (Tel: 01361 810253)
(2) Contact : Fay Mackay (Tel: 01896 850264)
Leaflets: Publications list: MI in Roxburgh & Berwick.

## 359 Cawdor Heritage Group

Collection covers the Cawdor area. It includes 300+ photographs 1890s-; maps 18C-; information on farming, trades, Cawdor castle & estate incl. a forestry worker's diary 1914-1970; memorabilia; GEN: CEN, OPRs, MAR/BAP, IND, MI. Expect to have own premises in 1999.
(1) Chairman: J Rose-Miller (Tel: 01667 493218)
(2) President: D Morrison (Tel: 01667 456271)
Charges: Search charges.
Leaflets: Booklets list from 1999.
Reprographics: Photocopies A4 (b&w, col).

## 360 Central Scotland Family History Society

Members undertake research into their family histories. Society covers the greater Stirling area.
(1) Secretary: Carol Sergeant (Tel: 01324 554874)
Leaflets: Publications list.

## 361 Clackmannanshire Field Studies Society
## Email: lindsay.corbett@stir.ac.uk

Small collection of photographs, slides, videos, maps plus records of society's projects.
(1) Chair: E K Roy (Tel: 01259 213954)
(2) Contact : L Corbett (Tel: 01259 215091)
Leaflets: Bi-annual newsletters from 1970 plus books by members published by Forth Naturalist & Historian list available.

## 362 Colinton Local History Society

Collection of members' research material, miscellaneous papers, oral tapes & c250 photographs 1850-.
(1) Studies Officer: Alistair Davidson (Tel: 0131 441 6607)
(2) Archive Officer: Frank Bennetts (Tel: 0131 441 1221)
Leaflets: Archive index.

## 363 Cullen, Deskford & Portknockie Heritage Group

Group members research the history of the area - farming, fishing, schools, churches, personalities; newspaper cuttings & photographic (300) collections.
(1) Contact : Len Hall (Tel: 01542 840927  Fax: 01542 840927)
(2) Contact : John Rennie (Tel: 01542 840199)
Reprographics: R5 (by arrangement).

## 364 Currie & District History Society

Collection of 500 photographs, 1000 negatives & 1000 slides 1890- covering the Currie district plus some miscellaneous papers & local maps. (NB the early John Tweedie material is in the Heriot Watt Univesity Archive).
(1) Hon Secretary: Mary Coghill (Tel: 0131 443 3297)
(2) Contact : Betty Dagg (Tel: 0131 449 2996)
Reprographics: Photographs & negatives, catalogue (paper & disc).

## 365 East Ayrshire Family History Society

Members undertake research into their family histories using facilities at the Dick Institute Library, Kilmarnock.
(1) Chairman: Jim Steel (Tel: 01563 524878)
(2) Vice Chairman: Thomas Shaw (Tel: 01563 530025)
Leaflets: Bi-annual journal, newsletter (members only).

## 366 East Linton Local History Society

Society members research the history of the area - farming, businesses, personalities, the East Linton artists; 300+ photographs & 200 postcards; GEN: MI.
(1) Secretary: Garry S Menzies (Tel: 01620 860741)

## 367 Fala, Soutra & District History & Heritage Society

Extracts from church & other records; photographs/slides early 20C-; archaeological excavations at Soutra medieval hospital for which reports (SHARP) are held.
(1) Contact : Jean Blades (Tel: 01876 833248)
Leaflets: SHARP Reports.

## 368 The Falkland Society

Small collection of books on the Falkland area plus 500+ photographs 20C.
(1) Contact : Pamela McIlroy (Tel: 01337 858017)
Finding aids: Material index.
Reprographics: R5 (by arrangement).

## 369 Ferryhill Heritage Society (Aberdeen)

Archival material on Ferryhill and surrounding area of Aberdeen (south of city centre), incl. Battle of Justice Mills, tramcars, mill wheel, Victorian architect Alexander Ellis plus photographic collection.
(1) Contact : Jacqueline Leith (Tel: 01224 213087)
(2) Contact : Violet McLeod (Tel: 01224 314279)
Leaflets: Society's newsletter & leaflets.
Reprographics: Photocopies & photographic service by arrangement.

## 370 Friockheim & District Historical Society

Collection of newspaper cuttings 1800-; 300 photographs (slides); videos featuring exhibition "Life past to Present" (1996) & Village Buildings Today (1998).
(1) Contact : Lindsay Smith (Tel: 01241 828464)
(2) Contact : Kerry Sidgwick (Tel: 01241 828574)

## 371 Glasgow Archaeological Society
*Tel: 0141 330 6751   Fax: 0141 330 4952*
**Email: c.primrose@lib.gla.ac.uk**

Collection of books (2300) and journals on archaeological subjects predominently Scottish 19-early20C. These will be accessible at Glasgow University Library from end of 1999. Archive material: minutes and correspondence of the Society from 1854. These can be consulted at the Glasgow University Archives, 13 Thurso Street, Glasgow.
(1) Secretary: Carol Primrose
(2) Archivist: L J F Keppie (Tel: 0141 330 4402)
Leaflets: Journal and bulletin of the Society. Dalrymple monograph series.

## 372 Great North of Scotland Railway Association
**Email: GBoardman@compuserve.com**

Association members undertake the study & collection of information, documents & illustrations covering the railway system of NE Scotland - GNER, LNER & BR.
(1) Secretary: G Boardman (Tel: 01343 820811)
Leaflets: Booklets, drawings of locomotives, rolling stock & stations. Quarterly journal for members.

## 373 Kincardine Local History Group

Notes on the history of Kincardine & Tulliallan; early maps; 1500 photographs & 2000 slides of district.
(1) Contact : Charles O'Donnell (Tel: 01259 731022)
Finding aids: Photographic collection indexed.
Reprographics: Photocopies & photographic service by arrangement.

## 374  Kinross Historical Society

Collection comprises locally written books, miscellaneous papers, texts of lectures/monographs, maps, slides, postcards & photographs. (Society will have its own premises late 1999).
(1) Contact : N H Walker (Tel: 01577 863499)

## 375  Lanarkshire Family History Society (formerly Hamilton & District FHS)

Society promotes the study of family history in Lanarkshire.
(1) Secretary: Allan Colthart (Tel: 01698 424526)

## 376  Largs & North Ayrshire Family History Society

Members undertake research into their family histories. Publication programme underway.
(1) Contact : W Gibb (Tel: 01475 675228)
(2) Contact : H Noble (Tel: 01475 672083)

## 377  Larkhall Heritage Group

Collection of photographs 1890s- incl. street scenes & the coal mining & railway past. 1860 maps.
(1) Contact : John Milligan (Tel: 01698 886776)
(2) Contact : Ann Rankin (Tel: 01698 885995)
Leaflets: Larkhall's Building Societies & railways.

## 378  Lesmahagow Parish Historical Association

The Archive holds a wide ranging collection of articles, journals, OS & early maps, 1500 photographs 1890s-, genealogical files of local families plus GEN: CEN, OPRs, MAR/B/BAP, ER, MI, DIR, IGI.
(1) Archivist: Robert McLeish (Tel: 01555 893859)
(2) Secretary: Jean Watters (Tel: 01555 892305)
Leaflets: Publications list.
Reprographics: R1, R5 (by arrangement).

## 379  The Lothians Family History Society
## Email: anne_agnew@onlin.rednet.co.uk

Society promotes the study of family history in the Lothians.
(1) Secretary: Liz Cowie (Tel: 0131 660 2134)
(2) Chair: Anne Agnew (Tel: 0131 660 1933)

## 380  Old Edinburgh Club

Society for the study of the history of Edinburgh. Publishes an occasional journal, "The Book of the Old Edinburgh Club".
(1) Secretary: Wendy Turner (Tel: 0131 247 4131)

## 381 Pictish Arts Society

Undertakes research into dark ages of Pictish history & culture.
(1) Archivist: I Craddock (Tel: 0131 552 1223)
Leaflets: Pictish Arts Journal & newsletters (members only).

## 382 Prestwick History Group

Collection of 1000 photographs & 3000 slides covering the Preswick & Monkton area 1988-, plus 155 tape recordings made by the Group 1985-, newspapers 1984- and miscellaneous papers.
(1) Contact : Alisdair W R Cochrane (Tel: 01292 470234)

## 383 Roslin Heritage Society

Collection of information on bleachfields 1719-1850, gunpowder works 1804-1954; carpet factory 1860-1960; farming; Rosslyn castle & chapel. Much of the material can be consulted at Midlothian Libraries, Local Studies Dept.
(1) Contact : George Campbell (Tel: 0131 440 2230)
(2) Midlothian Local Studies Officer: Marion Richardson (Tel: 0131 271 3980)

## 384 Troon & District Family History Society

Members undertake research into their family histories. Society has developed links with N of Ireland FH Society.
(1) Contact : Cliff Hewitt (Tel: 01292 312730)

# HELP FROM PRIVATE SOURCES

A significant amount of original archive and manuscript material remains in the ownership of private individuals, businesses and other organisations. A researcher should contact the National Register of Archives (Scotland) (NRA(S)) for assistance when wishing to find out where these are located. The NRA(S), a branch of the National Archives of Scotland (NAS), has been in existence for over fifty years, giving advice to private owners of historical papers in Scotland, and assisting researchers in gaining access to them.

There are now more than 3700 surveys on the Register, some of only a few pages, others extending to hundreds of pages. They are available for consultation in the Search Rooms of the NAS with the most complete and up-to-date version of the Register available at West Register House (see Directory entry). An index to the titles of surveys is available, and summaries are published in the *Annual Report of the Keeper of the Archives of Scotland* which can be consulted at the National Library of Scotland (NLS) and larger libraries in Scotland. In some cases, the National Register of Archives in London has compiled reports, while finding aids compiled by the private owners or their lawyers have been copied.

There are partial source lists on a number of topics such as architecture, art, medicine and technology. However NRA(S) source lists only cover the first 1000 surveys. NRA(S) surveys are gradually being transferred to an electronic version of the Register which can searched in both Search Rooms. Indexes of persons and places are available on the Historical Monuments Commission web-site at www.hmc.gov.uk.

The principal area where the NRA(S) can assist researchers is with their knowledge of the records still held by private owners, and how such owners can best be approached if access is required. It should be borne in mind that the existence of a survey does not imply that access will be granted. Permission remains at the discretion of the owner. Researchers must scrupulously observe any restriction owners may place on publication.

The NRA(S) has set down some 'golden rules' which they ask researchers to observe. They should

1. write to the NRA(S) giving as accurately as possible references to the material they wish to see;
2. as far as possible, read all available background material before a visit is arranged, thereby avoiding repeat visits;
3. give full information on why they wish to consult the papers, the nature and reasons for their particular area of research, and whether they intend to publish or paraphrase the material to be consulted;
4. give maximum advance notice for requests to consult papers in private ownership, and be prepared to be flexible with regard to arrangements for visits;
5. not seek to consult private papers for information which is readily available from public sources. The NRA(S) will point researchers in the right direction where public sources can be contacted;
6. some owners may charge an administration fee for arranging access;

7. properly acknowledge in any publication assistance given - the Registrar will be able to give advice on this.

An organisation which offers a service to the family historian is the Church of Jesus Christ of Latter Day Saints (LDS), probably better known as The Mormons, operating from their base in Salt Lake City, Utah, USA. Virtually every leading library and family history society will have versions of their International Genealogical Index (IGI). These provide information abstracted from the statutory registers of births, marriages and deaths from 1855 and the preceding Old Parish Registers (OPRs). This information is available on microfiche and CDROM. In addition a comprehensive index (surname, place and birthplace) to the 1881 census, and, the 'census as enumerated' is on microfiche.

The LDS 'Family Search' software allows the names of a husband and wife to be entered, with the search of the database producing a family group, not restricted to a single year. Minor variations in spelling, so often met with in Scotland, are taken into account. This is more comprehensive than information that would be obtained from the General Register Office (GRO) on-line index, which shows results of a search for a single year only. The web-site address for pages supported by the LDS is www.ancestry.com. These pages include a large amount of information including email addresses for help and support.

The LDS operate Family History Centres in the larger towns in Scotland. They are run by volunteers, with opening time varying from centre to centre. There is no charge for the use of the facilities in the Centres, although donations will be accepted. It is recommended that appointments be made to ensure that space is available and the required information is obtainable. The Scottish Centres are located in Aberdeen (01224 692 206), Dumfries (01387 254 865), Dundee (01382 451 247), Edinburgh (0131 337 3049), Glasgow (0141 357 1024), Inverness (01463 231 220), Paisley (0141 884 2780), Kilmarnock (01563 526 560), and Kirkcaldy (01592 640041).

# THE ELECTRONIC AGE

Since the first edition of *Exploring Scottish History* in 1992 we have entered the electronic age. Computers are everywhere - in the home, at work and in the resource centres. We can 'write' to each other by Email, access databases of ever increasing sizes, surf the Internet. The digitising of some records (see below) is now underway, which will permit them to be consulted at home. The high cost of bringing this about with current and anticipated technological developments will mean that only often consulted material will be available on-line. Many newspapers and genealogical records have been available on microfilm or microfiche for some years, but it will be some time before they will be able to be consulted on the 'small screen' at home. Perhaps, in the distant future, some of the younger readers of this book will not need to leave their home 'keyboard' when researching and publishing the results of their endeavours.

In Scotland two major electronic databases are being compiled as a result of money received from the National Lottery and matching contributions from the participating organisations. The first of these, launched in November 1996, was the **Scottish Cultural Resources Access Network** (SCRAN). It was founded by a partnership of the National Museums of Scotland (NMS), the Scottish Museums Council (SMC) and the Royal Commission on the Ancient & Historical Monuments of Scotland (RCAHMS). When the five-year contract finishes SCRAN will continue as a self-financing organisation. The second organisation is **The Scottish Archive Network**. It was officially launched by the National Archives of Scotland (NAS), formerly known as the Scottish Record Office (SRO), in January 1999. The principal participating organisations are the NAS and Genealogical Society of Utah, with active support and co-operation by 41 archives in Scotland. In the Directory these archive centres are indicated by a hash sign (#) placed before the entry number of the organisation.

SCRAN will provide easy access to 1.5 million text records of historic monuments and of artefacts held in museums, galleries and archives, plus, related multimedia resources and essays. The partners and other institutions located throughout Scotland will supply the original material. SCRAN will be accessible on the Internet and its resources available on CDROM. Much of the output will be aimed at the educational sector and available for consultation in libraries and eventually in the home. It will mean that a visual introduction to many historical topics and artefacts to be seen at institutions across the country will be available to everyone. Many historical researchers will have the choice of looking at original historical material and/or seeing the digitised version on their PC screen.

SCRAN projects are wide ranging and when looking through descriptions of the first 150 in the pipeline we find a number that will provide both background and more detailed information for social, local and family historians:
 Connecting Threads - Spinning, Weaving, Dyeing in the History of the Isle of Arran.
Farming & Dairying in Galloway features local agricultural artefacts.
The Sites to See - images of all Historic Scotland's properties open to the public.
Annan: Victorian Boom Town records Annan's Victorian built environment heritage.
Glasgow Museums Basic Records - 51000 records from all the Glasgow Museums.
Roy's Military Survey Map of Scotland from the British Library.

A History of the Scottish People 1450-1800 - a CDROM format for primary and secondary schools. It will cover economic, social, cultural and political developments.
The Churches of Scotland: Archaeology, History, and Architecture. Information on 10000 Scottish churches and sites.
Cromarty: Architecture & People. Records of fifty buildings in, and the development of the burgh.
Aberdeen City Photographic Project. Life in Aberdeen, from buildings to industries, seen through the lenses of photographers from pioneers to present day practitioners.
North British Locomotive Company Collection based on the Mitchell Library collection.

The Scottish Cultural Resources Access Network (SCRAN) can be contacted at: Abden House, 1 Marchhall Crescent, Edinburgh EH16 5HW. Tel: 0131 662 1211. Fax: 0131 662 1511. Email: scran@scran.ac.uk. Web: www.scran.ac.uk/

The Scottish Archive Network will create an electronic network and search room that will link every major Scottish archive and make information in them available throughout Scotland and further afield. The project is divided into three parts. The most important for history researchers will be the electronic search room which will include the top level finding aids (the catalogues or lists that describe the overall holdings) plus detailed catalogues if available, of the National Archives of Scotland and the co-operating archives. The 'frequently asked questions' section will include information on how to trace local history and family trees. There will be a 'shop window' for publications produced by the participating archives as well as news about and links to them. Links to related sites such as SCRAN and libraries will be provided. Archive users will also be able to 'talk' to each other and swap information and experiences.

The second part of the project is the automation of the Register of Testaments, or the Wills of Scots from 1500 to 1875. The aim is to automate the indexes and to link the index entry to the electronic image of the testament to which it refers. It will be a considerable undertaking with about 475000 index entries covering persons, places, occupations and dates to be digitised. The electronic image of a will be available in the NAS Historical Search Room, with a hardcopy obtainable on payment of a fee.

The development of the existing electronic catalogues in the NAS is the third part of the project. NAS has already automated many of its catalogues and they can be searched electronically to file, bundle or item level. These also will be made available to the network.

In addition NAS will be a member of the European Union Archive Network which includes the National Archives of Sweden and Italy plus the International Institute of Social History, Amsterdam. This project will open up access to top-level catalogues of the partner organisations.

NOTE. As can be seen these projects will take some considerable time before they will be ready for consultation on the Internet. It is hoped that Internet access will be possible by the end of 1999, a truly significant start to the new Millennium for history researchers in Scotland. News of this will be given in the press, the Scottish Local History Forum Journal and Journals of Family History Societies.

The Scottish Archive Network can be contacted at: National Archives of Scotland, Thomas Thomson House, Edinburgh EH1 3YY. Tel: 0131 535 1380. Fax: 0131 535 1390. Email: ibarnes@sro.gov.uk

In 1998 the General Register Office (GRO) in Edinburgh entered the electronic age by launching a web-site. By contacting www.origins.net researchers will be able to access the New Register House indexes system. This covers the statutory index of births, marriages and deaths (1855 to date), the Old Parish Register (OPR) indexes of baptisms and marriages (1553 to 1854) and all Scotland indexes to the 1881 and 1891 census records. For details of charges and access contact the GRO - the addresses is given in the Directory entry.

Many offices for the Registration of Births, Marriages and Deaths in Scotland have direct or shared links to the GRO network. Two of the larger local registration offices, Glasgow (Park Circus) and Dundee, and one of the smallest, Lochgilphead, are included in the Directory. The other registration offices that have (December 1998) a direct access to the GRO are: Aberdeen, Ayr, Dumfries, Elgin (includes Buckie, Forres and Keith), Inverness (includes Dingwall, Fort William and Thurso), and Lerwick. There are twenty-six registration offices with shared connections to the GRO. These are: Arbroath, Banff, Bathgate, Cambuslang, Carluke, Dumbarton, East Kilbride, Eastwood, Edinburgh (India Buildings, Victoria Street), Falkirk, Glasgow (Martha Street), Greenock, Hamilton, Inverurie, Irvine, Johnstone, Kirkwall, Lanark, Larkhall, Motherwell, Paisley, Perth, Renfrew, Rutherglen, Stenness and Stonehaven. On occasions researchers could experience delays in making connections from these offices with shared connections. Researchers can obtain the address of these offices from telephone directories. Prior contact is advisable in order to obtain information on the days and times the use of the facility will be available and the costs involved.

Many of the larger and some quite small organisations featured in the Directory are connected to the Internet, with Email and web-site addresses indicated. It is possible that, in the future, some of these addresses will be shortened and others lengthened to give direct access to separate sections of, or, services provided by an organisation. In most cases the information provided on the Internet would be of a general nature describing the services provided by the organisation. Some organisations will, through time, provide more detailed information about their collections and their contents.

An example of this is provided by contacting the web-site address www.nms.ac.uk/ which connects to the National Museums of Scotland. Information is provided on many of the museum collections, including pictures and details of their histories, held at various sites. There is an extensive education section aimed at getting schools to bring classes along to the museums. It includes information on events and how to get in touch with museum staff. More information on the collections in the museums will eventually appear as a SCRAN project - the National Museums of Scotland is one of the SCRAN partners.

As has been seen above in the case of the Scottish Archive Network's automation of the Register of Testaments, the cost of transferring or copying original documents so that they can featured on a web-site is extremely expensive. Only some of the most frequently consulted material will come available on-line. For the foreseeable future researchers will always have to visit the appropriate resource centres when undertaking any social, local or family history project in depth.

# PRINCIPAL REPOSITORIES ELSEWHERE
# IN THE UNITED KINGDOM
# AND IRELAND

Some archive material covering Scotland is to be found in national archives of the United Kingdom and occasionally in Ireland. For example, researchers into aspects of military history will have seen, when looking through the Directory, that the material in Scottish archives is patchy, especially that of a 'genealogical' nature. The principal national repositories, listed below, may have material of interest to some Scottish researchers. Similar organisations in Scotland may be able to give advice on what these institutions might hold in relation to a researcher's particular project.

**British Library, Manuscripts Collection**, 96 Euston Road, London NW1 2DB
Tel: 0171 412 7513          Fax: 0171 412 7787
Email: mss@bl.uk          www.bl.uk/collections/manuscripts/

**British Library, Newspaper Library**, Colindale Avenue, London NW9 5HE
Tel: 0171 412 7353          Fax: 0171 412 7379
Email: newspapers@bl.uk

**British Library Sound Archive**, 96 Euston Road, London NW1 2DB
Tel: 0171 412 7440          Fax: 0171 412 7441
Email: nfa@bl.uk

**Family Records Centre**, 1 Myddleton Street, London EC1R 1UW
Tel: 0181 392 5300          Fax: 0181 392 5307
Email: certificate.service@ons.gov.uk www.open.gov.uk/pro/frc.htm

*Jointly run by the Public Record Office and the Office for National Statistics. Holds indexes to statutory registers of births, marriages and deaths in England and Wales since 1837; wills and administrations before 1858 (Canterbury) and non-parochial registers 1567-1858. Has an on-line link with the General Register Office, Edinburgh.*

**General Register Office (Northern Ireland)**, Oxford House, 49-55 Chichester Street, Belfast BT1 4HL
Tel: 01232 252021          Fax: 01232 252044
                              www.nics.gov.uk/nisra/gro/
*Holds the statutory registers of marriages in Northern Ireland from 1845 and births and deaths since 1864.*

**House of Lords Record Office**, House of Lords, London SW1A 0PW
Tel: 0171 219 3074          Fax: 0171 219 2570
Email: hlro@parliament.uk          www.parliament.uk/

*Some three million documents are preserved including the records of both Houses of Parliament dating back to the sixteenth century.*

**Imperial War Museum**, Department of Documents, Lambeth Road. London SE1 6HZ
Tel: 0171 416 5221
Email: docs@iwm.org.uk
Fax: 0171 416 5374
www.iwm.org.uk/

*Records all aspects of the two World Wars and other military operations involving Britain since 1914.*

**Institution of Civil Engineers**, 1-7 Great George Street, London SW1P 3AA
Tel:0171 222 7722
Email: archive@ice.org.uk
Fax: 0171 976 7610
www.ice.org.uk/

**Institution of Mechanical Engineers**, Information and Library Service,
1 Birdcage Walk, London SW1H 9JJ
Tel: 0171 973 1265
Email: k_moore@imeche.org.uk
Fax: 0171 222 8762
www.imeche.org.uk/

**National Archives of Ireland**, Bishop Street, Dublin 8, Ireland
Tel: 00353 1 407 2300
Fax: 00353 1 407 2333
www.kst.dit.ie/nat-arch/

**National Army Museum**, Department of Archives, Photographs, Film & Sound,
Royal Hospital Road, Chelsea, London SW3 4HT
Tel: 0171 730 0717
Email: nam@ enterprise.net
Fax: 0171 823 6573
www.failte.com/nam/

**National Library of Ireland**, Kildare Street, Dublin 2, Ireland
Tel: 00353 1 661 8811
Fax: 00353 1 676 6690
www.hea.ie/natlib/homepage.html

**National Library of Wales**, Department of Manuscripts and Records, Aberystwyth SY23 3BU
Tel: 01970 623816
Email: ymh.lc@llgc.org.uk
Fax: 01970 625713
www.llgc.org.uk/

**National Maritime Museum**, Manuscripts Section, Greenwich, London SE10 9NF
Tel: 0181 312 6691
Email jf48@dial.pipex.com
Fax: 0181 312 6632
www.nmm.ac.uk/

**National Portrait Gallery Archive**, St Martin's Place, London WC2H 0HE
Tel: 0171 306 0055
Fax: 0171 306 0056
www.npg.org.uk/archive.htm

**Principal Registry of the Family Division**, Somerset House, Strand, London WC2R 1LP
Tel: 0171 936 7000

*Holds copies of wills admitted to probate in England and Wales and all grants of probate and administration since 1858.*

**Public Record Office**, Ruskin Avenue, Kew, Richmond, Surrey  TW9 4DU
Tel: 0181 876 3444                    Fax: 0181 878 8905
Email: enquiry.pro.rsd.kew@gtnet,gov.uk        www.open.gov.uk/pro/prohome.htm

**Public Record Office of Northern Ireland**, 66 Balmoral Avenue, Belfast  BT9 6NY
Tel: 01232 251318                    Fax: 01232 255999
Email: proni@nics.gov.uk            proni.nics.uk/

*A large amount of historical and archive material covering Northern Ireland before
1922 will be found in the National Archives of Ireland and the National Library of
Ireland.*

**Royal Air Force Museum**, Department of Research & Information Services,
Grahame Park Way, Hendon, London  NW9 5LL
Tel: 0181 205 2266                    Fax: 0181 200 1751
                                      www.rafmuseum.org.uk/

**Royal Commission on Historical Manuscripts**, Quality House, Quality Court,
Chancery Lane, London  WC2A 1HP
Tel: 0171 242 1198                    Fax: 0171 831 3550
Email: nra@hmc.gov.uk                www.hmc.gov.uk/

**Tate Gallery Archive**, Millbank, London  SW1P 4RG
Tel: 0171 887 8831                    Fax: 0171 887 8007

**Ulster Historical Foundation**, 12 College Square East, Belfast  BT1 6DD
Tel: 01232 332288                    Fax: 01232 239885
Email: enquiry@uhf.org.uk            www.uhf.org.uk

*It can provide information on family history resource centres in Northern Ireland and
the Irish Republic*

For names and addresses of record centres and archives in England & Wales refer
to *Record Repositories In Great Britain* (10th edition 1997) published by the PRO.

As many of the above repositories operate a booking system and require
researchers to have a reader's ticket it is essential that contact is made with them in
advance of any proposed visit. Most publish guides and other information covering
their collections, services and opening times.

**NOTE:** Telephone numbers in London and Northern Ireland will change during 2000.

# INDEX

The index contains the names of all organisations and their subsidiaries listed in the Directory, along with alternative forms of name.

Names beginning Mc are filed as Mac.

The reference number given against each entry in the index refers to the number of the entry in the Directory; it is not a page number.

| | |
|---|---|
| 602 Squadron Museum | 190 |
| Aberdeen & North East Scotland Family History Society | 1 |
| Aberdeen Art Gallery | 4 |
| Aberdeen City Archives & Town Clerk's Library | 2 |
| Aberdeen City Archives: Old Aberdeen House Branch | 3 |
| Aberdeen City Council: Museums & Art Galleries Section: Aberdeen Art Gallery | 4 |
| Aberdeen City Council: Reference & Local Studies Department | 5 |
| Aberdeen Journals Ltd | 6 |
| Aberdeen Maritime Museum: Lloyds Register of Shipping Library | 7 |
| Aberdeen University Library: Department of Special Collections & Archives | 8 |
| Aberdeen University Library: Queen Mother Library | 9 |
| Aberdeen University Library: Taylor Library | 10 |
| Aberdeen University: Centre for Scottish Studies | 11 |
| Aberdeen University: Department of Geography | 12 |
| Aberdeenshire Heritage: Arbuthnot Museum | 323 |
| Aberdeenshire Library & Information Service: Brander Library | 244 |
| Aberdeenshire Library & Information Service: Ellon Library | 176 |
| Aberdeenshire Library & Information Service: Fraserburgh Library | 184 |
| Aberdeenshire Library & Information Service: Inverbervie Library | 245 |
| Aberdeenshire Library & Information Service: Inverurie Library | 251 |
| Aberdeenshire Library & Information Service: Kemnay Library | 264 |
| Aberdeenshire Library & Information Service: Local Studies Department | 312 |
| Aberdeenshire Library & Information Service: Macduff Library | 295 |
| Aberdeenshire Library & Information Service: Peterhead Library | 324 |
| Aberdeenshire Library & Information Service: Stonehaven Library | 345 |
| Aberdeenshire Library & Information Service: Strichen Library | 349 |
| Abertay Historical Society | 81 |
| Advocates Library | 97 |
| Airdrie Library | 21 |
| Alexandria Library/Heritage Centre | 22 |
| Allan Ramsay Library | 283 |
| Andersonian Library: Special Collections Section | 226 |
| Angus Council Archives | 301 |
| Angus Council: Arbroath Library | 27 |
| Angus Council: Brechin Library | 47 |
| Angus Council: Carnoustie Library | 55 |

| | |
|---|---:|
| Angus Council: Forfar Library | 179 |
| Angus Council: Monifeith Library | 300 |
| Angus Council: Montrose Library | 302 |
| Angus Council: Montrose Museum and Art Gallery | 303 |
| Angus Council: Signal Tower Museum | 28 |
| Angus Council: The Meffan | 180 |
| Angus Folk Museum | 189 |
| Arbroath Library | 27 |
| Arbuthnot Museum | 323 |
| Archdiocese of Glasgow | 191 |
| The Architectural Heritage Society of Scotland | 98 |
| Argyll & Bute Archives | 292 |
| Argyll & Bute Library Service: Local Collection | 92 |
| Argyll & Sutherland Highlands Regimental Museum | 339 |
| Auld Kirk Museum | 275 |
| Ayrshire Archaeological & Natural History Society | 31 |
| Ayrshire Archives | 32 |
| Ayrshire Collection | 266 |
| Ayrshire Sound Archive | 33 |
| Bank of Scotland Archive | 99 |
| Bank of Scotland Museum | 100 |
| Baptist Union of Scotland | 192 |
| Barra & Vatersay Historical Society | 254 |
| Barrhead Community Museum | 36 |
| BBC Resources, Information & Archives Scotland | 193 |
| Benbecula Community Library | 256 |
| Bennie Museum | 37 |
| Bernera Local History Society | 258 |
| Berwick-upon-Tweed Record Office | 38 |
| Biggar Museum Trust (I) | 40 |
| Biggar Museum Trust (II) | 41 |
| Black Watch Regimental Museum | 317 |
| Blairgowrie Genealogy Centre & Blairgowrie, Rattray & District Local History Trust | 43 |
| Bo'ness Library | 45 |
| Bonnyrigg & Lasswade Local History Society | 46 |
| Border Television Library | 52 |
| Borders Family History Society | 358 |
| Brander Library | 244 |
| Brechin Library | 47 |
| British Geological Survey | 101 |
| British Golf Museum | 334 |
| Brookwood Library | 194 |
| Brora Library | 49 |
| Buckie District Fishing Heritage | 50 |
| Burns Cottage | 34 |
| Bute Museum, Buteshire Natural History Society | 327 |
| The Cameronians (Scottish Rifles) | 239 |
| Carluke Parish Historical Society | 54 |
| Carnoustie Library | 55 |
| Castle House Museum | 93 |

| | |
|---|---|
| Castlebay Community Library | 255 |
| Cawdor Heritage Group | 359 |
| Central Scotland Family History Society | 360 |
| Centre for Scottish Studies | 11 |
| Chartered Institute of Bankers in Scotland | 102 |
| Clackmannan Libraries Archives & Walter Murray Local Studies Collection | 24 |
| Clackmannanshire Field Studies Society | 361 |
| Clan Cameron Museum | 333 |
| Clan Donald Centre Library | 263 |
| Clan Donnachaidh Museum | 325 |
| Clan MacMillan Centre | 281 |
| Clark (Edward) Collection | 133 |
| Clydebank Central Library : Local Studies Department | 57 |
| Clydebank Museum | 56 |
| The Cockburn Association (The Edinburgh Civic Trust) | 103 |
| Colinton Local History Society | 362 |
| Comann Eachdraidh Bharraigh Agus Bhatarsaidh - Barra & Vatersay Historical Society | 254 |
| Comann Eachdraidh Lios Mor - Lismore Heritage Society | 290 |
| Comhairle Nan Eilean Siar (formerly Western Isles Council): Community Library [Castlebay] | 255 |
| Comhairle Nan Eilean Siar (formerly Western Isles Council): Community Library [Liniclate] | 256 |
| Comhairle Nan Eilean Siar (formerly Western Isles Council): Stornoway Library | 347 |
| The Corstorphine Trust: Local History Section | 104 |
| Costume Society of Scotland | 268 |
| Council for Scottish Archaeology | 105 |
| Cramond Heritage Trust | 106 |
| Crichton Royal Museum | 75 |
| Cromarty Courthouse | 59 |
| Cullen, Deskford & Portknockie Heritage Group | 363 |
| Cumbernauld Central Library | 61 |
| Cumbria Archive Service | 53 |
| Currie & District History Society | 364 |
| Customs & Excise | 257 |
| Dalkeith History Museum Workshop | 67 |
| Dalkeith History Society: Dalkeith History Museum Workshop | 67 |
| David Livingstone Centre | 44 |
| Denny Ship Model Experiment Tank Archives | 71 |
| Dingwall Library | 68 |
| Dollar Museum | 69 |
| Drymen & District Local History Society | 70 |
| Dumbarton Public Library | 72 |
| Dumfries & Galloway Council Archives | 73 |
| Dumfries & Galloway Family History Society | 74 |
| Dumfries & Galloway Health Board Archives: Crichton Royal Museum | 75 |
| Dumfries & Galloway Libraries: Local Studies Collection | 76 |
| Dumfries Museum | 77 |
| Dunbar & District History Society | 78 |

| | |
|---|---|
| Dunblane Cathedral City Museum | 80 |
| Dundee Arts & Heritage: McManus Galleries | 82 |
| Dundee City Archives | 83 |
| Dundee City Council: Local Studies Library | 84 |
| Dundee Registration Office (Births, Deaths & Marriages) | 85 |
| Dundee University Archives | 86 |
| Dunfermline Museum | 89 |
| Dunning Parish Historical Society | 91 |
| Dunoon & Cowal Heritage Trust: Castle House Museum | 93 |
| E A Hornel Art Gallery & Library | 272 |
| Easdale Island Folk Museum | 310 |
| East Ayrshire Council Library Service: Ayrshire Collection | 266 |
| East Ayrshire Council Library Service: Local Archives | 62 |
| East Ayrshire Family History Society | 365 |
| East Dunbartonshire Libraries: Brookwood Library | 194 |
| East Dunbartonshire Libraries: Reference & Local Studies Library | 274 |
| East Dunbartonshire Museums: Auld Kirk Museum | 275 |
| East Linton Local History Society | 366 |
| East Lothian Antiquarian & Field Naturalists' Society | 79 |
| East Lothian Council Library Service: Local History Centre | 237 |
| East Lothian Museums Service | 238 |
| East Renfrewshire Cultural Services: Local History Collection | 195 |
| The Economic & Social History Society of Scotland | 13 |
| Edinburgh Academy | 107 |
| Edinburgh Archaeological Field Society | 108 |
| Edinburgh Architectural Association | 109 |
| Edinburgh City Archives | 110 |
| Edinburgh City Corporate Services Library | 111 |
| Edinburgh City Libraries | 112 |
| Edinburgh City Libraries: Scottish Library | 113 |
| Edinburgh City Museums: Huntly House & People's Story | 114 |
| Edinburgh City Museums: Museum of Childhood | 115 |
| Edinburgh City Museums: Queensferry Museum | 331 |
| Edinburgh City Museums: The Writers' Museum | 116 |
| The Edinburgh Civic Trust | 103 |
| Edinburgh College of Art | 126 |
| Edinburgh University Library: Main Library | 117 |
| Edinburgh University Library: New College Library | 118 |
| Edinburgh University: Moray House Archive | 119 |
| Edinburgh University: School of Scottish Studies - Library & Archives | 120 |
| Edward Clark Collection | 133 |
| Elgin Museum | 174 |
| Ellon Library | 176 |
| Evening Times | 209 |
| Fala, Soutra & District History & Heritage Society | 367 |
| Falconer Museum | 181 |
| The Falkland Society | 368 |
| Falkirk Council Library Services: Bo'ness Library | 45 |
| Falkirk Council Library Services: Falkirk Library | 177 |
| Falkirk Council Library Services: Grangemouth Library | 232 |
| Falkirk Library | 177 |

Falkirk Museums: History Research Centre 178
Ferryhill Heritage Society (Aberdeen) 369
Fettes College Archives 121
Fife Archaeology Unit: Fife Sites & Monuments Record 230
Fife Council Central Area Libraries: Local History Collection 270
Fife Council East Area Libraries: Local History Collection 63
Fife Council Museums (East) 64
Fife Council Museums (West): Dunfermline Museum 89
Fife Council West Area Libraries: Local History Department 90
Fife Council: Law & Administration Archive Records Centre 297
Fife Family History Society: Family History Room 298
Fife Folk Museum 65
Fife Health Board: Purchaser Group Library 66
Forfar Library 179
Fort William Library 182
Forth Naturalist & Historian 340
Fraserburgh Library 184
Free Church College Library 122
Friockheim & District Historical Society 370
Galashiels & District Local History Association: Old Gala Club 186
General Register Office for Scotland (GRO) 123
Girvan & District Historical Society 188
Glasgow & West of Scotland Family History Society 196
Glasgow Archaeological Society 371
Glasgow Art Gallery & Museum 197
Glasgow Caledonian University Library: Special Collections & 198
Archives
Glasgow City Archives 199
Glasgow City Libraries & Archives: Glasgow Collection 200
Glasgow Collection 200
Glasgow Museums: Museum of Transport 201
Glasgow Registration Office 202
Glasgow University Library: Local History Section 203
Glasgow University Library: Special Collections Department 204
Glasgow University: Archives & Business Records Centre (including 205
Scottish Brewing Archive)
Glasgow University: Hunterian Museum: Roman Scotland Archive 206
Gordon Highlanders Museum 14
Gorebridge & District Local History Society 231
Grampian Television Library 15
Grampian Transport Museum 23
The Grand Lodge of Antient Free & Accepted Masons of Scotland: 124
The Grand Lodge of Scotland Museum & Library
Grangemouth Library 232
Great North of Scotland Railway Association 372
Greater Glasgow Health Board Archive 207
GRO (General Register Office for Scotland) 123
Gullane & Dirleton History Society 236
Hamilton & District FHS 375
Hawick Archaeological Society: Historical Collection 242
Hawick Museum & Gallery 243

| | |
|---|---|
| The Hay Fleming Reference Library | 335 |
| Heatherbank Museum of Social Work | 208 |
| The Herald & Evening Times | 209 |
| Heriot-Watt University Archive | 125 |
| Heriot-Watt University: Edinburgh College of Art | 126 |
| Heriot-Watt University: Scottish Borders Campus | 187 |
| Highland Council Archive Service | 246 |
| Highland Council Museum Service: The Whyte Photographic Collection | 247 |
| Highland Folk Museum | 269 |
| Highland Health Board Archives | 248 |
| Highland Libraries: Brora Library | 49 |
| Highland Libraries: Dingwall Library | 68 |
| Highland Libraries: Fort William Library | 182 |
| Highland Libraries: Inverness Public Library | 249 |
| Highland Libraries: Thurso Library | 350 |
| Highland Libraries: Wick Library | 356 |
| Historic Resources Centre | 25 |
| Historic Scotland Library | 127 |
| History Research Centre | 178 |
| HM Customs & Excise | 233 |
| Hornel (E A) Art Gallery & Library | 272 |
| Hunterian Museum: Roman Scotland Archive | 206 |
| Huntly House & People's Story | 114 |
| Institute of Chartered Accountants of Scotland | 128 |
| Inverbervie Library | 245 |
| Inverness Museum and Art Gallery | 250 |
| Inverness Public Library | 249 |
| Inverurie Library | 251 |
| Isle of Arran Heritage Museum | 253 |
| Isle of Islay Museum | 257 |
| Isle of Mull Museum (Library & Archive) | 262 |
| Jordanhill Campus Library | 227 |
| Kemnay Library | 264 |
| Kilmartin House Centre for Archaeology & Landscape Interpretation | 267 |
| Kincardine Local History Group | 373 |
| Kinross Historical Society | 374 |
| Kintyre Antiquarian & Natural History Society | 51 |
| Kirkcaldy Museum & Art Gallery | 271 |
| Kirkliston Local History Archive Trust | 276 |
| Laird Forge | 252 |
| Lanark Library: Reference & Local Studies Dept. | 280 |
| Lanark Museum | 279 |
| Lanarkshire Family History Society (formerly Hamilton & District FHS) | 375 |
| Largs & District Historical Society | 282 |
| Largs & North Ayrshire Family History Society | 376 |
| Larkhall Heritage Group | 377 |
| Lasswade (& Bonnyrigg) Local History Society | 46 |
| Leadhills Miners Library & Reading Institute: Allan Ramsay Library | 283 |
| Lesmahagow Parish Historical Association | 378 |
| Liddesdale Heritage Centre | 307 |

Liniclate Community Library 256
The Linlithgow Story Museum 288
Lismore Heritage Society 290
Livingstone (David) Centre 44
Lloyds Register of Shipping Library 7
Lochgilphead Registrar's Office 293
Lorn Archaeological & Historical Society 311
Lossiemouth Fisheries & Community Museum 294
Lothian Health Services Archive 129
The Lothians Family History Society 379
Low Parks Museum 240
Macaulay Land Use Research Institute Library 16
Macduff Library 295
McLean Museum and Art Gallery 234
McManus Galleries 82
Main Library 117
Mallaig Heritage Centre 296
Map Library 138
The Meffan 180
Meteorological Office 130
Midlothian Council Libraries: Local Studies Centre 291
Milngavie & Bearsden Historical Society 210
Moffat Museum 299
Monifeith Library 300
Montrose Air Station Museum (Trust) 304
Montrose Library 302
Montrose Museum and Art Gallery 303
The Moray Council Museums Service: Falconer Museum 181
The Moray Council: Local Heritage Centre 175
Moray House Archive 119
Motherwell Heritage Centre 305
Murray (Walter) Local Studies Collection 24
Museum of Childhood 115
Museum of Fire 131
Museum of Flight Library 94
Museum of Islay Life 257
Museum of Lead Mining (formerly Scottish Lead Mining Museum) 352
Museum of Transport 201
Nairn Literary Institute Library 306
Napier University Library: Craiglockhart Campus Library 132
Napier University Library: Edward Clark Collection 133
NAS (National Archives of Scotland) 134
National Archives of Scotland (NAS) formerly Scottish Record Office 134
(SRO)
National Gallery of Scotland: Library 135
National Library of Scotland: Main Library 136
National Library of Scotland: Manuscripts Division 137
National Library of Scotland: Map Library 138
National Monuments Record of Scotland (NMR(S)) 149
National Museums of Scotland Library: Royal Museum of Scotland 139

| | |
|---|---|
| National Museums of Scotland Library: Scottish United Services Museum | 140 |
| National Museums of Scotland: Scottish Agricultural Museum | 141 |
| National Museums of Scotland: Scottish Life Archive | 142 |
| The National Trust for Scotland | 143 |
| The National Trust for Scotland: E A Hornel Art Gallery & Library | 272 |
| The National Trust for Scotland: Pollok House | 211 |
| New College Library | 118 |
| New Lanark Conservation Trust Library | 278 |
| Newton Stewart Museum | 308 |
| NMR(S) (National Monuments Record of Scotland) | 149 |
| North Ayrshire Libraries: Local History Library | 30 |
| North Ayrshire Museum | 329 |
| North Highland Archive | 357 |
| North Lanarkshire Council Archives | 60 |
| North Lanarkshire Council: Motherwell Heritage Centre | 305 |
| North Lanarkshire Libraries: Airdrie Library | 21 |
| North Lanarkshire Libraries: Cumbernauld Central Library | 61 |
| North Lochs Historical Society | 259 |
| Northern College: Aberdeen Campus Library | 17 |
| Northern Health Services Archives | 18 |
| Old Aberdeen House Branch | 3 |
| Old Edinburgh Club | 380 |
| Old Gala Club | 186 |
| Orkney Library & Archive Service | 277 |
| Pairc Historical Society | 260 |
| Paisley Museum | 315 |
| Paisley University: Local/Special Collection | 313 |
| People's Palace | 212 |
| People's Story | 114 |
| Perth & Kinross Council Archive | 318 |
| Perth & Kinross Libraries: Local Studies Section | 319 |
| Perth Museum & Art Gallery | 320 |
| Peterhead Library | 324 |
| Pictish Arts Society | 381 |
| Pollok House | 211 |
| Prestwick History Group | 382 |
| Queen Mother Library | 9 |
| Queen's Own Highlanders | 29 |
| Queensferry Museum | 331 |
| Ramsay (Allan) Library | 283 |
| RCAHMS (Royal Commission on the Ancient and Historical Monuments of Scotland) | 149 |
| Reid Library | 20 |
| Renfrewshire Council Library Service: Local Studies Library | 314 |
| Renfrewshire Council Museum Service: Paisley Museum | 315 |
| RIAS (Royal Incorporation of Architects in Scotland) | 151 |
| The Robert Gordon University: Architecture & Surveying Library | 19 |
| Roman Scotland Archive | 206 |
| Roslin Heritage Society | 383 |

Rowett Research Institute: Reid Library 20
The Royal Bank of Scotland Archives 144
Royal Botanic Garden Library 145
Royal Burgh of Lanark Museum Trust: Lanark Museum 279
Royal College of Nursing Archives 146
Royal College of Physicians & Surgeons of Glasgow 213
Royal College of Physicians of Edinburgh 147
Royal College of Surgeons of Edinburgh 148
Royal Commission on the Ancient and Historical Monuments of 149
Scotland (RCAHMS)
Royal Faculty of Procurators: Library 214
Royal Highland & Agriticultural Society of Scotland: Library 150
The Royal Highland Fusiliers Regimental Museum 215
Royal Incorporation of Architects in Scotland (RIAS) 151
Royal Museum of Scotland 139
Royal Observatory 152
Royal Pharmaceutical Society of Great Britain 153
The Royal Scots Regimental Museum Library 154
Royal Scottish Academy Library 155
Royal Scottish Geographical Society 216
Royal Society of Edinburgh 156
The Saltire Society 157
Saughton House Library 167
Savings Bank Museum 328
School of Scottish Studies - Library & Archives 120
Scotland Street School - Museum of Education 217
Scotland's Lighthouse Museum: Library & Study Centre 185
The Scots at War Trust 158
Scotsman Publications: Library 159
Scottish Agricultural Museum 141
Scottish Borders Archive & Local History Centre 330
Scottish Borders Campus 187
Scottish Borders Council Museums & Galleries: Hawick Museum & 243
Gallery
Scottish Brewing Archive 205
Scottish Catholic Archives 160
Scottish Church History Society 161
The Scottish Civic Trust 218
Scottish Daily Record & Sunday Mail Editorial Library 219
Scottish Film & Television Archive 220
Scottish Fisheries Museum 26
Scottish Genealogy Society 162
Scottish History Society 163
Scottish Industrial Heritage Society 221
Scottish Jewish Archives Centre 222
Scottish Lead Mining Museum 352
Scottish Life Archive 142
Scottish Maritime Museum: Denny Ship Model Experiment Tank 71
Archives
Scottish Maritime Museum: Laird Forge 252
Scottish Military Historical Society 229

| | |
|---|---|
| Scottish Mining Museum | 309 |
| Scottish Museums Council: Information Centre | 164 |
| Scottish National Gallery of Modern Art | 165 |
| Scottish National Portrait Gallery | 166 |
| Scottish Natural History Library | 265 |
| Scottish Office Library & Information Service: Saughton House Library | 167 |
| Scottish Office Library & Information Service: St Andrew's House Library | 168 |
| Scottish Office Library & Information Service: Victoria Quay Library | 169 |
| Scottish Record Office (SRO) | 134 |
| Scottish Society of the History of Medicine | 321 |
| Scottish Sunday Mail (& Daily Record) Editorial Library | 219 |
| Scottish Television Library Services: Film & Videotape Library | 223 |
| Scottish Theatre Archive | 204 |
| Scottish United Services Museum | 140 |
| Scottish Urban Archaeological Trust (SUAT) | 322 |
| Scottish Working People's History Trust | 170 |
| Shetland Archives | 284 |
| Shetland Family History Society | 285 |
| Shetland Library | 286 |
| Shetland Museum | 287 |
| Signal Tower Museum | 28 |
| Signet Library | 171 |
| Skye & Lochalsh Area Museum Service: Dualchas | 326 |
| Smith Art Gallery & Museum | 341 |
| The Society of Antiquaries of Scotland | 172 |
| South Ayrshire Libraries: Scottish & Local History Library | 35 |
| South Lanarkshire Council: Archives & Information Management Service | 95 |
| South Lanarkshire Libraries | 96 |
| South Lanarkshire Libraries: Lanark Library: Reference & Local Studies Dept. | 280 |
| South Lanarkshire Libraries: Local Studies Department | 241 |
| South Queensferry History Group | 332 |
| Springburn Museum | 224 |
| SRO (Scottish Record Office) | 134 |
| St Andrew's House Library | 168 |
| The St Andrews Preservation Trust Museum | 336 |
| St Andrews University Library: Special Collections Department | 337 |
| Stevenson College: Library | 173 |
| Stewarton & District Museum | 338 |
| The Stewartry Museum | 273 |
| Stirling Council Archives Services | 342 |
| Stirling Council Library Service: Local History Collection | 343 |
| Stirling University Library | 344 |
| Stonehaven Library | 345 |
| Stonehouse Heritage Group | 346 |
| Stornoway Library | 347 |
| Stranraer Museum | 348 |
| Strathclyde Police Museum | 225 |

Strathclyde University: Andersonian Library: Special Collections Section    226
Strathclyde University: Jordanhill Campus Library    227
Strathnaver Museum    39
Strichen Library    349
SUAT (Scottish Urban Archaeological Trust)    322
Summerlee Heritage Park    58
Tay Valley Family History Society    87
Taylor Library    10
Thurso Library    350
The Trades House of Glasgow    228
Troon & District Family History Society    384
Tweeddale Museum    316
Uig Heritage Centre    261
Ullapool Museum & Visitor Centre    351
University of Abertay Dundee: Library    88
Victoria Quay Library    169
W H Welsh Educational & Historic Trust    48
Walter Murray Local Studies Collection    24
West Dunbartonshire Libraries: Alexandria Library/Heritage Centre    22
West Dunbartonshire Libraries: Clydebank Central Library : Local Studies Department    57
West Dunbartonshire Libraries: Dumbarton Public Library    72
West Highland Museum    183
West Kilbride Museum Trust    353
West Linton Historical Association    354
West Lothian History & Amenity Society Library    289
West Lothian Library Service: Local History Collection    42
Western Isles Council: Community Library [Castlebay]    255
Western Isles Council: Community Library [Liniclate]    256
Western Isles Council: Stornoway Library    347
Westray Heritage Centre    355
The Whyte Photographic Collection    247
Wick Library    356
The Writers' Museum    116

# THE SPONSORS

Three organisations have sponsored and collaborated in the publication of this book. They have all been involved in publishing books of interest to historical researchers in addition to their other activities.

The **Scottish Library Association** (SLA) was founded in 1908 to promote libraries and librarianship in Scotland. Today it has over 2500 members who cover all aspects of library and information work.

The Association publishes a bi-monthly journal *Scottish Libraries*, and a wide range of publications, and promotes Local History Weeks throughout Scotland. In addition it provides training and continuing education courses for members.

Through its members the Association has wide links with public libraries, local history groups, schools and resource services, universities and health boards. It also has a website at www.slainte.napier.ac.uk/ which gives information on libraries, their services and current library promotions and initiatives.

Further information can be obtained from the Scottish Library Association, 1 John Street, Hamilton ML3 7EU. Tel: 01698 458888; Fax: 01698 458899 or Email: sctlb@leapfrog.almac.co.uk

The **Scottish Records Association** (SRA) was established in 1977 to arouse interests in, and awareness of, historical records relating to Scotland. It provides information on them and promotes discussion on their custody, preservation, accessibility and use. It organises an annual conference, visits to archives and publishes newsletters, accession bulletins and *Scottish Archives*, Scotland's only archival journal. Social and local history often features in conference papers and in *Scottish Archives*. These papers provide valuable pointers to a rich variety of record sources.

All these activities make the Association a unique forum where the views and needs of custodians of records (owners, archivists, and librarians) and their users (academic, social, local and family historians, geographers and genealogists) are aired and discussed. The SRA does not undertake research on any topic.

Information on the SRA's publications or membership can be obtained from the Scottish Records Association, c/o Glasgow City Archives, Mitchell Library, North Street, Glasgow G3 7DN.

The **Scottish Local History Forum** (SLHF) was established in 1983 to bring people together, not only the professional and amateur historian who make contributions to the study of social, local and family history, but also those people who use historical information in connection with education, tourism and community work, or as part of a modern leisure activity.

It endeavours to promote local history at both local and national level and helps with the establishment and development of groups and societies throughout Scotland. It publishes a journal, *Scottish Local History*, three times a year and organises an Autumn Conference, which takes place at differing venues.

For further information on the Forum and its Journal contact Murray Blair, Hon. Treasurer, 29 Glenpark Avenue, Glasgow G46 7JE (Tel: 0141 638 0155).

## ACKNOWLEDGEMENTS

The Sponsors wish to thank the following people and organisations who made significant contributions towards the publication of this book and especially to all those people who completed questionnaires and provided such comprehensive summaries of their collections and archives.

To the planning and editorial group - Michael Cox, Scottish Local History Forum, compiler of the Directory, who, together with Alan Reid and Brian Osborne, Scottish Library Association, contributed articles. Grateful thanks are extended to Norman Newton and Mike Seton for their contributions which together point the way to anyone wishing to find out and write about their Scottish history.

The support and assistance from the Secretary, Tristram Clarke, and members of the Scottish Records Association was most welcome. The help and advice given by Alan Borthwick of the National Archives of Scotland, former Chairman of the Scottish Local History Forum, and his colleagues, Ishbel Barnes (Scottish Archive Network) and Alison Lindsay (photographs) was most appreciated. Thanks are extended to Sandy Buchanan for supplying information on SCRAN; Gordon and David Killicoat for family history information and to Scott Ballantyne for the cover design.

Grateful thanks are extended to Ann Steele of the SLA, who co-ordinated the operation, together with her colleagues who undertook the often frustrating task of deciphering the handwriting on so many of the questionnaires, and, that of the compiler, when inputting information to the database, and, to Gordon Dunsire of Napier University, Edinburgh, for undertaking the programming for the database as well as the formatting and production of camera ready copy for the printers.

The sponsors also wish to thank the National Archives of Scotland and Robson McClean WS (Burgess Ticket) for allowing the reproduction of the photographs and to Polygon for permitting the use of the map featured in *Tracing Your Scottish Ancestry* (1996) by Kathleen B Cory. Every effort has been made to seek the permission of the copyright holders to reproduce photographs used in this publication, and, as no directory compiled over period of almost a year can be fully accurate when published, apologises are extended to organisations where factual errors are found.